HATE CRIMES

HATE CRIMES

VOLUME 1

Understanding and Defining Hate Crime

Barbara Perry, General Editor
Brian Levin, Volume Editor

PRAEGER PERSPECTIVES

Westport, Connecticut
London

Library of Congress Cataloging-in-Publication Data

Hate crimes / Barbara Perry, general editor.
      p. cm.
  Includes bibliographical references and index.
  ISBN 978–0–275–99569–0 (set : alk. paper) — 978–0–275–99571–3
(vol. 1 : alk. paper) — 978–0–275–99573–7 (vol. 2 : alk. paper) — 978–0–275–99575–1
(vol. 3 : alk. paper) — 978–0–275–99577–5 (vol. 4 : alk. paper) — 978–0–275–99579–9
(vol. 5 : alk. paper)
  1. Offenses against the person. 2. Hate crimes. 3. Violent crimes. 4. Genocide.
I. Perry, Barbara, 1962–
  K5170.H38   2009
  364.15—dc22   2008052727

British Library Cataloguing in Publication Data is available.

Library of Congress Catalog Card Number: 2008052727
ISBN: 978–0–275–99569–0 (set)
       978–0–275–99571–3 (vol. 1)
       978–0–275–99573–7 (vol. 2)
       978–0–275–99575–1 (vol. 3)
       978–0–275–99577–5 (vol. 4)
       978–0–275–99579–9 (vol. 5)

First published in 2009

Praeger Publishers, 88 Post Road West, Westport, CT 06881
An imprint of Greenwood Publishing Group, Inc.
www.praeger.com

Printed in the United States of America

The paper used in this book complies with the
Permanent Paper Standard issued by the National
Information Standards Organization (Z39.48–1984).

10 9 8 7 6 5 4 3 2 1

*This book is dedicated to my extraordinary mother and father,
and their parents, whose eloquence produced an appreciation
for empathy combined with intellect in service to community.
It is also dedicated to my beautiful wife and children,
who look for goodness in people.
Last, to my colleagues, who support my work
in researching hate and extremism.*

CONTENTS

SET INTRODUCTION

Barbara Perry
General Editor

The twentieth century appeared to close much as it had opened—with sprees of violence directed against the Other. The murder of Matthew Shepard, the lynching of James Byrd, the murderous rampage of Benjamin Smith, and post-9/11 anti-Muslim violence all stand as reminders that the bigotry that kills is much more than an unfortunate chapter in U.S. history. Racial, gender, ethnic, and religious violence persist. It is a sad commentary on the cultural and social life of the United States that a series such as this remains timely as we enter the twenty-first century. The dramatic cases cited earlier are but extreme illustrations of widespread, daily acts of aggression directed toward an array of minority communities. I use the term *communities* purposefully here since these acts are less about any one victim than about the cultural group they represent. Hate crime is, in fact, an assault against all members of stigmatized and marginalized communities.

Clearly this is not a new phenomenon, even in the United States. It is important to keep in mind that what we currently refer to as hate crime has a long historical lineage. The contemporary dynamics of hate-motivated violence have their origins in historical conditions. With respect to hate crime, at least, history does repeat itself, as similar patterns of motivation, sentiment, and victimization recur over time. Just as immigrants in the 1890s were subject to institutional and public forms of discrimination and violence, so, too, were those of the 1990s; likewise, former black slaves risked the wrath of the Ku Klux Klan (KKK) when they exercised their newfound rights in the antebellum period, just as their descendants risked violent reprisal for their efforts to win and exercise additional rights and freedoms in the civil rights era; and women who demanded the right to vote on the eve of the twentieth century suffered the same ridicule and harassment as those who demanded equal rights in the workplace later in the century. While the politics of difference that underlie these periods of animosity may lie latent for short periods of time, they nonetheless seem to remain on the simmer, ready to resurface whenever a new threat is perceived—when immigration levels increase; or when relationships between groups shift for other political, economic, or cultural reasons; or in the aftermath of attacks like those on 9/11. Consequently, hate crime remains a crucial indicator of cultural fissures in the United States and around the globe. This set, then, remains similarly relevant in the current era.

Hate Crimes offers interested readers a comprehensive collection of original chapters surveying this phenomenon we have come to know as hate crime. Interestingly, the field of hate crime studies is interdisciplinary, so the contributors here represent a variety of disciplines, including law, sociology, criminology, psychology, and even public health. Moreover, since it is also a global phenomenon, we have invited not just American scholars, but international contributors as well. This comparative/cross-cultural approach adds an important element to the set. It reminds readers that hate crime is a universal problem and that approaches taken elsewhere might be of use to North Americans.

The volumes included in this set have been divided into five distinct focal areas. Volume 1, *Understanding and Defining Hate Crime*, is edited by Brian Levin of California State University, San Bernardino. He has collected a series of chapters that lay a strong foundation for the volumes that follow. The pieces here provide an introduction to what it is we mean by the term *hate crime*. There is ongoing debate about such things as whether the term is even appropriate, what behaviors ought to be included in our understanding of hate crime, and what classes of victims should be included. The relevant chapters, then, offer diverse definitions, ranging from legal to sociological approaches.

One consequence of the varied and divergent definitions used to conceptualize bias-motivated crime is that the confusion also complicates the process of gathering data on hate crime. Berk, Boyd, and Hamner (1992) astutely observe that "much of the available data on hate motivated crime rests on unclear definitions; it is difficult to know what is being counted as hate motivated and what is not" (p. 125). As a result, while both academic and media reports make the claim that ethnoviolence represents a "rising tide," the truth is that we don't know whether in fact this is the case or not (Jacobs & Potter, 1998). Thus Levin also includes a number of chapters that attempt to address the issue of data collection and measurement of hate crime.

The limitations of definition and measurement highlighted previously help to explain the limited attempts thus far to theorize hate crime. In the absence of empirical information about bias-motivated violence, it is difficult to construct conceptual frameworks. Without the raw materials, there is no foundation for theorizing. Additionally, the relatively recent recognition of hate crime as a social problem (Jenness & Broad, 1998) also contributes to the lack of theoretical accounts. This volume, however, includes chapters that begin to offer compelling models to help us make sense of hate crime.

The second volume, *The Consequences of Hate Crime*, is a particularly valuable contribution to the literature on hate crime. Editor Paul Iganski of Lancaster University in the United Kingdom has brought together a unique collection of chapters that explore both the individual and the social impacts associated with this form of violence. Running through much of the literature—even through court decisions on hate crime—is the assumption that such offences are qualitatively different in their effects, as compared to their non-bias-motivated counterparts. Specifically, Iganski (2001) contends that there are five distinct types of consequences associated with hate crime: harm to the initial victim; harm to the victim's group; harm to the victim's group (outside the neighborhood); harm to other targeted communities; and harm to societal norms and values. The first of these has been the subject of considerable scholarly attention. Research suggests that first and foremost among the impacts on the individual is the physical harm: bias-motivated crimes are often characterized by extreme brutality (Levin & McDevitt, 1993). Violent personal crimes motivated by bias are more likely to involve extraordinary levels of violence. Additionally, the empirical findings of studies of the emotional, psychological, and behavioral impacts of hate crime are beginning to establish a solid pattern of more severe impact on bias crime victims, as compared to nonbias victims (see, e.g., Herek, Cogan, & Gillis, 2002; McDevitt et al., 2001). Several chapters in this volume explore these individual effects.

Additionally, however, this volume includes a number of chapters that begin to offer insights into other often overlooked consequences of hate crime: community effects. Many scholars point to the "fact" that hate crimes are "message crimes" that emit a distinct warning to all members of the victim's community: step out of line, cross invisible boundaries, and you, too, could be lying on the ground, beaten and bloodied (Iganski, 2001). Consequently, the individual fear noted previously is thought to be accompanied by the collective fear of the victim's cultural group, possibly even of other minority groups likely to be victims. Weinstein (as cited by Iganski, 2001) refers to this as an *in terrorem* effect: intimidation of the group by the victimization of one or a few members of that group. It is these effects that contributors such as Monique Noelle and Helen Ahn Lim address.

Barbara Perry, editor of volume 3, *The Victims of Hate Crime*, introduces this volume with the caveat that little empirical work has been done on the distinct experiences of different groups of hate crime victims. Much of the literature has more or less assumed a homogeneous group known as "victims." However, this occludes the fact that the frequency, dynamics, motives, and impacts of bias-motivated violence differ across target communities. Thus the volume draws on emerging theoretical and empirical work that explores manifestations of hate crime within diverse communities. Especially novel here is the inclusion of pieces that address hate-motivated crime directed toward women and the homeless community. Consideration of these groups, in particular, forces us to expand our traditional characterization of hate crime victims, which is often restricted to race, religion, ethnicity, or sexual orientation.

Volume 4, *Hate Crime Offenders*, brings us to a consideration of the second half of the equation: perpetrators of hate crime. Randy Blazak from Portland State University has gathered an intriguing collection of chapters. The authors here have been set the task of responding to Blazak's opening question, Who are the hate mongers? Many would respond to this question by reference to members of the KKK or a skinhead group, for example. This is a very common myth. In fact, fewer than 5 percent of identifiable offenders are members of organized hate groups. Recognizing this, Blazak has asked his contributors to explore both individual perpetrators and those involved in hate groups. Thus this is an engaging and diverse collection of chapters, which explore issues ranging from women's involvement in hate crime, to typologies of hate crime offenders, to white power music. He even includes an interview with a hate offender.

Frederick Lawrence, editor of volume 5, *Responding to Hate Crime*, has solicited work from his contributors that gives us food for thought with respect to how we might respond to hate crime. Clearly there are diverse approaches available: legislation, social policy, community organizing, or education, to name just a few. In the extant scholarship, there have been relatively few concentrated analyses of such efforts to respond to or prevent bias-motivated crimes. In large part, such recommendations come by way of a conclusion and are thus not fully developed. Hence the chapters in Lawrence's volume explicitly present interventions intended to ameliorate the incidence or impact of hate crime. While the emphasis is on criminal justice responses (legislation, policing, prosecution), Lawrence also includes chapters that explore preventative measures, restorative justice initiatives, and the role of organizations like the Southern Poverty Law Center.

I speak for all of the editors when I say that we are very pleased to have been asked to develop this collection of hate crime literature. It was a unique opportunity to share emerging perspectives and analyses with a diverse audience. It is hoped that what we offer here will provide the insights that readers are seeking, but also inspiration for further explorations and interventions into this disturbing class of violence.

REFERENCES

Berk, R., Boyd, E., & Hamner, K. (1992). Thinking more clearly about hate-motivated crimes. In G. Herek & K. Berrill (Eds.), *Hate crimes: Confronting violence against lesbians and gay men* (pp. 123–143). Newbury Park, CA: Sage.

Herek, G., Cogan, J., & Gillis, R. (2002). Victim experiences in hate crimes based on sexual orientation. *Journal of Social Issues, 58,* 319–339.

Iganski, P. (2001). Hate crimes hurt more. *American Behavioral Scientist, 45,* 626–638.

Jacobs, J., & Potter, K. (1998). *Hate crimes: Criminal law and identity politics.* New York: Oxford University Press.

Jenness, V., & Broad, K. (1998). *Hate crimes: New social movements and the politics of violence.* New York: Aldine de Gruyter.

Levin, J., & McDevitt, J. (1993). *Hate crimes: The rising tide of bigotry and bloodshed.* New York: Plenum.

McDevitt, J., Balboni, J., Garcia, L., and Gu, J.,. (2001). Consequences for victims: A comparison of bias- and non-bias motivated assaults. *American Behavioral Scientist, 45,* 697–713.

INTRODUCTION

Brian Levin

It is with great pride that I present *Understanding and Defining Hate Crime*, the first volume of the five-volume set *Hate Crimes*. Never before has such a noteworthy collection of international scholars been assembled in one book collection to present original work on this important topic. The contributors to this particular volume have written countless books and articles on the topic and presented advanced research to audiences around the world. In addition to their stellar academic achievements, these contributors offer a unique practical perspective as well. They have collected and analyzed official national data, worked for government agencies, tracked hate groups, interviewed victims and offenders, addressed courts and legislatures, trained practitioners, and appeared in newspapers and documentaries internationally.

The theme of this introductory volume explores important foundational issues related to history, theory, definitions, and measurement. While the term *hate crime* is relatively new, the issue of prejudice and violence has an eternal quality to it. As North America and Europe, where much of our readership is based, becomes increasingly diverse, understanding the dynamics of hate violence is more relevant than ever. Moreover, there has been a tremendous expansion not only of scholarship and data, but also of real-world information, which has emerged with the institutionalization of hate crime responses over the past two decades.

This volume begins with my analysis of the complex relationship between law and racial violence over the course of American history in "The Long Arc of Justice: Race, Violence, and the Emergence of Hate Crime Law."

The incomplete journey of American law from brutal enforcer of slavery to its current aspiration of guardian against hate crime is a remarkable one that holds important foundational lessons for the present. Similarly, Carolyn Turpin-Petrosino's chapter, "Historical Lessons: What's Past May Be Prologue," perceptibly analyzes a seemingly unbroken and diverse chain of hate violence across a span of centuries. Scholar's scholar Jack Levin (no relation) and Gordana Rabrenovic, in "Hate as Cultural Justification for Violence," cogently trace how bigoted violence draws sustenance from a widespread, though often ignored, underlying culture of prejudice. Barbara Perry's discussion of foundational theory in "The Sociology of Hate: Theoretical Approaches" provides important straightforward insight into the role that hate violence has in reinforcing destructive intergroup hierarchies. David Gadd and Bill Dixon's "Posing the 'Why' Question: Understanding the Perpetration of Racially Motivated Violence and Harrassment" looks to perpetrators themselves to shed light on the reasons behind hate incidents in this important research out of England.

The middle three chapters of the book examine crucial elemental issues relating to hate's hard core. All three chapters are authored by distinguished scholars whose research into hate movements has involved direct communication with present and former hatemongers. Mark S. Hamm's chapter, "From the Klan to Skinheads: A Critical History of American Hate Groups," offers a comprehensive and fascinating glimpse of hate movements through seven historical periods. Heidi Beirich, of the renowned Southern Poverty Law Center, and Kevin Hicks's "White Nationalism in America" explores how a stealthy version of racism is gaining ground in contemporary society by targeting fears of a nation in decline. Randy Blazak deftly confronts and tries to resolve key definitional and measurement issues relating to extremism in "Toward a Working Definition of Hate Groups."

While not about hate groups, Susie Bennett, James J. Nolan, and Norman Conti's chapter, "Defining and Measuring Hate Crime: A Potpourri of Issues," addresses the conflicts and efforts that make defining and counting hate crimes a much more complicated endeavor than many might think. Nolan should know something about this as he was previously responsible for the collection and tabulation of the Federal Bureau of Investigation's national hate crime data. A decade ago, Jessica S. Henry coauthored a controversial and widely cited article that challenged the way we punish and count hate crimes in the United States. She has refocused her critical lens on the unintended harmful consequences of inconsistent definitions and measurement in "Hate Crimes Laws: A Critical Assessment."

For additional perspective, I chose two scholars to end the book whose research area is outside the disciplines of criminal justice and sociology. Historian Timothy Pytell analyzes the worst manifestation of mass hate in his chapter "Weighing Genocide." Communication scholar and former journalist

Sara-Ellen Amster traces the role that mass communication tools have played in spreading the message of domestic hate movements in "From *Birth of a Nation* to Stormfront: A Century of Communicating Hate."

After representing his organization in a U.S. Supreme Court *amici* brief supporting the constitutionality of hate crime, I met with civil rights legend Rev. C.T. Vivian at his southern home. I told Reverend Vivian how honored I was to talk to a man who bravely faced down a baton-wielding Alabama sheriff in Selma to secure voting rights for the disenfranchised. He told me that as dangerous as it was, his bravery was easy in one respect, as the battle lines decades ago were clear. A large part of the next effort for civil rights, he told me, would be informational, as the remaining roots of prejudice had to be exposed for them to be eliminated. This diverse and well-researched book is a tribute to him and other pioneers and a continuing, though far safer, part of the same effort.

CHAPTER 1

THE LONG ARC OF JUSTICE: RACE, VIOLENCE, AND THE EMERGENCE OF HATE CRIME LAW

Brian Levin

They had for more than a century before been regarded as beings of an inferior order, and altogether unfit to associate with the white race, either in social or political relations; and so far inferior, that they had no rights which the white man was bound to respect; and that the negro might justly and lawfully be reduced to slavery for his benefit. He was bought and sold, and treated as an ordinary article of merchandise and traffic, whenever a profit could be made by it. This opinion was at that time fixed and universal in the civilized portion of the white race. It was regarded as an axiom in morals as well as in politics, which no one thought of disputing, or supposed to be open to dispute; and men in every grade and position in society daily and habitually acted upon it in their private pursuits, as well as in matters of public concern, without doubting for a moment the correctness of this opinion.

Chief Justice Roger Taney's majority opinion,
Scott v. Sanford (1857, p. 407)

But we do need to remind ourselves that so many of the disparities that exist in the African American community today can be directly traced to inequalities passed on from an earlier generation that suffered under the brutal legacy of slavery and Jim Crow.

Segregated schools were, and are, inferior schools; we still haven't fixed them, 50 years after *Brown v. Board of Education* (1954), and the inferior education they provided, then and now, helps explain the pervasive achievement gap between today's black and white students.

> Legalized discrimination—where blacks were prevented, often through violence, from owning property . . . meant that black families could not amass any meaningful wealth to bequeath to future generations. That history helps explain the wealth and income gap between black and white, and the concentrated pockets of poverty that persists in so many of today's urban and rural communities.
>
> Presidential candidate Barack Obama, "A More Perfect Union," Address, March 18, 2008; Philadelphia, PA.

In twenty-first-century America, the relatively new concept of hate crime is rightfully viewed under a contemporary prism. This includes a focus on a range of different prejudices analyzed across numerous fields of study. While the disciplines of psychology, public policy, criminology, political science, sociology, and even genetics have offered valuable insight into the nature of hate crimes and society's response to them, they frequently leave something valuable out of the discussion. What is often ignored is the context of how our oldest legal foundations made the state a primary party to both the perpetration and continuation of racial violence, well before the term *hate crime* ever entered into the English lexicon.

Notwithstanding the obvious differences in scope, timing, government sanction, and terminology, bigoted violence today serves the same purpose that it did in prior centuries. Dr. Barbara Perry's (2001) assessment of contemporary hate crime as an enforcer of social order on the basis of characteristics such as race concludes that it is "a mechanism of power intended to sustain somewhat precarious hierarchies, through violence and threats of violence (verbal and physical). It is generally directed toward those whom our society has traditionally stigmatized and marginalized" (p. 3).

Bigoted violence today enforces unjust social hierarchies in much the same way that slavery and other racially based human rights deprivations did in the past. The result, then, was a racially stratified society built on precepts of inferiority and compelled by a fierce combination of an unrelenting legal system and brutal violence. As centuries slowly turned, so did the role of law. Law shifted from an oppressive instrument of race-based violence and deprivation to an imperfect protector of civil rights. This rich but often disturbing evolution of legal history has created a template not only for the creation of modern hate crime law, but also for its continuing expansion to include other protected groups beyond race.

Generically, *hate crime* refers to discriminatory criminal acts committed because of someone's actual or perceived membership in a particular socially identifiable status group. Status characteristics are those material attributes, like race or gender, that are common to identifiable classes of people that society recognizes through law, science, tradition, or custom. Hate crime laws and other modern legal protections on the basis of status came about only after a lengthy history during which such markers were used as a pretext for unfair treatment and the deprivation of rights (B. Levin, 2002).

Discrimination refers to treating similarly situated classes of people differently without a legal or sufficient basis because of those characteristics (B. Levin, 2002). Central to the original concept of discrimination law is not the elimination of every act of differential treatment among people, but rather certain invidious differential treatments for illegitimate reasons (Ely, 1980). While some critics decry contemporary hate crime laws as a new phenomenon of divisive "identity politics" and the latest incarnation of legal "moral pork barrel," these laws are a subset of much older civil rights and antidiscrimination laws (Jacobs & Potter, 1998; Jenness & Broad, 1997).

THE PLACE OF RACE

Race is a ubiquitous but inexact way of grouping people together into socially definable groups by certain physical traits and geographic ancestry. Despite major societal advances across several fronts and the unraveling of the flawed precepts underlying racist theories, racial victimizations remain the most frequent type of hate crime (Federal Bureau of Investigation [FBI], 1992–2008). Contemporary discussions on the significance of race have been complicated by a brutal history, ambiguous definitions, malevolent and shifting applications, and conflicting scholarly theories across different disciplines. Even within various disciplines, like genetics, a vigorous debate continues as to whether race is relevant or conversely merely a biased anachronistic social construct.

Sociologist Tomas Almaguer (1994) contends that "race is fundamentally a socially conferred status whose anthropological and biological underpinnings are dubious at best, how and where racial lines are drawn is an open question and the possibility for contestation always exists" (p. 9). Some researchers maintain that despite flaws and past misuse, race still has scientific relevance. Race, they contend, is a proxy for understanding how certain underlying genetic traits, like disease risk, progressed over time in distinct groups with certain ancestral and geographic histories. Opponents, like the *New England Journal of Medicine*, counter that such invocations of race are now unnecessary, as modern science allows for direct analysis of more relevant and specific genetic markers. Another counterargument against reliance on rigid racial distinctions is the fact that modern genetics has established that for many, despite outward appearances, ancestry is frequently mixed (Wade, 2002).

Even with modern science indicating significant widespread similarities across population groups, old prejudices, stereotypes, and disproved race "science" continue to persist in segments of mainstream culture, particularly with regard to the alleged racial inferiority of African Americans. However, race in prior periods was also an exclusionary tag that broadly applied against those whose differences today are viewed primarily in nonracial terms. Some groups such as Latinos and Jews were, and by many current hardened bigots are, viewed as *racial* outcasts. Currently African Americans are the most commonly targeted group for hate crime, with Latinos and Jews constituting the most common targets for ethnic and religious hate crime, respectively.

While these shifting race notions alone were not and are not the only factor in anti-Semitism, such racial designations contributed significantly to their lower status and resultant residual prejudice. Anti-Semitism in Europe over the past 500 years has seen peaceful periods interrupted by mass slaughters, forced conversions, and expulsions in virtually every century. The underlying foundations of anti-Semitism involve a combination of exclusionary notions of religious prejudice for Jews' failure to embrace Christianity, their perceived spread of impure racial traits, and challenges to their patriotism from false political and economic conspiracy theories. Anti-Semitism was never as entrenched in the United States as it was in Europe, but the underlying notions migrated across the Atlantic, albeit in diluted form.

Still, in the United States, for Jews and many others, like Latinos, who were closer to the "white" end of the social hierarchy, racial barriers were often less uniformly and rigidly applied. Native Americans and Asians, however, who lacked European cultural and religious markers, were often placed lower on the scale (Almaguer, 1994). While this chapter focuses on race, various other distinctions have also been similarly used to the detriment of individuals throughout American history.

THE STRUCTURE AND EXTENT OF CIVIL RIGHTS LAWS

One of the primary ways that group-based barriers to meaningful societal participation have fallen has been the enactment of civil rights laws. Race is arguably the oldest and most frequently protected status category under these laws. Structurally, civil rights laws, of which hate crime laws are a subset, consist of all or some of the following components: a protected group, a covered activity, and a prohibition on some type of detrimental conduct. One example is a law that criminalizes racially based voting interference through violence or physical threat. In actual practice, there are numerous factors and questions that complicate matters.

One important issue is determining the extent to which various circumstances or rights require legal coverage. American law, for example, broadly, though not completely, protects the right to work and vote, but these rights are not unlimited. Someone can be denied the vote based on such factors as criminal record, residency, and age. Similarly, a person can be denied certain employment based on merit and a variety of elements that are not offered statutory protection.

There is also the matter of balancing conflicts between various stakeholders. First, the Supreme Court has developed a distinct set of rules that severely restrict the government's ability to treat people differently based on race, although there are exceptions such as limited affirmative action to achieve diversity, research, and census enumeration. The government has greater ability to make distinctions based on gender and even more latitude to make distinctions among other groups. However, the Supreme Court has held that the 14th Amendment's equal protection guarantee precludes group-based animus by government as a rationale for differential treatment of even the least legally protected groups (Ely, 1980; Romer v. Evans, 1996).

When the participants are nongovernmental actors, courts have been forced to balance the conflicting rights of private parties. As shown in the pyramid of hate (see Figure 1.1), prejudicial behavior occurs across a spectrum that includes legal acts that fail to rise to the level of hate crime.

Figure 1.1 Pyramid of Hate

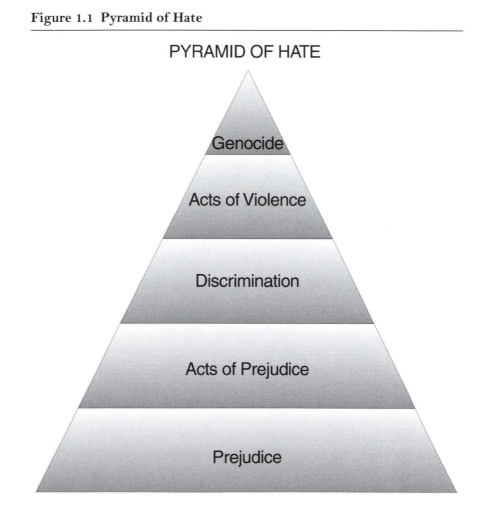

Avoidance and private disparagement are among the more passive acts, followed by more overtly offensive conduct like directed, but nonthreatening, verbal insults. In the United States, the First Amendment generally protects an individual's freedom to nonviolently associate and express beliefs, with limited exceptions such as in the areas of employment, housing, and commerce. However, the expression of abstract forms of racial and other types of hatred is, in most noncommercial circumstances, considered protected speech. Similarly, membership in a nonviolent hate group is protected association. These rights are guarded despite the fact that such protections arguably allow harm to society at large and to members of targeted groups in particular. The conflict between eliminating discrimination, on one hand, and protecting disfavored speech and association, on the other, has been a reoccurring issue for the courts (B. Levin, 2002).

The protection of offensive speech and disfavored association is based on a variety of justifications. One is that the government should, to the extent possible, foster a marketplace of ideas where people can evaluate an array of positions on their own. Another rationale is that the government should avoid interference with certain fundamental individual liberties, such as speech, because of the risk of abuse and a disparity in the balance of power. Similarly, it is likely that unpopular ideas and groups would bear the brunt of enforcement. As legal scholar David Cole (1992) explains, "If the history of political struggles teaches us anything, it is that the majority will most often seek to regulate the speech of the politically powerless" (p. S32).

Some manifestations of prejudice, however, cross the line from speech into conduct. Proceeding up the pyramid of prejudice are actionable, though nonviolent forms of discrimination that deprive people of such things as employment or housing opportunities. Most often, these acts are matters for civil court adjudication, though there is sometimes an overlap with criminal law. When applicable, civil remedies can include injunctions to stop the prohibited conduct, money damages to those victimized, and the introduction of revised institutional training, policies, and procedures. The Supreme Court has held that the First Amendment guarantee of speech and association does not preclude Congress from prohibiting discrimination. The post–Civil War 13th and 14th amendments have been interpreted by the Supreme Court to give Congress greater ability to protect people from discrimination on the basis of race. However, the Court has also held that Congress has some authority to prevent discrimination against a variety of other groups when there is a clear connection to interstate commerce. Congress derives its authority to punish these manifestations of discrimination from its powers under the Constitution's commerce clause to regulate business activities that have an interstate component. In today's interconnected nation, this regulatory authority is quite broad, though not unlimited. States, however, have much wider latitude than the federal government to protect various status groups with their civil and criminal laws (Higginbotham, 1996; B. Levin, 2002; United States. v. Morrison, 2000).

Other forms of prejudice enter into the realm of criminal conduct. The crimes of physical violence and property damage pose distinct issues that differentiate themselves from less obvious manifestations of prejudice. First is the issue of redundancy: most underlying acts, like assault, are already punished by criminal law, irrespective of the perpetrator's motivation. The counterargument is that hate crimes have distinct risks, motives, and harms that make them unique and worthy of separate designation. The situational nexus, target, risk, motive, and severity of seemingly similar conduct are often used to make distinctions relating to criminal punishment. In addition, there is recognition that these crimes broadly affect communities across fragile intergroup lines in distinct ways. Some argue that while state hate crime laws are permissible, the effort for federal hate crime laws is redundant because nearly every state has one.

In addition, there is debate on how antidiscrimination efforts fit into the criminal law arena. Civil antidiscrimination prohibitions are designed to improve increased access by all to various beneficial opportunities. Criminal laws, however, are designed to eliminate, or at least discourage, the effects of antisocial behavior across the board, rather than to equitably redistribute them across the population. Since assaults and vandalisms are already covered by criminal statutes, there are those who argue that what is really being targeted is the expressive idea behind the crime, rather than the crime itself. The counterargument is that intergroup violence has a sweeping discriminatory and terroristic effect on members of targeted groups, who may curtail their participation in an array of activities and interactions out of fear. As law professor James Weinstein (1992) observed,

> The effect of Kristallnacht[1] on German Jews was greater than the sum of the damage to buildings and assaults on individual victims. Unlike vandalism in response to a football game, hate crimes can have a powerful *in terrorem* effect, particularly for members of minority groups who have been or currently are victims of racist violence. (p. 10)

PROMISES BROKEN

The origins of modern hate crime and other antidiscrimination laws are rooted in post–Civil War federal enactments designed to combat the continuing effects of outlawed slavery. Among these were various criminal laws that punished conspirators or governmental actors who deprived others of civil rights. These laws, along with the 13th Amendment's abolition of slavery and the 14th Amendment's guarantee of equal legal protection, were intended to reverse the previous decade's Dred Scott decision. That 1857 decision eliminated Congress's authority to regulate slavery and relied in large part on the entrenched acceptance of racial inferiority as a primary justification. The decision embraced slaves' status as property and dismissed the notion that blacks could be citizens who could have their rights recognized (Higginbotham, 1996; Scott v. Sanford, 1857).

Ironically, the Ku Klux Klan was founded during the same month, December 1865, that the 13th Amendment was ratified. (Chalmers, 1981). The 14th Amendment, ratified in 1868, conferred citizenship on former slaves but did so without explicitly relying on race. As constitutional scholar John Hart Ely (1980) observed, "the decision not to limit the amendment to race, and thus to leave open at least the possibility of a line of growth, seems rather clearly to have been conscious" (p. 149). The amendment conferred dual state and national citizenship on those born within the United States and on naturalized immigrants. The amendment also guaranteed equal protection of the laws, while also protecting the privileges and immunities of citizenship from undue interference by either state or national government. Both the concepts of protection from governmental discrimination and protection from undue governmental interference with fundamental rights, like freedom of speech, are rooted in this amendment (Ely, 1980; Higginbotham, 1996; B. Levin, 2002).

Initially, it was the violence of the Ku Klux Klan that served as a counterweight to the new civil rights legal protections. However, as the Klan soon ebbed, it was the legal system itself that again proved to be the most formidable impediment to the civil rights of blacks and others. State and local Jim Crow laws mandating segregation and unequal treatment of African Americans were enacted. Starting in Tennessee in 1869, these new laws spread throughout the South to destroy emerging federal protections. In the years after the Civil War, the Supreme Court eviscerated the effectiveness of new federal civil rights laws, while also upholding Jim Crow segregation, differential treatment among the races, and the notion of black inferiority. This restrictive interpretation of civil rights protections in a series of cases had widespread significance as it was also extended to laborers, women, and immigrants (B. Levin, 2002).

The Supreme Court's stunning rejection of civil rights protections, however, was perhaps most apparent in appalling cases of racial violence. In 1872 the Court invalidated guilty verdicts in a federal case against two Kentucky white supremacists who hacked four innocent family members to death four years earlier as part of a plan for a wider race war. The case was tried in federal court because Kentucky state law barred the admission of statements by black witnesses. In *Blyew v. United States* (1872), the Court, relying on contorted reasoning, held that the Civil Rights Act of 1866 should operate on behalf of the white defendants, rather than the deceased victims and witnesses—as Congress had intended.

Any doubt as to the Supreme Court's abandonment of blacks to the scourge of racial violence was put to rest in two pivotal 1876 companion cases related to the worst racial massacre of the Reconstruction era. In *United States v. Reese* (1876), the justices invalidated sections of the Enforcement Act of 1870, which punished state officials who obstruct the voting rights of blacks. The Court summarily ruled that Congress lacked the legislative authority to do so. In its holding in *United States v. Cruikshank* (1876), released the same day, the Court dismissed the last remaining indictments of three whites convicted of using violence to prevent blacks from voting. A total of 97 indictments were initially issued, but only 3 had resulted in a conviction. Both cases arose out of the Easter 1873 Colfax massacre in Louisiana, where 100 black state militia members were killed by organized white supremacists while guarding a courthouse. The killings of the militia members by the Klan-inspired White League followed a disputed gubernatorial election. The Supreme Court invalidated the last federal law on the topic, the Civil Rights Act of 1875, in 1883. No other piece of civil rights legislation would be enacted until the late 1950s (Civil Rights Cases, 1883; B. Levin, 2002).

RACE VIOLENCE AT THE DAWN OF A NEW CENTURY

The demise of the Klan by the 1870s did not spell the end of racial violence. A chilling type of spontaneous racial violence emerged that lasted well into the twentieth century: lynching. American lynchings were usually exercises of public mob torture killings, through which victims were mutilated, burned, or hung. Victims were targeted on the accusation of a crime or perceived violation of social mores. From the revolutionary period until the late 1800s, frontier vigilantes undertook most lynching, before being replaced by racists. Of the 4,743 American lynchings, 3,446 victims were African American (Foner & Garraty, 1991). From 1890 to 1930, antilynching laws were enacted in 16 states, but enforcement was limited. Efforts by the National Association for the Advancement of Colored People (NAACP) to pass federal antilynching legislation commenced in 1918. While antilynching bills passed the House of Representatives in 1922, 1937, and 1940, they ultimately failed because of Senate opposition. The case of Leo Frank, a Jewish northerner lynched in Georgia in 1915 after his sentence was commuted by the governor, led to the establishment of the Jewish Anti-Defamation League (ADL). The ADL would play a pivotal role in the establishment of hate crime laws decades later (Foner & Garraty, 1991; B. Levin, 2002).

Mass race riots were yet another form of racist violence directed against African Americans across the United States. From Oklahoma to Florida, to Illinois and elsewhere, 23 murderous race riots erupted from 1910 to 1920 alone. A single race riot in East St. Louis, Illinois, resulted in 47 deaths, with some victims being burned to death in the street. In the aftermath of racial mob violence, Illinois targeted bigoted expression. It became the first state to enact a group libel law that criminalized bigoted, "defamatory" statements relating to racial, religious, or ethnic groups. Some other states followed Illinois's lead, but not the federal government (B. Levin, 2002; Walker, 1994).

While group libel laws survived a Supreme Court test in 1952, they were rarely used, and Illinois rescinded its law by 1961. Constitutional scholars contend that subsequent Supreme Court First Amendment rulings would wholly invalidate such laws today (Beauharnais v. Illinois, 1952; Walker, 1994). Even though group libel type laws are no longer viable in the United States, they are quite common in Canada, the United Kingdom, Germany, France, Australia, and elsewhere in Europe. In other Western nations, expressions of "incitement to racial hatred" and "Holocaust denial" are criminal offenses, but enforcement is somewhat limited (B. Levin, 2002).

The reemergence of the Ku Klux Klan in the United States from 1915 to 1925 also influenced state criminal civil rights legislation. In contrast to the post–Civil War Klan, the Second Era Klan was a national phenomenon as it aggressively targeted new groups in its circle of hatred: Roman Catholics, Jews, and new immigrants. The Second Era Klan was the most successful incarnation of any hate group in America's history. By 1925 the Klan grew to 4.5 million members and included prominent politicians as well as many Protestants in America's heartland. (Chalmers, 1981). Among future leaders who were ensnared by the Klan during this period were Supreme Court Justice Hugo Black and President Harry S. Truman. Both later disavowed their earlier membership (B. Levin, 2002).

A variety of laws targeting the Klan were enacted in states with large politically active Roman Catholic and Jewish populations, mostly in the Northeast and Great Lakes region. Among these were antimasking laws and an unusual New York State law. New York's law not only banned masks, but also forced certain "oath-bound" organizations categorized as illegitimate by legislative decree to register with the state and disclose their membership. The Supreme Court, in 1928, upheld New York's restrictions on disfavored organizations in *Bryant v. Zimmerman* (1928). Ironically, the Court would reverse itself three decades later. In *NAACP v. Alabama* (1958), an anti-Klan civil rights group successfully fought a state effort to compel disclosure and apply other restrictions on private organizations (B. Levin, 2002; Walker, 1994).

THE CIVIL RIGHTS ERA

The civil rights era of the 1950s and 1960s resulted in the greatest renewal of civil rights protections since the post–Civil War period. A chain of court decisions, presidential edicts, and legislation materially advanced antidiscrimination efforts for the first time in decades. The unanimous May 17,

1954, Supreme Court decision in *Brown v. Board of Education* invalidated racial discrimination and segregation in public schools. While there were scattered judicial victories advancing civil rights over the previous half century,
they all operated under the restriction that racial discrimination and segregation were constitutional under the 13th and 14th amendments.

The *Brown* decision was the first decision to invalidate that rule, established in the 1896 *Plessy v. Ferguson* case. Relying in part on a rejection of
social equality and an explicit embrace of notions of racial inferiority, the
Plessy court approved of governmentally sanctioned separation of the races
under the "separate, but equal" theory. Homer Plessy, the original plaintiff,
was segregated into a "colored" railcar, despite the fact that he was only of
one-eighth African blood (Plessy v. Ferguson, 1896).

The forced segregation of the *Plessy* era was almost always unequal, as
blacks were barred from meaningful participation in the main political,
financial, commercial, and educational institutions of the time. As a technical
matter, the Brown ruling only directly applied to public school segregation.
However, the fact that the *Plessy* segregation doctrine had been unequivo-
cally overturned meant that governmentally sanctioned racial discrimination
in other areas would be invalidated as those cases came to court.

Before the passage of new criminal laws in 1968, however, came renewed
but somewhat limited criminal enforcement of some old ones by federal authorities. During most of the period, federal prosecutors were forced to rely
on the same two post–Civil War era statutes enacted during the first era of
Klan violence. Those companion statutes are 18 U.S.C. §241, which prohibits
conspiracies to violate protected rights, and 18 U.S.C. §242, which punishes
government officials who interfere with civil rights. While initially intended
to protect emancipated slaves, they do not explicitly mention race. The two
1968 laws, 18 U.S.C. §245 and 42 U.S.C. §3631, explicitly prohibit race and
other status-related crimes, but only when they interfere with the particular
rights listed in the statutes such as housing (B. Levin, 2002).

During the civil rights era, a reinvigorated Ku Klux Klan was implicated
in many of the dozens of racial killings and bombings that took place across
the American South. The overall prosecution record was often disappointing,
with some cases going unsolved, others ending in state court acquittals, and
still others ending with limited punishment after federal prosecution. Some
homicide prosecutions in Mississippi and Alabama would be delayed for decades. The upswing in 1960s enforcement of civil antidiscrimination laws
and criminal civil rights statutes resulted in crucial tests before the Supreme
Court. The Supreme Court's decisive support of civil rights protections,
particularly those involving Klan violence, stood in stark contrast to their
hostile rulings of a century prior. On the civil side, the Court upheld Congress's use of the Constitution's commerce clause to outlaw discrimination
with respect to business and public accommodation. In the criminal arena,

the Supreme Court decisively upheld the federal government's authority to prosecute violent interference with rights.

Two horrific racial violence cases involving four Klan murders during the summer of 1964 wound their way through the federal courts. Three of those murdered were young civil rights workers James Chaney, a black native Mississippian, and white northerners Andrew Goodman and Michael Schwerner. The convictions in the case, of Klansmen and their co-conspirator Neshoba County deputy sheriff Cecil Price, were the first time a Mississippi jury ever convicted Klansmen or police for the killing of an African American or civil rights worker (Bullard, 1993). Less than one month after the Mississippi trio were killed, a Klan "security force" hunting for civil rights workers on a highway outside of Athens, Georgia, mistakenly ambushed three unarmed black army reservists in the area for military exercises. Lieutenant Colonel Lemuel Penn, an education administrator from Washington, D.C., was killed by a shotgun blast to the neck. Various defendants in the Neshoba, Mississippi, killings and the Penn case unsuccessfully challenged the use of federal criminal civil rights laws up to the U.S. Supreme Court (U.S. v. Guest, 1966; U.S. v. Price, 1966). The national media coverage afforded Klan violence and police brutality against innocent African Americans furthered efforts at statutory reform. The Justice Department's reliance on century-old statutes during the period induced the agency to assist in the promulgation of the Civil Rights Act of 1968, which included new criminal provisions—including 18 U.S.C. §245.

Since 1968, the most frequently charged federal criminal civil rights law applicable to hate crime is 18 U.S.C. §245, "Federally Protected Rights" (the acronym U.S.C. refers to the *United States Code*, where all federal legislation can be found). The law prohibits interference with voting, obtaining government or federally funded benefits or services, accessing federal employment, or participation in a federal jury. Among other things, the law also punishes interference with six other federally protected activities, but only when they are committed on the basis of race, color, religion, or national origin. Those protected activities include enrollment in public education, participation in state programs, obtaining private or state employment, participation in state and local jury service, interstate travel, and the benefits of various types of public accommodations (18 U.S.C. §245). While police-reported cases remained relatively stable, the number of hate crime cases opened by the Federal Bureau of Investigation (FBI) from 2000 to 2005 declined by 60 percent, and the number of agents assigned to hate crime declined by 20 percent (Shukovsky, Johnson, & Lathrop, 2007).

CITY AND STATE INITIATIVES EMERGE AGAINST HATE CRIME

The effort against discriminatory violence shifted in the closing decades of the twentieth century. With the decline of the Klan by the late 1970s, bigoted violence and the resulting response to it changed. First, there was renewed recognition that racial violence was not a uniquely southern problem, but one for increasingly diverse metropolitan areas in the North and West as well. Second, unlike previous eras, much of the momentum against violent bigotry involved efforts at the state and local government levels. Third, while state laws in the early 1980s initially protected primarily on the basis of race, ethnicity, and religion, there was a subsequent expansion by over half of the states to cover categories such as sexual orientation, gender, and disability.

By the early 1980s, municipal police agencies in Boston, New York, and Chicago developed special units, data collection, and training following incidents of racial and anti-Semitic crimes. Starting with Maryland, state police agencies in the Northeast and New England regions became the first to develop specialized response, training, and reporting procedures (B. Levin, 2002).

Human relations and civil rights organizations also played a key role in nascent data collection and monitoring efforts. Starting in 1979, private monitoring organizations, such as the National Anti-Klan Network and the Southern Poverty Law Center's Klanwatch, focused renewed national attention on a resurgence of bigoted violence. In 1979 the ADL published its first comprehensive national annual audit of anti-Semitic incidents. County and municipal human relations commissions as well as advocacy organizations representing such groups as Asian Americans and gays and lesbians, among others, soon followed with their own data collection and outreach efforts. In 1983 the U.S. Commission on Civil Rights issued a report urging further examination of bias-motivated violence. Academic research showing that hate crime was underreported and more severe than previously thought also influenced policy. The consortiums that developed between law enforcement; civil rights groups; victims' rights organizations; and religious, gay, ethnic, and other advocacy groups resulted not only in better data collection and response to victims, but an emphasis on legislative reform as well (B. Levin, 1999, 2002).

In 1981 the ADL drafted model legislation to combat institutional vandalism against houses of worship, cemeteries, and public institutions. The ADL also drafted a model penalty enhancement statute, based in part on federal law, that increased penalties for those who commit certain underlying crimes because of someone's actual or perceived race, religion, or national origin. ADL's model was amended to include sexual orientation later in the decade and gender in 1996 (Anti-Defamation League, 1991; Rosenberg & Lieberman, 2008). By 1985 Rhode Island, Connecticut, New York, Illinois, Massachusetts, Pennsylvania, Oregon, and Washington State had broad criminal laws that punished those who committed crimes on the basis of race, national origin/ethnicity, and religion. Rhode Island had an additional law that protected legal immigrants, while Washington State's law covered disability and Illinois covered creed (National Institute against Prejudice and Violence [NIPV], 1988). By 1991, 28 states had hate crime laws, increasing to 41 by the year 2000 (B. Levin, 1999, 2002; NAPV, 1988).

PUNISHMENT FOR HATE: THE SUPREME COURT DECIDES

The issue of enhanced punishment for crimes of racial bias reached the Supreme Court four times in 10 years. First, the U.S. Supreme Court established rules relating to when a person's hateful beliefs can be used in death penalty cases. In *Barclay v. Florida* (1983), the U.S. Supreme Court upheld the death sentence of a black defendant given by a judge who relied on the defendant's racial motivation for committing random murder. In *Dawson v. Delaware* (1992), the Supreme Court overturned a death sentence that was imposed in part on the basis of a convict's membership in a white supremacist group in a murder case in which his racist beliefs and associations were not relevant to the crime. The Court found that a defendant's abstract racist ideology was an impermissible basis to impose criminal punishment.

In the 1992 case of *R.A.V. v. St. Paul*, the Supreme Court unanimously invalidated a 1989 municipal "hate speech" ordinance used to prosecute a teenage skinhead for burning a cross in the yard of an African American family. The law selectively punished hate symbols only when used to express specific hateful viewpoints, but not others. The justices were sharply divided as to the overall extent of the city's authority (R.A.V. v. St. Paul, 1992). All nine justices agreed that the statute's sweep was too broad by punishing protected speech and symbols used to evoke anger or resentment. Since *Beauharnais*, the Court has regularly held that the First Amendment protects offensive speech and political discourse that fails to rise to the level of a threat, immediate incitement to criminality, or solicitation of a crime. Four of the justices supported the position that it was constitutional to punish expression whose severity went beyond merely offending someone. Since threats and so-called fighting words were traditionally declared to be unprotected by the First Amendment and thus punishable, these justices maintained that it was constitutional for the government to selectively punish certain types of bigoted expression within these unprotected categories.

The prevailing opinion, authored by Associate Justice Antonin Scalia, held differently. The five majority justices ruled that even traditionally unprotected areas of speech are afforded a baseline of protection that prevents the government from selectively punishing certain viewpoints, but not others. They held that punishing certain types of threatening cross burnings, such as those based on racial supremacy, but not others, such as those degrading the mentally ill, violated that principle. The *R.A.V.* decision invalidated hate speech laws in which the criminality hinged solely on the idea expressed through the use of a particular symbol. The ruling also had the additional effect of invalidating speech codes at public universities throughout the United States. In 2003 the Court, however, reasserted the authority of government to punish cross burnings intended to intimidate others (Virginia v. Black, 2003).

The Court's unanimous 1993 decision in *Wisconsin v. Mitchell* upheld the constitutionality of broadly applicable penalty enhancement laws for hate crime. Specifically, the enhancement law at issue punished an offender's discriminatory selection of a victim or property based on the status characteristics of another person, including race, religion, color, national origin, and ancestry. Todd Mitchell was a 19-year-old African American Kenosha, Wisconsin, resident. Mitchell was angered over a scene in the movie *Mississippi Burning*, in which an African American child was beaten by white supremacists as he knelt to pray. Mitchell incited a crowd to viciously beat Gregory Riddick, an innocent, white, 14-year-old passerby. He was convicted of aggravated battery, party to a crime, and sentenced to two years for the underlying assault. He was also assessed another two-year term under the state's hate crime penalty enhancement law for intentionally selecting his victim on account of race, for a total of four years incarceration out of a possible seven-year term (B. Levin, 1999; Wisconsin v. Mitchell, 1993).

In reversing the Wisconsin Supreme Court, the U.S. Supreme Court, in an opinion by then Chief Justice William Rehnquist, cited three basic reasons for affirming the statute. First, while the government may not punish abstract beliefs, it has wide latitude to address motive. Motive is the reason why a person commits a crime. Second, the Court further found that penalty enhancement laws, unlike the statute at issue in *R.A.V.*, were aimed at discriminatory conduct and did not prevent or punish merely hateful expression. In *R.A.V.*, the actual criminality depended not on the hostile use of a particular symbol, but on whether a designated disfavored viewpoint was conveyed by its use. Last, the Court addressed the severity of hate crimes' harms, stating that they are "thought to be more likely to provoke retaliatory crimes, inflict distinct emotional harm on their victims and incite community unrest" (Wisconsin v. Mitchell, 1993, pp. 487–488).

Research has established that hate crimes, in contrast to crime in general, are more likely to involve excessive violence, threats, multiple offenders, serial attacks, greater psychological trauma to victims, a heightened risk of social disorder, and a greater expenditure of resources to resolve (B. Levin, 1999). In comparison to crime generally, hate crimes are seven times as likely to involve attacks against persons. Hate crimes are three times as likely to cause injury and more likely to involve hospitalization (Harlow, 2005; B. Levin,

Figure 1.2 National Crime Victimization Survey (NCVS) Hate versus Nonhate Crime: Violence

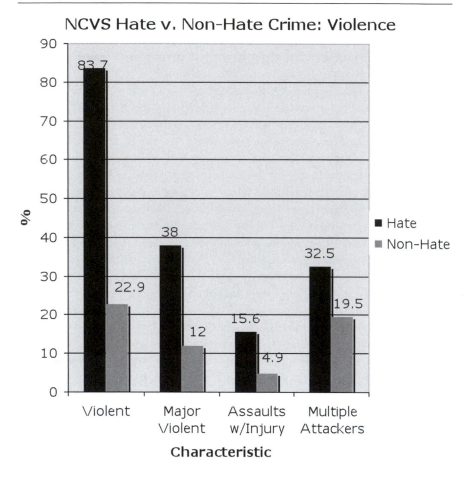

1992–1993; J. Levin & McDevitt, 1993). These crimes are also more likely to involve incidents with multiple offenders (see Figure 1.2).

NEW FEDERAL HATE CRIME REPORTING AND LEGISLATIVE INITIATIVES

Nationally, four new pieces of hate crime legislation were introduced starting in 1990. The first was the Hate Crime Statistics Act, signed into law by President Bush in April 1990. The act, similar to some state laws, initially required the attorney general to collect data voluntarily submitted by the states on crimes motivated by race, religion, sexual orientation, and ethnicity. It was subsequently amended to include disability. The FBI counted, 7,624 hate crime incidents in 2007, of which 50.8 percent were racially motivated. African Americans, who constitute only 12.4 percent of the American population, have consistently been overrepresented as both victims and, to a much lesser extent, offenders since the early 1990s, when national reporting commenced (FBI, 1992–2008). In 2007 antiblack motivation accounted for almost 35 percent of all incidents and about 69 percent of the racially motivated ones. African Americans accounted for 20.8 percent of attackers in all reported hate crimes. Antiwhite attacks accounted for over 10 percent of all hate crime attacks, while 62.9 percent of known offenders were white (FBI, 1992–2008).[2]

Out of 16,000 law enforcement agencies in the nation, 13,241 "participated" in the data collection program in 2007, but only 2,025 actually reported incidents within their jurisdiction. The results varied significantly by state, with New Jersey reporting more hate crime than the combined total of about one dozen other states. The vastly uneven reporting among states probably results not only in an overall undercount, but also in an underrepresentation of those incidents involving African Americans. The three states with the highest proportions of African American citizens, Mississippi, Louisiana, and Georgia, were notable for their lack of reporting, with a combined total of only 44 hate crimes (FBI, 1992–2008; U.S. Census Bureau, 2006–2008).

While blacks, whites, Jews, gays, and Latinos have occupied roughly the same rankings over the past decade as the most frequently targeted victim groups, attacks against far less frequent targets, such as the disabled, appear to be increasing in the most recent periods. Reported attacks to the FBI against the disabled registered significant increases over earlier years, but it is difficult to discern how much of this may reflect increased data collection efficiencies. After the 9/11 terrorist attacks, reported anti-Arab and Islamophobic hate crime soared before a sustained decline to moderately elevated levels by 2007 (FBI, 1992–2008). In some major metropolitan areas, like Los Angeles County, intraminority group attacks, such as those by and between blacks and Latinos, dominate the racial hate crime figures, even though many cases of gang violence are actually excluded (Los Angeles County, 2007). While the number of hate groups has recently increased and some highly publicized crimes sometimes involve hate group members, the number of individuals in these groups are near historic lows. Modern hate crime incidents are much more likely to involve informal associations of young people who are seeking thrills or protecting turf than they are to involve hardened hatemongers (McDevitt, Levin, & Bennett, 2002).

A 2005 Bureau of Justice Statistics (BJS) national household victimization survey also indicated that hate crimes were vastly underreported by and to police. That report found that about 3 percent of all violent crime were hate crimes. Of 191,000 hate crime incidents annually, 92,100, or 43.8 percent, were reported to police, with 17,680, or 8.4 percent, of the total being reported by victims as being confirmed by the police. However, the number of "confirmed" cases surveyed was more than double what was actually reported by police agencies to the FBI during the same reporting period. The BJS study also found a slightly higher level of incidents, 55.4 percent, to be racially motivated (Harlow, 2005).

NEW CRIMINAL MEASURES

In 1994 the Hate Crime Sentencing Enhancement Act was passed. The statute, a penalty enhancement law, increases the sentence for underlying federal offenses by about 30 percent when the fact finder establishes beyond a reasonable doubt that the target is intentionally selected because of the race, color, religion, national origin, ethnicity, gender, disability, or sexual orientation of another (28 U.S.C. §994). The law's practical limitation is that it is only applicable to a relatively small number of substantive underlying federal offenses. In 1996 Congress enacted new legislation broadening coverage and increasing the penalties for church arsons after a series of well-publicized church fires (18 U.S.C. §248).

Initially introduced in 1998, the Matthew Shepard Local Law Enforcement Hate Crime Prevention Act of 2007 failed to come to a full vote. Most observers believe the law will pass in subsequent legislative sessions because of the Democratic majority in Congress. Support for the bill began after a string of nationally publicized hate murders, which included the dragging murder of James Byrd in Jasper, Texas, and the homophobic killing of Wyoming college student Matthew Shepard. The bill would alter the main federal criminal civil rights statute, 18 U.S.C. §245, in two significant ways. First, the bill would extend federal legal protection on the basis of gender, disability, and sexual orientation. However, these categories would only be covered in cases involving interstate commerce because of federal jurisdictional requirements in the Constitution. The other criminal reform the bill provides is a major broadening of the circumstances protected for racially motivated crime, where the federal government has far greater authority. Currently, 18 U.S.C. §245 requires that prosecutors establish both that the victim was attacked because of his or her status and because of his or her exercise of a particular protected activity listed in the statute (B. Levin, 1999). See Table 1.1 for a summary of current hate crime laws.

While there has been a significant expansion in state hate crime law coverage beyond the initially protected categories of race, ethnicity, and religion, race crimes continue to dominate. Over the last two decades, new categories have been added. Of the 45 states with hate crime laws, 28 cover gender, 32 states cover sexual orientation and disability, and fewer than 10 cover transgendered status (Rosenberg & Lieberman, 2008). Even within states that cover newer categories, enforcement varies. Gender, disability, and, to a lesser extent, sexual orientation in nonurban areas tend to generate far fewer reported cases

Table 1.1 Hate Crime Laws

Statute	Description
Federal	
18 USC §241	Punishes conspiracies that interfere with civil rights. No racial motivation needed.
18 USC §242	Punishes government officials who use their authority to interfere with civil rights.
18 USC §245	Punishes interference with particular enumerated rights on the basis of race, color, religion, or national origin.
42 USC §3631	Punishes interference with housing rights on the basis of race, color, religion, sex, or national origin.
Hate Crime Sentencing Enhancement Act (HCSEA)	Increases the penalties by approx. one-third for underlying federal offenses committed on the basis of race, color, religion, national origin, ethnicity, gender, disability, or sexual orientation.
18 USC §247	Increases the coverage and penalties under federal law for attacks against houses of worship.
State	
Hate crime penalty enhancement laws	Increases the sentences for underlying crimes when a fact finder establishes beyond a reasonable doubt that a victim or property is selected on the basis of group characteristics.
Hate crime stand alone laws	Punishes violence, threats, and or property destruction on the basis of group characteristics without the necessity of charging another offense.
Cross burning statutes	Punishes the hostile use of a burning cross on the property of another without the owner's permission.

than older covered categories. Most recently, there has been an increased effort to add homelessness as a category, as over one-half dozen states have seen bills introduced since 2006. The effort comes as recent data suggest that unprovoked, nonrobbery homicides of homeless people for the period 2004–2006 were triple that of all the hate crime homicides tabulated by the FBI for their covered categories (National Coalition for the Homeless, 2007).

As America diversifies, intergroup relations and its legal system have advanced to the point where an African American has been elected president, and violent prejudice is not nearly as entrenched as it has been in past centuries. However, if intergroup violence is a barometer of the continuing reach of ignorance, stereotypes, and prejudice, there is still much work to be done. Hate crime and discrimination, while diminished, remain daily occurrences that continue to exact a toll not only on victims, but on the intergroup bonds that cement civil society. Dr. King's inspiring vision of this continuing effort as a journey is as true today as it was four decades ago: "The arc of the moral universe is long, but it bends toward justice" (King & Washington, 1986, p. 52).

NOTES

1.   Kristallnacht, or "night of broken glass," was a massive two-day coordinated exercise of Nazi terror and rioting that took place on November 9–10, 1938, against Germany's Jewish community. At its conclusion, 91 were killed; thousands of people and possessions were seized; and thousands of synagogues, homes, and businesses were attacked or destroyed. Shortly thereafter, World War II and the Nazi Holocaust began (Gilbert, 2006).

2.   The offender data appear to include Hispanic in the white offender data but not in the "antiwhite" attacks.

REFERENCES

Almaguer, T. (1994). *Racial fault lines: The historical origins of white supremacy in California*. Berkeley: University of California Press.
Anti-Defamation League. (1991). *Hate crime statutes: A 1991 status report*. New York: Author.
Barclay v. Florida, 463 U.S. 939 (1983).
Beauharnais v. Illinois, 343 U.S. 250 (1952).
Blyew v. United States, 80 U.S. 581 (1872).
Brown v. Board of Education, 347 U.S. 483 (1954).
Bryant v. Zimmerman, 278 U.S. 63 (1928).
Bullard, S. (Ed.). (1993). *Free at last: A history of the civil rights movement and those who died in the struggle*. Montgomery, AL: Southern Poverty Law Center.
Chalmers, D. M. (1981). *Hooded Americanism*. New York: Franklin Watts.
Civil Rights Cases, 109 U.S. 3 (1883).
Cole, D. (1992, July 29). Free speech because of inequality, not in spite of it. *Legal Times*, p. S32.
Dawson v. Delaware, 503 U.S. 159 (1992).
Ely, J. (1980). *Democracy and distrust: A theory of judicial review*. Cambridge, MA: Harvard University Press.
Enforcement Act, 16 Stat. 140 (1870).
Federal Bureau of Investigation. (1992–2008). *Hate crimes in the United States: 1991–2007*. Washington, DC: U.S. Department of Justice.

Foner, E., & Garraty, J. (Eds.). (1991). *The readers companion to American history.* Boston: Houghton Mifflin.

Gilbert, M. (2006). *Kristallnacht: Prelude to destruction.* London: HarperCollins.

Harlow, C. W. (2005, November). *Hate crime reported by victims and police* (NCJ No. 209911). Washington, DC: Bureau of Justice Statistics.

Hate Crime Sentencing Enhancement Act, 28 U.S.C. § 994 (1994).

Hate Crime Statistics Act, 28 U.S.C. § 534 (1990).

Higginbotham, A. L. (1996). *Shades of freedom.* New York: Oxford University Press.

Jacobs, J., & Potter, K. (1998). *Hate crimes: Criminal law & identity politics.* New York: Oxford University Press.

Jenness, V., & Broad, K. (1997). *Hate crimes: New social movements and the politics of violence.* Hawthorne, NY: Aldine de Gruyter.

King, M., & Washington, J. (Ed.). (1986). *A testament of hope: The essential writings and speeches of Martin Luther King.* New York: HarperCollins.

Levin, B. (1992–1993). Bias crimes: A theoretical and practical overview. *Stanford Law & Policy Review, 4,* 165–180.

Levin, B. (1999). Hate crime: Worse by definition. *Journal of Contemporary Criminal Justice, 15,* 6–21.

Levin, B. (2002). From slavery to hate crime laws: The emergence of race and status-based protection in American criminal law. *Journal of Social Issues, 58,* 227–245.

Levin, J., & McDevitt, J. (1993). *Hate crimes: The rising tide of bigotry & bloodshed.* New York: Plenum.

Los Angles County. (2007). *Hate crime report: 2006.* Los Angeles: Author.

Matthew Shepard Local Law Enforcement Hate Crime Prevention Act, S. 1105 (2007).

McDevitt, J., Levin, J., & Bennett, S. (2002). Hate crime offenders: An expanded typology. *Journal of Social Issues, 58,* 303–317.

NAACP v. Alabama, 357 U.S. 449 (1958).

National Coalition for the Homeless. (2007). *Hate, violence and death on Main Street: A report on hate crimes and violence against people experiencing homelessness, 2006.* Washington, DC: Author.

National Institute against Prejudice and Violence. (1988). *Striking back at bigotry.* Baltimore: Author.

Obama, B. (2008, March 18). *Remarks by Barack Obama: "A more perfect union."* Retrieved April 14, 2008, from http://www.csmonitor.com/2008/0319/p25s01-uspo.html

Perry, B. (2001). *In the name of hate: Understanding hate crimes.* New York: Routledge.

Plessy v. Ferguson, 163 U.S. 537 (1896).

R.A.V. v. St. Paul, 505 U.S. 377 (1992).

Romer v. Evans, 517 U.S. 620 (1996).

Rosenberg, D., & Lieberman, M. (2008). *Hate crime laws: 2000.* New York: Anti-Defamation League.

Scott v. Sanford, 60 U.S. 393 (1857).

Shukovsky, P., Johnson, T., & Lathrop, D. (2007, April 25). FBI opening far fewer civil rights inquiries. *Seattle Post Intelligencer.* Retrieved April 14, 2008, from http://seattlepi.nwsource.com/national/313178_fbicivilrights26.html

United States v. Cruikshank, 92 U.S. 542 (1876).

United States v. Guest, 383 U.S. 745 (1966).

United States v. Morrison, 529 U.S. 598 (2000).

United States v. Price, 383 U.S. 787 (1966).

United States v. Reese, 92 U.S. 214 (1876).

U.S. Census Bureau. (2006–2008). *American fact finder*. Retrieved April 14, 2008, from http://factfinder.census.gov/home/saff/main.html?_lang=en

U.S. Religious Landscape Survey. (2008). *Pew Forum on Religion & Public Life*. Retrieved April 14, 2008, from http://religions.pewforum.org/reports

Virginia v. Black, 538 U.S. 343 (2003).

Wade, N. (2002, July 30). Race is seen as real guide to track roots of disease. *New York Times*, p. F1.

Walker, S. (1994). *Hate speech: The history of an American controversy*. Lincoln, NE: Bison Books.

Weinstein, J. (1992). First amendment challenges to hate crime legislation. *Criminal Justice Ethics, 11*, 6–18.

Wisconsin v. Mitchell, 508 U.S. 476 (1993).

CHAPTER 2

HISTORICAL LESSONS: WHAT'S PAST MAY BE PROLOGUE

Carolyn Turpin-Petrosino

The federal government's definition of hate crime is as follows: "a criminal offense against a person or property motivated in whole or in part by an offender's bias against a race, religion, disability, ethnic origin or sexual orientation" (U.S. Department of Justice, n.d., para. 2). What makes hate crime distinct from other crime categories is its impact on a free society. The perpetrator sees the victim as inherently inferior and unworthy of the equality, justice, or freedom guaranteed by the Constitution due to his or her race, religion, sexual orientation, or other status condition. Should hate crimes achieve their intended collective effects, the civil rights of whole segments of the U.S. population would be compromised.

What has society learned about the problem of hate crime? The purpose of this chapter is to provide a historical perspective of hate crime in the United States. Given the scope of this topic, I focus here on the broad similarities between historical and modern hate-motivated acts and related factors. Finally, this chapter will explore the question, Is the past prologue for hate crimes? Are modern and future hate crimes a function of historical hate crime patterns?

A HATE CRIME IS A HATE CRIME IS A . . .

On a beautiful autumn afternoon, a group of individuals going about their daily routine was suddenly and viciously attacked in their own community by those who viewed them as disturbingly different and threatening. The aim of the attackers was to send a message: these individuals were not welcomed here, even in their living separately from the majority, because of their "difference," "inferiority," and "dangerousness," (Carnes, 1995). The attack nearly accomplished the murder of most of the male members of the group, including children.

This incident occurred on October 30, 1838, in Caldwell County, Missouri. The victims were Mormons. The perpetrators were local militiamen, who carried out the orders of Governor Boggs to "exterminate or drive out the Mormons from the State" (Carnes, 1995, p. 26). This event occurred over 150 years ago, yet it possesses characteristics of modern-day hate crimes. In fact, there are many historical incidents that resemble the hate crimes of today. The targeting of others due to their race, ethnicity, religion, or other perceived differences has been common throughout American history (Feagin, 2001; Perlmutter, 1992).

THE SEVENTEENTH THROUGH THE NINETEENTH CENTURIES: WHEN HATE CRIMES WERE NOT

Many bias-motivated acts were not considered illegal during earlier times (Jordan, 1968; Miller, 1979; Petrosino, 1999; Stampp, 1956; Steinfield, 1973; Takaki, 1994a, 1994b; Wells-Barnett, 1969). The reasons for this include the absence of constitutional—or statutory—protections, or other legal rights of the victims; the denial of their very personhood; and the direct involvement of governments and other authorities in historical hate acts (Petrosino, 1999). One of the ironies in recorded history is that while acts such as assault, theft, murder, and rape were crimes under the common law, these same acts were less likely to be viewed as criminal when motivated by racism, ethnocentrism, or classism (Hoffer, 1992; Jordan, 1968). Few would argue that the common law was constructed to protect the poor to the same extent as white property-owning males (Mann, 1993; Perlmutter, 1992; Steinfield, 1973; Takaki, 1994a, 1994b; Walker, Spohn, & DeLone, 1996).

The historical incidents that were selected for this review possess characteristics similar to those found in modern hate crimes. They include the following: (1) victims are more likely to be members of racial or ethnic minority groups (Bureau of Justice Assistance, 1997; Hamm, 1994); (2) victim groups are disadvantaged economically and politically relative to the majority group (Hamm, 1993); (3) prevailing cultural values and traditions situate victim groups as suitable for discriminatory and unequal treatment (Perry, 2001); and (4) for the perpetrator, victim groups represent a serious threat to his or her quality of life (i.e., economic stability and/or physical safety; Levin & McDevitt, 1993; Ridgeway, 1990). An additional criterion was added to underscore the power imbalance between victims and perpetrators: would the legal authorities of that time respond to the bias-motivated acts in a similar fashion if the victims were white Anglo-Saxon Protestants and the attackers were racial and/or ethnic minorities? The incidents selected occurred during the seventeenth, eighteenth, and nineteenth centuries and are drawn from the historical experiences of racial and ethnic minorities in America. Hate crimes were not solely experienced by members of these groups, but their victimization is well documented due to its constancy.

The following section describes the sample incidents and the prevailing social climates surrounding them. They are drawn from four time periods: pre–Civil War, post–Civil War, civil rights, and post–civil rights eras.

THE HISTORICAL EVOLUTION OF HATE CRIME

Pre–Civil War (1600s–1865)[1]

Many historians describe the early contacts between Europeans and Native Americans as nonviolent. However, the nature of these contacts changed with the increasingly self-serving acts of white colonists and early American leaders (Sanders, 1978; Spindler, 1972; Steinfield, 1973; Tebbel & Jennison, 1960). As Native Americans resisted white encroachment, interferences, and deceptive practices, they were depicted as dangerous and barbaric people (Harjo, 1998; Riding In, 1998). This increasingly negative imagery of Native Americans was supported by Jacksonian ideology, which shaped cultural values, social practices, and political thought from the 1820s to 1860s. Berlet and Lyons (2000) describe Jacksonian perspectives as advocating "an inclusive class ideology of White male egalitarianism with the hard racism of exclusion, terror, and suppression toward people of color" (p. 42). This social climate would facilitate egregious bias-motivated acts against Native Americans.

The Near-Genocide of the Yuki and Cheyenne Indians

The Yuki of northern California numbered approximately 5,000 when first encountered by white settlers in 1848. At this point in American history, atrocities were routinely committed against Native Americans by white settlers, local authorities, and the U.S. Cavalry in the form of kidnapping, theft, fraud, forced indentured servitude, sexual assault, starvation, and murder (Hendricks, 2006; Riding In, 1998). Targeting the Yuki for similar treatment, therefore, was not unusual. Military records indicate interest in their extermination to increase white settlements in the area (Gundersen & Smelser, 1994; Miller, 1979). Upon the execution of planned attacks, authorized by California's governor Peter Burnett, the Yuki lost 90 percent of their population in a 32-year period (Chalk & Jonassohn, 1990). The Cheyenne were victims of similar acts, as described in the 39th *U.S. Congressional Record*, 2nd session, Senate Report 156. The following is an account of a mass murder that occurred on November 28, 1864, as told by eyewitness Robert Bent (Brown, 1970):

> When the troops fired, the Indians ran. . . . I think there were six-hundred Indians in all . . . about sixty [men]. . . . I saw five squaws under a bank for shelter . . . but the soldiers shot them all. . . . There seemed to be indiscriminate killing. . . . There were some thirty or forty squaws collected in a hole for protection; they sent out a little girl about six years old with a white flag . . . ; she had not proceeded but a few steps when she was shot and killed. . . . I saw one squaw cut open with an unborn child. . . . I saw the body of a leader, with the privates cut off, and I heard a soldier say he was going to make a tobacco pouch out of them. (p. 73)

Given the antagonistic relationship between whites and Native Americans, and the emphasis on white expansionism, these acts appear to be racially motivated. Evidence of racial animus toward Native Americans permeated white American culture at that time, and these brutal acts clearly indicate a potent disregard of the victims' humanity (Berthrong, 1963). In fact it was not until 1891 that the U.S. Supreme Court declared that Indians were *human beings* (Kennedy, 1959).

Transporting and Holding Black Slaves

Historical perceptions of Africa and African people were articulated through a Eurocentric perspective until the latter part of the twentieth century (Fredrickson, 1991; Jordan, 1968; Pieterse, 1992). When the focus on the New World became economically driven and slavery was introduced as a significant means to pursue that end, the utility of a particular African image became necessary. African skin color and non-Christian religious practices made it simpler for the British and others to view Africans as uncivilized heathens and to associate blackness with negativity, evil, and foulness (Jordan, 1968). Soon, it became rational to associate heathenism—with its inferences of inferiority—with blackness. This constructed image of Africans provided justification for the eventual institutionalization of enslavement.

By 1625 being African became synonymous with being enslavable. The perception of the African as inferior did not change once they were brought to the colonies. From their earliest experiences in colonial America—even predating institutionalized slavery—Africans were treated in a debased and discriminatory manner. With the advent of legalized African slavery in the colonies and the enactment of the Black Codes beginning in 1640, blacks became distinguished from all other groups in America (Morris, 1996). These collective initiatives reinforced the racial animus and prejudiced attitudes held toward this group.

The transoceanic voyage from the west coast of Africa to the Caribbean and then to the colonies proved to be extraordinarily brutal for slaves. The following account is an observer's description of the nature of the Middle Passage voyage (Perlmutter, 1992):

> The sense of misery and suffocation was so terrible that in the 'tweendecks—where the height was sometimes only eighteen inches, so that the unfortunate slaves could not turn around, were wedged immovably in fact, and chained to the deck by the neck and legs—that the slaves not infrequently would go mad before dying or suffocating. In their frenzy some killed others in the hope of procuring more room to breathe. (p. 18)

Conservative estimates place the death toll during the voyages at approximately 100,000 (Higginbotham, 1978). Once slavery was well established, it received the legal status of *perpetual* (Jordan, 1968), making the loss of freedom lifelong and complete. The status of children born to slaves was clarified when slavery was defined by law as an *inherited* condition (Higginbotham, 1978). Slaveholders employed various techniques to coerce blacks to accept their condition. Although maintaining institutionalized slavery was difficult, the economic rewards it yielded encouraged those involved to commit whatever acts were necessary to sustain it (Gundersen & Smelser, 1994).

The New York Draft Riots

The New York City Draft Riots of 1863, which were caused by a confluence of factors including new federal policies and laws, also involved racially motivated violence (Murdock, 1967). Within a short span of time, proslavery supporters in New York witnessed the enactment of the Emancipation Proclamation (September 1862) and the Enrollment Act of Conscription (March 1863). Together, these laws sought to change the legal status of blacks in America from enslaved to free. The conscription law, which particularly impacted those in lower socioeconomic classes, required white males to fight in the Civil War for black liberty. Since blacks were not citizens in 1863 (that would not occur until 1868), they were exempt from the draft. These two laws added to the already existing racial tensions between Irish and German immigrants and free blacks. What resulted was the Draft Riots, several days of racial violence including the vicious murder of at least 11 blacks and the wanton destruction of property, which symbolized black progress (Harris, 2003). Black men were particularly targeted. Some were beaten, stabbed, hanged, and their bodies then burned. Since the Irish were among the poorest white immigrants who were particularly threatened by the prospect of competing for jobs with newly freed blacks, they were the principal perpetrators of the carnage that took place.

Kearneyism

Asian laborers were invited to the United States to assist in the construction of the transcontinental railroad and to work Hawaiian sugar plantations (Healey, 1995). Initially viewed as an industrious people, the images of Asians soon deteriorated. Ideas advocated by the eugenics movement (which occurred between the 1880s and the 1940s) centered on racial classifications, and non-European groups, such as Asians, did not fair well in these schemes. Some contended that the adult Mongoloid was equivalent to an adolescent Caucasian (Gould, 1981). In fact, many stereotypes used to depict Native Americans and Africans were used against Asians (Takaki, 1994b):

> White workers called the Chinese "nagurs" [*sic*], and a magazine cartoon depicted a Chinese man as a bloodsucking vampire with slanted eyes, a pigtail, dark skin, and thick lips. Like blacks, the Chinese were described as heathen, morally inferior, savage, childlike, and lustful. Chinese women were condemned as a "depraved class" and said to resemble Africans. (p. 66)

Several states enacted laws during the 1800s to constrain Asian liberties. These statutes initially segregated them and culminated in an effort to banish Asians from the United States. The pervasiveness of anti-Asian attitudes during this period is also well documented. Even President Theodore Roosevelt (1901–1909) believed America should be preserved as a heritage for whites and that Asians should not live here (Takaki, 1994b). The Native Sons of the Golden West, a nativist organization that sought to minimize the presence of racial minorities in California, is credited with the following statement (Chronister, 1992): "that the state of California should remain what it had always been and God himself intended it shall always be—the White Man's Paradise . . . the 31st star shall never become dim or yellow" (pp. 40–41).

Asian unemployment surged at the completion of the railway but was short-lived. Many took jobs that whites declined, or they started their own businesses. While Asians found steady work, white unemployment was a growing problem. Labor leader Denis Kearney and others inflamed anti-Asian sentiments by consistently arguing that Chinese workers caused white unemployment (Steinfield, 1973). The scapegoating of Asians by Kearney, along with preexisting norms of prejudice and racism, created an atmosphere that prompted spontaneous acts of racially motivated violence against Asians. During this period, Asians were robbed, assaulted, and murdered, and Asian-owned businesses were vandalized or destroyed. But, because Asians lacked basic civil liberties, little was done through the courts to respond to their victimization. The murder of Asians became so casual that the print media frequently chose not to report its occurrence (Steinfield, 1973; Takaki, 1994b).

Post–Civil War (1865–1949)

Lynching

The history of lynching in American and its relevance to modern hate crime has been underemphasized. Named for Charles Lynch, who popularized the act during the eighteenth century, lynching, or lynch law, involved the unlawful killing of an individual thought to have violated important social norms and/or the law. These extralegal acts were usually carried out publicly by mobs. Although whites were occasionally lynched, blacks were disproportionately targeted. The victimization rate of blacks in southern states was 350 percent greater than that of whites (Cutler, 1969; Dennis, 1984; Foner and Garraty, as cited in Levin, 2002; Wells-Barnett, 1969).

Black lynching in southern states escalated following emancipation in response to federal government efforts to remove legal constraints on black participation in political, social, and economic systems. Historical records reflect how easily blacks were selected for lynching (Wells-Barnett, 1969): "John Hughes of Moberly (Missouri) and Isaac Lincoln of Fort Madison (S. Carolina) and Will Lewis in Tullahoma, Tenn. suffered death for no more serious charge than that they were 'saucy' to white people" (p. 17). The casual nature of black lynching reveals the ubiquitous nature of the racial animus existing at that time.

Perlmutter (1992) states that "lynching was so common it was impossible to keep accurate accounts" (p. 151). The following is an eyewitness report of a July 15, 1921, lynching in Moultrie, Georgia that was published in a local newspaper (Steinfield, 1973):

> Williams was brought from Moultrie on Friday night by sheriffs. . . . Saturday court was called. . . . The trial took half an hour. Then Williams, surrounded by fifty sheriffs armed with machine guns, started out of the courthouse door toward the jail. . . . 500 poor pecks rushed the sheriffs, who made no resistance. . . . They tore the negro's clothing off. . . . The negro was unsexed, as usual, and made to eat a portion of his anatomy. . . . The negro was chained to [a] stump. . . . The pyre was lit and a hundred men, women, old and young . . . joined hands and danced around the negro while he burned. (pp. 40–42)

Ku Klux Klan Violence (First and Second Eras)

The Civil War (1861–1865) confronted Southern slavery and its ending brought the first efforts to dismantle it. But the idea of black freedom, equality, and black participation in the political process via Reconstruction was repugnant to many white Southerners. To hinder these developments the Ku Klux Klan formed in 1866 in Pulaski, Tennessee. A secret society, the Klan utilized terroristic and violent tactics to stop blacks from exercising newly gained civil liberties and to restore white control over every major aspect of black life. Black community leaders as well as sympathetic whites where particularly targeted. In pursuing these activities, the Klan laid the foundation for the white supremacist movement in the United States. Historically, the Klan demonstrated three distinct periods of onset activity, which occurred in 1866, 1915, and 1954. During the first period, the Klan is suspected of murdering over 1,500 blacks in Georgia alone (Berlet & Lyons, 2000). The second period saw the Klan develop the largest and most diverse membership, attracting individuals from various education and socioeconomic levels. Klan membership peaked at nearly 5 million during this period (Dobratz & Shanks-Meile, 1997; Potok, 2001). Despite the Klan's ability to wield political influence—even on the national level—and obtain a measure of respectability in the eyes of many, its members frequently engaged in violent bias-motivated behavior. Only now, Roman Catholics, Jews, and other whites who were empathetic to the plight of blacks were added as legitimate targets.

Historical Incident: Anti-Semitism and the Leo Frank Lynching

Anti-Semitism predates the discovery of the New World, therefore these attitudes existed in America since its beginning. The scapegoating of Jews, the establishment of Jewish quotas, portraying Jewish religious practices as sinister, and committing discriminatory acts against them were commonplace. The resurgence of the Ku Klux Klan, beginning in 1915, saw the targeting of Jews residing in the South and Midwest. "A whole new breed of hatemonger developed on the American scene [at that time] that thrived on the spread of hate propaganda against Jews" (Steinfield, 1973, p. 162).

The National Pencil Company in Atlanta, Georgia was the site of the rape and murder of 14-year-old employee Mary Phagan. Despite dubious evidence, Jewish owner Leo Frank was charged with her murder and placed on trial. Local newspapers waged blatant anti-Semitic campaigns against Frank during the trial. Conviction followed, and Frank was sentenced to death. His sentence was later commuted to life by Georgia's governor; an action not well received by many. On August 16, 1916, while Frank was housed in Milledgeville Prison, a group of 25 men entered, overpowered guards, and removed him. After driving to Marietta, Georgia, Frank was lynched by hanging. His murder is representative of the stark determination of those motivated by anti-semitism and hatred.

Historical Incident: Residential Move-In Violence

Beginning in the 1890s, blacks began to leave the rural areas of the South for northern cities. A half million relocated during World War I, and approximately 6 million more followed just after the war, and through the 1960s (Meyer, 2000). Along with the potential for a better life, migration also meant that their racial victimization would no longer occur just in the South. Most blacks settled in major metropolitan areas in the North that were largely racially segregated. Black families made economic gains, but seeking better neighborhoods meant moving into predominately white residential areas, which was met with great resistance.

When white initiatives, such as opportunistic zoning regulations, improvement associations, and race-restrictive covenants, failed to maintain segregated neighborhoods, threats and violence became the next strategy. Black families were frequently subjected to racially motivated harassment and intimidation. Meyer (2000) provides an account of the notes received by a black family that moved into a white area of Brooklyn:

> If you move into that house, one warned, it will be the worst days [*sic*] work that you ever did. . . . You should know better than to move where you are not wanted. Another letter came from the Klan. There are five of us for each Nigger on Staten Island. (p. 34)

Detroit saw appalling racially motivated violence as black families attempted to settle into better appointed neighborhoods occupied by white families. Meyer notes (2000, p. 37), "In early July, a mob of about 1,000 whites gathered to taunt the family of John Fletcher, which had recently moved to a white block on the city's west side. Demonstrators yelled, 'lynch him. Lynch him." Chicago violence was far worse than that which occurred in New York and Detroit. Fifty-eight racially motivated bombings occurred in the city between 1917 and 1921.

Civil Rights Era (1950–1979)

Prior to *Brown v. the Board of Education* (1954), Black life was encumbered by two U.S. Supreme Court decisions: *Dred Scott v. Sandford* (1857) and *Plessy v. Ferguson* (1896). In the *Scott* decision, the Court established that people of African descent could never be citizens of the United States and were little more than objects of property. Approximately 40 years later, the *Plessy* decision established the legal doctrine of separate but equal, prescribing segregated public facilities. Together, these decisions codified and affirmed white supremacy and black inferiority in America. However, the *Brown* decision upended both *Scott* and *Plessy*. The Supreme Court decision in *Brown* announced that segregation was inherently unequal and violated the equal protection clause of the 14th Amendment. Black citizens have rights and are warranted the protection provided in the 14th Amendment. The modern civil rights movement thus began—as well as the reawakening of hate-motivated crimes.

But backlash from *Brown* took many forms, such as the publication of the 1956 Southern Manifesto. Signed by 100 U.S. senators and congressmen from 11 southern states, the manifesto stated that the Supreme Court went beyond its mandate in reaching the *Brown* decision. It went on to state that the signing members of the manifesto were committed to "resist forced integration by any lawful means" (Dudley, 1996, p. 70). The fear that integration would lead to "racial mixing" and, in turn, the demise of the white race was common among many whites in the United States. Alabama governor John Patterson reiterated his commitment to fight the *Brown* decision in his 1959 inaugural speech (Dudley, 1996):

> I will oppose with every ounce of energy I possess . . . any mixing of the white and Negro races in the classrooms of this state. . . . Any attempt by the federal government or anyone else to integrate the schools of this state by force would cause turmoil, chaos and violence. (p. 78)

These pivotal Supreme Court decisions that first denied and then established the civil rights of black Americans reflect the turbulence surrounding the very idea of black equality in America.

Historical Incident: The War against Integration

With the *Brown* decision and the start of the civil rights movement, racially motivated crimes increased between 1954 and 1965. Much of the violence was Klan activity and included, according to the U.S. Justice Department, "seventy bombings in Georgia and Alabama, 30 Negro church burnings in Mississippi, the sadistic castration of a black man in Birmingham, ten racial killings in Alabama, plus the . . . murders of three civil rights workers in Mississippi" (Sims, 1996, p. 95). This spree of Klan violence is identified as the third onset period of the Klan. The Mississippi White Knights were responsible for the most egregious terrorist attacks during this period. Klan leaders urged members to engage in strategic attacks against civil rights participants. Consequently, "there were 80 racially motivated assaults, including 35 shootings, 20 church arsons, and five murders" (p. 235) [Bullard, 1993; Chalmers, 1981] as cited in Levin, 2002).

Post–Civil Rights Era (1980 to Present)

The 1980s saw a surge in hate crime activity across the country and a growth in neo-Nazi skinheads and other white supremacist groups. It is during this period in the post–civil rights era that bias-motivated crimes are first referred to as hate crimes. A proposal of the federal bill for the Hate Crime Statistics Act of 1990 coined the term, which was later popularized by the media (Jacobs & Potter, 2000). This criminal activity, newly identified as hate crimes or bias crimes, was made more visual by the Justice Department's hate crimes report, titled *Hate Crime Statistics*. This annual publication of hate crime incidence was now required as a result of the Hate Crime Statistics Act.

Hate crimes during this period ranged from malicious damage to property, verbal threats, and intimidation to assaults and murder. In fact, many hate crimes of this period are similar to the residential move-in violence of the post–Civil War era. However, there are factors that distinguish hate crime trends of the post–civil rights period from those of previous periods: globalization, exploitation of the military, and the violent nature of youth in the hate movement.

Globalization

As early as the 1960s, leaders in the American Nazi Party met periodically with European national socialists. But today, the Internet makes contact between such groups effortless. According to some reports, members of U.S.-based hate groups are associating more frequently with their European counterparts (Anti-Defamation League, 1995; Southern Poverty Law Center, 2001). This interaction is encouraged by pan-Aryanism, an ideological belief in the hate movement that describes a common struggle among all whites against the destructive forces of Jews, racial minorities, and the evils of capitalism.

Exploitation of the Military

Recent high-profile hate crimes involving white supremacists who were also serving in the U.S. military revealed the recruitment efforts of hate groups near military bases (Holthouse, 2006). Currently the military touts a zero-tolerance policy regarding enlisted personnel participating in hate groups. This increased vigilance is a result of fallout from ex-serviceman Timothy McVeigh (Oklahoma City bomber) and enlisted men James Burmeister and Malcolm Wright (Ft. Bragg/Fayetteville murders) and their respective involvement in bias motivated murders, (Kifner, 2006; Potok, 2006). Nevertheless, Neo-Nazis, Klan, the National Alliance, and other similar groups seek to recruit individuals with a military background due to their extensive training (and potential access) to weaponry, explosives, and combat skills. These groups espouse the belief that a race war (a.k.a. Racial Holy War—*Rahowa*) will occur in the United States and that those in the hate movement will wage the war on behalf of the white race.

Violent Youth

According to the Bureau of Justice Statistics's National Incident-Based Reporting System, nearly 40 percent of hate crime offenders are under the age of 25. Neo-Nazi skinhead groups, who are among the most violent hate crime perpetrators (Dobratz & Shanks-Meile, 1997; Hamm, 1993), also have the youngest memberships (Hamm, 1993; Wooden, 1994).

Each of these post-civil rights hate crime characteristics evolved from social changes that manifested during this era, including advancements in information technology and an increasingly violent youth culture.

SIMILARITIES AND DIFFERENCES BETWEEN HISTORICAL AND MODERN HATE CRIMES

Before summarizing the common features of historical incidents, it is important to note what characterized the social conditions surrounding hate-motivated acts. These key factors are present in the social environment of both historical and modern hate crime acts. They include the presence of: (1) powerful groups with cultural, political, and economic advantages; (2) powerless groups lacking in the aforementioned resources; (3) a culture that devalues and/or subordinates the social status of powerless groups, while effectuating the superiority of powerful groups; (4) an underlying irrational fear of powerless groups, which are viewed as negatively impacting the quality of life of powerful groups; and (5) authorities that fail to understand and/or comprehensively address the issues underlying these dynamics, which inevitably lead to hate-motivated acts. The sample incidents from all four historic time periods reflect these conditions. But even with these consistent features, there are inter-period distinctions worth noting.

Summary: Pre–Civil War Hate-Motivated Acts

1. Victim groups were viewed as either interfering with or necessary to fulfill governmental policies. The intent to grow the nation geographically and economically placed the freedom and dignity of Native Americans, Africans, and Asians on a collision course with government objectives.
2. Majority groups generally supported these discriminatory government policies because such groups also adhered to the social norms and cultural beliefs of that era.
3. The combined effects of the preceding produced conditions amenable to the occurrence of bias-motivated acts that resulted in innumerable destructive outcomes, including the murders of many innocent persons. As a result, the so-called hate crimes from this period mostly resemble pogroms. Native Americans were almost totally obliterated, Africans endured perpetual bondage and spontaneous lynching, and Asians were intimidated and murdered because of their ability to survive economically.
4. These acts were carried out almost exclusively by governmental bodies or agents acting on behalf of local, state, or federal authorities and not extremist groups.

Summary: Post–Civil War Hate Crimes

1. Victim groups were targeted by smaller entities that were less likely to be directly connected to government authorities.

2. Perpetrators organized under the rubric of terrorism and white supremacy for the first time., The modern hate movement was born with the formation of the Ku Klux Klan in 1866.
3. The Klan formed in reaction to efforts by the federal government to provide equality to victim groups. This pattern was repeated in the resurgence of hate crime during the civil rights period.
4. Hate crimes committed during this period resembled terrorism as perpetrators utilized violence or threats of violence to achieve their objectives.
5. Finally, the intent of hate crime is not genocidal—as was found in the pre–Civil War era—but rather to intimidate, control, and oppress victim groups.

Summary: Civil Rights Era Hate Crimes

1. The hate crimes committed during this period, particularly as a result of the civil rights movement, revealed the conspicuous involvement of law enforcement authorities. Several bombings and murders directly involved local officials and government agents (e.g. Neshoba County, Mississippi law enforcement and other personnel were involved in the murder of civil rights workers Schwerner, Chaney, and Goodman).
2. With law enforcement officials either taking an active role in hate crimes or protecting perpetrators, the level of vulnerability for victim groups was more pronounced. In these instances, the law enforcement community victimized targeted citizens, rather than protect them.

Summary: Post–Civil Rights Era Hate Crimes

1. With the availability of lethal weaponry, including assault weapons, how-to books on killing methods and implements, paramilitary training camps, and dangerous explosives and ammunition, today's hate crime perpetrator can accomplish a high level of destruction in a brief period of time.
2. The U.S. military is occasionally used as a means to train and equip individual white supremacists.
3. This period sees the involvement of younger and more violent hate crime perpetrators than what occurred during earlier times.

CONCLUSION: IS THE PAST PROLOGUE?

Things that are prologue introduce or lead to something more important. The historical examples reviewed in this chapter indicate that past patterns of bias-motivated acts and the conditions that facilitated them not only serve as a prologue for modern hate crime, but are predictive of future hate crime. Social conditions evidenced in the past is well etched into the social, cultural, and political fabric of American society and proofed by unequivocal results: first, the continual existence of hate crime now has 350-year-old history in the United States; second, the composition of perpetrator-victim groups remains relatively unchanged over time; and third, the general factors that motivate hate crime also remain stable in spite of social progress.

Even so, the past is capable of teaching, of warning, as long as there is motivation to learn. This history teaches the following basic lessons:

Lesson 1: Racism and anti-Semitism fuel the hate movement. From the earliest beginnings of America, a white-racist ideology was developed and maintained by all those who profited from it (Barkan & Cohn, 1994; Feagin, 2001, Schmaltz, 1999). These attitudes (and more) continue today and must be recognized by society, rather than ignored.

Lesson 2: The agenda of the hate movement is persistent and political. It has been since the forming of the Ku Klux Klan, the beginning of the modern hate movement. "As long as there is a white man in Georgia, there'll be a Ku Klux Klan in Georgia" (Sims, 1996, p. 258).

Lesson 3: The underlying fears that whites have regarding minorities resist multicultural education and cultural diversity initiatives. Despite the intent of such efforts, they have at times fueled resentment and perhaps increased racial tensions (Levin & McDevitt, 1993).

Lesson 4: *The hate movement is growing internationally and is attracting younger and more violent participants.* As observed by Mark Hamm (1994), "hate crime . . . must be conceptualized as an international youth movement toward racism" (p. 175).

Lesson 5: The potential lethality of hate crime acts must not be underestimated. Would-be hate crime perpetrators (as any other criminal) have access to a variety of dangerous tools in America, as mentioned previously. They are capable of causing serious bodily injury and death to multiple victims suddenly and without much warning.

If society continues to ignore the conditions that facilitate hate crimes, they will reoccur and worsen. Effective interventions can be developed and implemented. What is required is a commitment to intervene and disrupt the patterns that we have consistently viewed throughout history and continues today.

NOTE

1. The Civil War commenced in 1861, but 1865 is used to define a particular historical mind-set.

REFERENCES

Anti-Defamation League. (1995). *The skinhead international: A worldwide survey of neo-Nazi skinheads.* New York: Author.

Barkan, S. E., & Cohn, S. F. (1994). Racial prejudice and support for the death penalty by whites. *Journal of Research in Crime and Delinquency, 31,* 202–209.

Berlet, C., & Lyons, M. N. (2000). *Right-wing populism in America: Too close for comfort.* New York: Guilford Press.

Berthrong, D. J. (1963). *The Southern Cheyennes*. Norman: University of Oklahoma Press.

Brown, D. (1970). *Bury my heart at Wounded Knee: An Indian history of the American West*. New York: Holt, Rinehart & Winston.

Brown v. Board of Education, 347 U.S. 483 (1954).

Bullard, S. (Ed.). (1993). *Free at last: A history of the civil rights movement and those who died in the struggle*. Montgomery, AL: Southern Poverty Law Center.

Bureau of Justice Assistance. (1997). *A policymaker's guide to hate crimes* (BJA Monograph No. NCJ 162304). Washington, DC: U.S. Department of Justice Office of Justice Programs.

Carnes, J. (1995). *Us and them: A history of intolerance in America*. Montgomery, AL: Southern Poverty Law Center.

Chalk, P., & Jonassohn, K. (1990). *The history and sociology of genocide: Analyses and case studies*. New Haven, CT: Yale University Press.

Chronister, A. (1992). Japan-bashing: How propaganda shapes Americans' perception of the Japanese. Unpublished master's thesis, Lehigh University, Bethlehem, PA.

Cutler, J. E. (1969). *Lynch-low: An investigation into the history of lynching in the United States*. Chicago: Negro Universities Press.

Dennis, D. (1984). *Black history*. New York: Writers and Readers.

Dobratz, B. A., & Shanks-Meile, S. (1997). *White power, white pride! The white separatist movement in the United States*. Baltimore: The Johns Hopkins University Press.

Dred Scott v. Sandford, 60 U.S. 393 (1857).

Dudley, W. (Ed.). (1996). *The civil rights movement: Opposing viewpoints*. San Diego, CA: Greenhaven Press.

Feagin, J. R. (2001). *Racist America: Roots, current realities, & future reparations*. New York: Routledge.

Fredrickson, G. M. (1991). *White supremacy: A comparative study in American and South African history*. New York: Oxford University Press.

Gould, S. J. (1981). *The mismeasurement of man*. New York: W. W. Norton.

Gundersen, J. R., & Smelser, M. (1994). *American history at a glance* (5th ed.). New York: HarperCollins.

Hamm, M. S. (1993). *American skinheads: The criminology and control of hate crime*. Westport, CT: Praeger.

Hamm, M. S. (1994). Conceptualizing hate crime in a global context. In M. S. Hamm (Ed.), *Hate crime: International perspectives on causes and control* (pp. 173–194). Cincinnati, OH: Anderson.

Harjo, S. S. (1998). Redskins, savages, and other Indian enemies: An historical overview of American media coverage of Native peoples. In C. R. Mann & M. S. Zatz (Eds.), *Images of color images of crime* (pp. 30–46). Los Angeles: Roxbury.

Harris, L. M. (2003). *In the shadow of slavery: African Americans in New York City, 1626–1863*. Chicago: University of Chicago Press.

Hate Crime Statistics Act, 28 U.S.C. § 534 (1990).

Healey, J. F. (1995). *Race, ethnicity, gender and class: The sociology of group conflict and change*. Thousand Oaks, CA: Sage.

Hendricks, S. (2006). *The unquiet grave: The F.B.I. and the struggle for the soul of Indian country*. New York: Thunder's Mouth Press.

Higginbotham, A. L., Jr. (1978). *In the matter of color: Race and the American legal process: The colonial period.* New York: Oxford University Press.

Hoffer, P. C. (1992). *Law and people in colonial America.* Baltimore: The Johns Hopkins University Press.

Holthouse, D. (2006, Summer). A few bad men. *Intelligence Report,* pp. 1–6.

Jacobs, J. B., & Potter, K. (2000). *Hate crimes: Criminal law & identity politics.* New York: Oxford University Press.

Jordan, W. D. (1968). *White over black: American attitudes toward the Negro, 1550–1812.* Chapel Hill: University of North Carolina Press.

Kennedy, S. (1959). *Jim Crow guide to the U.S.A.: The laws, customs and etiquette governing the conduct of nonwhites and other minorities as second-class citizens.* Westport, CT: Greenwood Press.

Kifner, J. (2006, July 7). White supremacists enlisting in military, watchdog report says Aryan Nations graffiti in Baghdad. *San Francisco Chronicle,* p. A-9.

Levin, B. (2002). From slavery to hate crime laws: The emergence of race and status-based protection in American criminal law. *Journal of Social Issues, 58,* 227–246.

Levin, J., & McDevitt, J. (1993). *Hate crimes: The rising tide of bigotry and bloodshed.* New York: Plenum Press.

Mann, C. R. (1993). *Unequal justice: A question of color.* Bloomington: University of Indiana Press.

Meyer, S. G. (2000). *As long as they don't move next door: Segregation and racial conflict in American neighborhoods.* New York: Rowman & Littlefield.

Miller, Y. P. (1979). *Ukomno'm: The Yuki Indians of northern California.* Socorro, NM: Ballena Press.

Morris, T. D. (1996). *Southern slavery and the law, 1619–1860.* Chapel Hill: University of North Carolina Press.

Murdock, E. C. (1967). *Patriotism limited, 1862–1865: The Civil War draft and the bounty system.* Kent, OH: Kent State University Press.

Perlmutter, P. (1992). *Divided we fall: A history of ethnic, religious, and racial prejudice in America.* Ames: Iowa State University Press.

Perry, B. (2001). *In the name of hate: Understanding hate crimes.* New York: Routledge.

Petrosino, C. (1999). Connecting the past to the future: Hate crime in America. *Journal of Contemporary Criminal Justice, 15,* 22–47.

Pieterse, J. N. (1992). *White on black: Images of Africa and blacks in Western popular culture.* New Haven, CT: Yale University Press.

Plessy v. Ferguson, 163 U.S. 537 (1896).

Potok, M. (2001, Fall). The new internationalism. *Intelligence Report,* p. 1.

Potok, M. (2006, Summer). Extremism and the military. *Intelligence Report,* p. 1.

Ridgeway, J. (1990). *Blood in the face.* New York: Thunder's Mouth Press.

Riding In, J. (1998). American Indians in popular culture: A Pawnee's experiences and views. In C. R. Mann & M. S. Zatz (Eds.), *Images of color images of crime* (pp. 15–29). Los Angeles: Roxbury.

Sanders, R. (1978). *Lost tribes and promised lands: The origins of American racism.* Boston: Little, Brown.

Schmaltz, W. H. (1999). *Hate: George Lincoln Rockwell and the American Nazi Party.* Washington, DC: Brassey's.

Sims, P. (1996). *The Klan* (2nd ed.). Lexington: University Press of Kentucky.

Southern Poverty Law Center. (2001, Fall). Hands across the water. *Intelligence Report*, pp. 14–23.

Spindler, W. H. (1972). *Tragedy strikes at wounded knee and other essays on Indian life in South Dakota and Nebraska.* Vermillian: University of South Dakota Press.

Stampp, K. M. (1956). *The peculiar institution: Slavery in the ante-bellum south.* New York: Vintage.

Steinfield, M. (1973). *Cracks in the melting pot: Racism and discrimination in American history* (2nd ed.). New York: Glencoe Press.

Takaki, R. (1994a). *Issei and Nisei: The settling of Japanese America.* New York: Chelsea House.

Takaki, R. (1994b). *Journey to gold mountain: The Chinese in 19th-century America.* New York: Chelsea House.

Tebbel, J., & Jennison, K. (1960). *The American Indian wars.* New York: Harper & Row.

U.S. Department of Justice. (n.d.). *Hate crime—Overview, 2007.* Retrieved November 11, 2008 from http://www.fbi.gov/hq/cid/civilrights/overview.htm

Walker, S., Spohn, C., & DeLone, M. (1996). *The color of justice.* New York: Wadsworth.

Wells-Barnett, I. B. (1969). *Wells-Barnett: On lynchings: Southern horrors, a red record, mob rule in New Orleans.* New York: Arno Press.

Wooden, W. S. (1994). *Renegade kids, suburban outlaws.* New York: Wadsworth.

CHAPTER 3

HATE AS CULTURAL JUSTIFICATION
FOR VIOLENCE

Jack Levin and Gordana Rabrenovic

Until recently, the term *hate* referred to any intense dislike or hostility, whatever its object. In everyday conversation, for example, an individual might have said that he "hated" his teacher, the taste of liver, communism, or even himself. Thus, in this generic sense of the term, hate was employed to label an emotion or attitude that could be directed at almost anything: a person, a group, an idea, some other abstraction, or an inanimate object.

Beginning in the mid-1980s, however, in response to a series of racially inspired murders in New York City, the *term hate* also became used for the first time in a much more restricted sense to characterize an individual's negative beliefs and feelings about the members of some other group of people because of their race, religious identity, ethnic origin, gender, sexual orientation, age, or disability status (Jacobs & Potter, 1998; Jenness & Broad, 1997; Jenness & Grattet, 2004; Lawrence, 1999; B. Levin, 1992–1993; J. Levin & McDevitt, 1993). As incorporated into the concept of hate crimes—criminal offenses based on an individual's "difference"—this more limited usage came to overlap terms such as *prejudice, bias, bigotry, ethnocentrism,* and *ethnoviolence* (as in such more specific forms as racism, sexism, ageism, homophobia, and xenophobia; (see J. Levin & Paulsen, 1999; Perry, 2003; J. Levin & Rabrenovic, 2004b).

Hate is not the only concept in the lexicon of bigotry to have undergone a major shift in meaning. The term *prejudice* was similarly transformed in part as a result of the publication of Gordon Allport's classic book, *The Nature of Prejudice,* in 1954. Having its roots in the context of courtroom behavior, the original meaning of the term was employed to characterize the prejudgment or prejudice of a juror who evaluated a defendant before all of the facts of the case had been presented. Following Allport's treatment, however, the term *prejudice* lost its legalistic meaning and was instead defined in the literature of behavioral science as a hostile attitude directed specifically toward the members of an out-group (e.g., Asians, gays, Muslims, Latinos, and so on; Ehrlich, 1972; J. Levin & Levin, 1982).

Allport (1954) considered *discrimination* as the behavioral counterpart to hate and prejudice—as hurtful, harmful, destructive behavior toward others because they are perceived to be members of a particular out-group. Violence represents an extreme version of discrimination, but other examples include name-calling, vandalizing, threatening, firing, or refusing to have contact with individuals who are different. Not all instances of discrimination are hate crimes, but all cases of hate crimes are discriminatory.

The terms *hate* and *prejudice* are frequently employed interchangeably in the literature of the behavioral sciences and criminal justice. When slight differences in their treatment of bigotry do exist, prejudice tends to emphasize the cognitive aspects of hostile attitudes (i.e., stereotypic images), whereas hate tends to stress the emotional or affective component of attitudes.

ORDINARY VERSUS PATHOLOGICAL HATE

We might be tempted to characterize hate and prejudice as typically deviant, irrational, and pathological—as an aspect of the domain of a few "crazies" on the fringe of society whose psychosis is in urgent need of treatment by psychotherapy, psychotropic medications, or both. At the extreme, it is true that a relatively small number of cases of hate attacks have been inspired by the delusional thinking of the perpetrator. When hate becomes pathological, the perpetrator is convinced that he must rid the world of evildoers, those outsiders who are destroying his racial heritage, his culture, and his rightful place in society. Hatemongers who go on a rampage with a semiautomatic rifle and then take their own lives may be operating out of an extreme form of psychopathology (Levin & Arluke, 2007; Michener, 2003).

Yet hate hardly depends for its existence on individual pathology or abnormal psychology. Nor is it a form of deviance from the point of view of mainstream society. Even if the admission of being prejudiced is unacceptable, hate itself is typically normal, rational, and conventional. It is part of the culture—the way of life—of the society in which it exists, appealing typically to the most conventional and traditional of its members (Barnett, 1999; Feagin & Vera, 1995; Westie, 1964). When we conceive of hate as an aspect of culture, we regard it as part of the totality of an individual's learned and accumulated experiences, including beliefs, values, attitudes, roles, and material possessions (Hofstede, 1997). Hate intensifies as it incorporates widely shared myths and stereotypes and moves into the moral community of a group of people (Opotow & McClelland, 2007).

Even in such an extreme set of circumstances as the atrocities committed under Nazism, anti-Semitic acts were carried out and encouraged not only by ideological fanatics and delusional schizophrenics, but also by ordinary citizens. The power of Nazism was indeed strong, but it hardly prevented most ordinary citizens from making ethical decisions and functioning in a normal way (Barnett, 1999; Browning, 1992). For example, Polish authorities suggested for decades that the Nazis had been responsible for a 1941 massacre of the Jewish residents of the town of Jedwabne. New evidence argued that it was not Nazi soldiers, but ordinary Polish farmers who herded 1,600 of their Jewish neighbors into a barn and set it on fire (Stylinski, 2001).

Where it is cultural, sympathy for a particular hatred may become a widely shared and enduring element in the normal state of affairs of a group of people. Even more important, the prejudice may become systematically organized to reward individuals who are bigoted and cruel and to punish those individuals who are caring and respectful of differences (Katz, 1993). In such circumstances, tolerance for group differences may actually be regarded as rebellious or deviant behavior, and those who openly express tolerance may be viewed as rebels, in the negative sense of the term.

Those who sympathize with bigotry draw their hate from the culture, developing it from an early age. As a cultural phenomenon, racism—the particular hatred based on racial differences—is as American as apple pie. It has been around for centuries and is learned by every generation in the same way that our most cherished cultural values have been acquired: around the dinner table; through books and television programs; and from teachers, friends, and relatives (J. Levin, 2007; J. Levin & Levin, 1982).

In the American experience, white racism has a long and deep cultural history, being traceable back centuries to the impetus in the New World for enslaving large numbers of Africans, rather than white Europeans. Racism can therefore be seen not as a conscious conspiracy of powerful people or the delusional thinking of a few radical bigots, but rather as an important, if largely unconscious, aspect of America's historical experience and of our shared cultural order, arising from the taken-for-granted assumptions that Americans learn to make about themselves and others (Kovel, 1971; Lawrence, 1987; Smith, 1995).

CULTURAL HATE IS WIDELY SHARED

The cultural element of hate can be seen in its amazing ability to sweep across broad areas of a nation. Individuals separated by region, age, social class, and ethnic background all tend to share roughly the same hostile images of and feelings about various groups. In the United States, for example, some degree of antiblack, anti-Asian, and anti-Latino racism can be found among substantial segments of Americans—males and females, young and old, rich and poor—from New York to California, from North Dakota to Texas. In the aftermath of the September 11 attack on America, an anti-Muslim sentiment also become widely accepted by Americans coming from a wide range of social and ethnic backgrounds.

In Nazi Germany, Hitler's condemnation of the Jews similarly reflected not only his personal opinion, but also the beliefs of hundreds of thousands of German and Austrian citizens. While the police looked on approvingly, university students joined together to beat and batter their Jewish classmates. Faculty members and students voiced their demands to rid the universities of Jews and cosponsored lectures on the "Jewish problem." Because of their genuine conviction, thousands of German soldiers and police helped to murder Jews. Civil service bureaucrats aided in doing the paperwork to expedite carrying out Hitler's extermination program. Many important business, banking, and industrial firms cooperated in the task of enslaving and murdering Jewish citizens. Thousands of German physicians cooperated in sterilizing or eliminating the "undesirables." Finally, whereas the church in other European countries denounced racist anti-Semitism, Germany's religious leaders (both Roman Catholic and Protestant) failed to protest the final solution (Weiss, 1996).

At the cultural level, the emotional character of racial or religious hatred is reflected collectively in laws and norms that prohibit intimate contact between different groups of people. In the Deep South, Jim Crow laws created separate public facilities: "colored" and "white" restrooms, waiting rooms, water fountains, and sections on public buses. In the South African version of apartheid, blacks were similarly restricted to living in segregated communities and could work among whites only under the strictest supervision.

In Nazi Germany, the same sort of enduring sympathy for hate might be found among citizens concerning anti-Semitism. In explaining the particular stronghold of Hitler's "final solution," Goldhagen (1996) has argued that an "eliminationist anti-Semitism" was a long-standing feature of German culture that dated back centuries. The majority of ordinary German citizens believed that the Jews, ostensibly being responsible for all of their country's economic woes, had to be eliminated at any cost. Thus, rather than some dark and repulsive secret, gruesome stories about the Nazi's brutal anti-Jewish policies—the death camps, gas chambers, hideous experiments, and mass murders—were told and retold proudly across the land to ordinary German citizens, who were eager to hear them.

In German society—as in many other European countries—Jews were widely disliked for their failure to convert to Christianity and their rejection of Jesus as deity. But the cultural hate that spread throughout Germany in the 1930s was also racial. Jews were widely believed to be literally vermin—subhuman creatures disguised as human beings—who were responsible for every ill that plagued the German people. Jews could never be changed, even if they converted to Christianity, hence the need to eliminate them from the face of the earth.

Nazi anti-Semitism was located at the end of a continuum of cultural bigotry that seems to have helped determine the fate of Jews not only in Germany, but in other European countries as well. Nations such as Poland and Hungary, which had had a long-standing tradition of anti-Semitic attitudes and behavior, were also nations in which a large proportion of Jews were murdered; countries such as Denmark, Belgium, and Bulgaria, where a tradition of tolerance and respect for religious diversity was strong, were also countries where a relatively sizable proportion of Jews survived (Fein, 1979).

CULTURAL HATE TRANSCENDS GENERATIONS

At precisely the same time in the 1800s when it was on the decline in other western European countries, anti-Semitism increased rapidly among the populations of Germany and Austria. By the 1890s, anti-Jewish feelings had gained widespread acceptance throughout the same generation that would later bring Hitler to power. Nazism was initially only one of the political movements to espouse anti-Semitic policies. In 1919, political parties across the ideological spectrum merged to fight a more effective battle against the "rule of the Jews." Huge amounts of anti-Jewish political propaganda were disseminated to the masses (Weiss, 1996).

Moreover, even long after Hitler's death and the defeat of the Nazi movement during World War II, anti-Semitism continued to thrive and prosper. An analysis of anti-Jewish attitudes in East and West Germany found that strong anti-Semitism remained in West Germany even after "four decades of re-education . . . and a nearly total taboo on public expressions of anti- Semitism" (Watts, 1997, p. 219). A survey of German youngsters recently found that more than one-third believe that Hitler's regime had "a good side," and nearly 40 percent said that Nazism had its good points. In the former East Germany, where the economy continues to be shaky, 15 percent of all 14- to 16-year-old respondents thought that Nazism was a good idea (Helm, 2001).

On the other side of the racial ledger, it is also no coincidence that the country of Bulgaria, whose people actively defied Hitler to a greater extent than any other Nazi-allied country, has remained at peace with itself, despite a high unemployment rate and an ethnic mix that resembles that of its next-door neighbor, the former Yugoslavia. Just like its opposite, respect for differences often also has a cultural component.

CULTURAL HATE JUSTIFIES VIOLENCE

In the 1950s, Sykes and Matza developed a conceptual framework to explain how certain individuals drift in and out of delinquent behavior.

According to Sykes and Matza, delinquents generate a set of techniques of neutralization that they employ to justify behavior that violates cultural norms. These techniques—for example, believing that their victims deserve their maltreatment—temporarily suspend the perpetrators' attachment to mainstream culture and provide them with the freedom to transgress.

Hate is, in this respect, more powerful than any technique of neutralization. Unlike forms of criminal behavior that violate widely held cultural norms, hate is sanctioned in the dominant culture. As a result, there is no need for a hatemonger to suspend commitment to conventional standards of behavior. The perpetrator feels supported and encouraged; he or she sees no need to neutralize his or her hostilities; his or her justification is thoroughly accessible.

Hate provides a cultural justification in two ways. First, it *identifies the enemy*. Groups of youngsters who go out looking for an appropriate victim to bash or assault already know—based on accumulated immersion in the culture— exactly which groups are off limits and which groups can be attacked with moral impunity. Second, hate reemerges *after the fact* to excuse a perpetrator's infliction of pain and suffering. The cultural images and feelings again come into play to justify engaging in criminal behavior without suffering pangs of conscience, with moral impunity. The perpetrator has not attacked human beings; he has targeted subhuman or satanic forces, thus preventing them from eliminating the finest qualities of his cultural heritage. He has done a favor for his friends and family, who also may despise members of the targeted group but lack the resolve to actually attack. The perpetrator's hate may remain latent, but only until he has committed an act that begs for justification.

Even white supremacists who belong to organized hate groups may not always be as hate filled as we believe, at least not until they join. In her research into what motivates women who join white supremacist groups, sociologist Kathleen Blee (2003) discovered that many of her respondents became more hateful only after joining the movement. Their decision to take membership in a hate group was apparently inspired less by prejudice or hate and more by a desire for community, that is, to remain in good standing with their comrades. Teenagers who bash or assault their victims for the thrill similarly experience increasing prejudice after they have attacked. Initially, hate is not necessarily much of a contributing factor—they fear rejection by their friends, who think that hate and violence are pretty cool.

Hate, in the short term, is a dependent variable. It follows and is defined by a violent act. But over time, hate then becomes a contributing factor in allowing future acts of violence that can escalate into more serious continuing offenses. In *retaliatory hate crimes*, a vicious cycle of hate and violence emerges between groups. There may be economic and/or political reasons for a particular intergroup conflict, dating back to its initial period. Yet hate often keeps the conflict going so that warring parties refuse to negotiate. They reject the possibility of peaceful coexistence. In many cases, hate is the inter-vening variable between the desire for power, belonging, and socioeconomic status, on one hand, and continuing violence, on the other.

In *retaliatory* hate crimes, the villains become the victims, but those indi-viduals who were originally responsible for committing the offenses are not necessarily singled out for retaliation. Instead, the selection of targets can be arbitrary and random within the offending group. Any outsider will do as an appropriate target, whether or not he or she was originally involved in perpetrating a hate offense (J. Levin & McDevitt, 2002).

According to Michener (2003), the indiscriminate character of retaliation owes much of its existence to an evolutionary need for protection against groups of outsiders who, given the opportunity, would have eliminated their enemies. In what she refers to as *third-party revenge*, any transgression on the part of one outsider is treated as a transgression that any of them would commit. This permits scapegoating indiscriminately to any member of the out-group, whether or not the victim had been involved in perpetrating the original transgression. Michener also points out that positive attributes of outsiders are not similarly generalized. A decent and honorable or courageous act committed by an out-group member is usually treated as an idiosyncrasy—as an attribute that separates the "good outsider" from the rest of his or her group members. Moreover, the tendency to generalize bad characteristics only applies to outsiders, not to insiders. The thought hardly crosses the mind that an in-group member's bad behavior might be representative of a trait found widely in the group. The "one commits a violation, all commit a violation" rule seems to apply only to out-group members.

Third-party revenge allows the expression of hate in response to any hate attack perpetrated by the members of another group. The retaliatory aspect of such crimes—tit for tat—can become a vicious cycle of violence that esca-lates into intergroup warfare. What begins as an individual hate crime can easily become civil war.

INFANTILIZATION VERSUS DEHUMANIZATION

The particular character of hate that develops seems to depend at least somewhat on the forms of discrimination it is meant to encourage or justify. Outsiders who are expected to be submissive and subordinate to the interests of the dominant group are often *infantilized*. Their image is that of naive and misspoken children. Yet some forms of hostility are more life-threatening than others. Those outsiders who are regarded as posing a threat to the advantaged position of the dominant group may be treated not like chil-dren, but as animals or demons, as she-devils or vermin or children of Satan. Or they may be viewed simply as private property (J. Levin & Levin, 1982). In any case, they are more likely to be *dehumanized*.

The derivation of this notion in the American experience can be traced back to widespread stereotypic thinking among white colonists, in which Africans were regarded as apelike heathens and savages controlled almost completely by their senses, rather than by their intellect. Their savage behavior was reflected in "primitive" non-Christian religious beliefs and rituals and in allegations of their "uncivilized" cultural practices, including polygamy, infanticide, and ritualistic murder (Smith, 1995).

Although predating slavery, such dehumanizing ideas about blacks were quickly rediscovered by European colonists to justify placing abducted Africans onto crowded slave ships, where their maltreatment was so severe that many of them died of malnutrition and disease. Instead of dealing with the moral consequences of the forced enslavement of an entire group of people based strictly on skin color, the colonists denied the evil of the institution of slavery. Blacks were not seen as people; they were property.

Once they had reached the New World, the negative stereotyping of slaves included more infantilization than dehumanization. Blacks who consented to play the role of loyal and subservient slaves were generally regarded by their masters as children who needed the wise counsel and guidance of their superior white masters to survive. The image was that of Little Black Sambo, the musical but ignorant youngster who lacked the brains to come in out of the rain. From this point of view, slaves were not victimized or exploited; they were the beneficiaries of a way of life that would ensure their very survival. Enslavement was therefore seen as a morally righteous "white man's burden."

In the years following the end of the Civil War, however, the infantilized image of African Americans was transformed into a dehumanized hatred, on the basis of which murder and mayhem could be justified. No longer seen as valuable property, blacks had to fend for themselves. They were unable to rely on their masters to protect them from other racist whites. Rather than viewed as children, blacks were now regarded as dangerous animals, or even as sexual predators, lacking in human intelligence or spirituality, that needed to be tamed or killed (J. Levin & Levin, 1982).

Such negative images are often seen in warfare. The underlying causes of a conflict may be economic, but stereotyping has facilitated bloodshed. In Northern Ireland, for example, civil strife was routinely reinforced, for decades, by a set of stereotypes of Romans Catholics and Protestants that might be expected to describe racial differences alone, for example, that Roman Catholics have shorter foreheads, larger genitalia, and less space between their eyes than their Protestant neighbors (Levin, 1997).

ELIMINATING THE COMPETITION

Only the nastiest images of newcomers seem to spread during hard economic times, as the native-born population perceives that their financial position is being challenged. At times, certain prejudices become narrowly targeted. During the 1800s and early 1900s, when they came to the United States and competed for jobs with native-born citizens, Irish American newcomers were stereotyped by political cartoonists of the day as apes and crocodiles (Keen, 1986). During the same period, as soon as they began to compete with native-born landowners and merchants, Italian immigrants settling in New Orleans were widely depicted as dangerous members of organized crime who needed to be controlled (Gambino, 1977).

Chinese immigrants to nineteenth-century America tended to be regarded as "honest," "industrious," and "peaceful," so long as jobs remained plentiful. But when the job market tightened and the Chinese began to seek work in mines, farming, domestic service, and factories, a dramatic shift toward anti-Chinese sentiment emerged. They quickly became stereotyped as "dangerous," "deceitful," "vicious," and "clannish." Whites then accused the Chinese immigrants of undermining their standard of living (Sung, 1961). In a similar way, the depressions of 1893 and 1907 served to solidify the opposition to immigration from Italy, setting the stage for widespread acceptance of stereotypes depicting Italian Americans as "organ-grinders, paupers, slovenly ignoramuses, and so on" (La Gumina, 1973, p. 23).

Similarly, as income inequality has increased and Americans have become concerned about their own possible unemployment, immigrants from Latin American countries have been increasingly regarded as rapists, murderers, and terrorists. Actually, the crime rate among Latin American newcomers is substantially below that of native-born Americans (J. Levin & Rabrenovic, 2004b). Jobs are often but not always the primary nexus of competition between groups. In the history of American society, intergroup conflict has often taken the form of organized efforts to secure land and extend political boundaries. Hate and prejudice have developed to justify the ruthless, illegal tactics that were so frequently employed.

TAKING LAND THAT BELONGS TO OUTSIDERS

Throughout history, countries have fought over disputed land masses. The experience of Mexican Americans provides a case in point. After being stereotyped by Anglos as "treacherous, childlike, primitive, lazy, and irresponsible," Mexican Americans found themselves manipulated by politicians, lawyers, and land-grabbers alike (P. Jacobs & Landau, with Pell, 1971). Despite the 1848 Treaty of Guadalupe-Hidalgo, which guaranteed Mexicans the right of full citizenship, landowning Mexican families found their titles in jeopardy and their land and cattle stolen or taken from them by fraud. Unlike their Anglo counterparts, Mexican Americans could not count on the courts for protection Native Americans were severely mistreated at the hands of land-hungry white Americans, who eagerly accepted the view that

Indians were "treacherous and cruel savages who could never be trusted." (P. Jacobs & Landau, with Pell, 1971). The negative stereotype served a purpose: as long as the Indians were needed for their agricultural expertise, their military assistance, or their skill as trappers, white Americans tended to see them in a favorable light and to permit their culture to maintain itself, but when large-scale campaigns became directed toward securing the lands occupied and settled by Native Americans, the negative image emerged in full force. If the central business of the Indian savage was to torture and slay, then the central business of the white man must be gradually to eliminate the Indian savage (P. Jacobs & Landau, with Pell, 1971).

In some cases, the process of elimination was anything but gradual. By 1825, some 13,000 Cherokees maintained their homes in the southeastern region of the United States. They occupied 7 million acres of land, owned prosperous farms, and were at peace. This situation was radically altered by the discovery of gold in the hills of Georgia. To gain possession of the rich Cherokee-owned lands, white Americans, with the help of the Georgia legislature, President Andrew Jackson, the U.S. Congress, the Supreme Court, and the military, found it "necessary" to drive the Cherokees beyond the Mississippi. In the Cherokee removal of 1838, Native Americans were rounded up and taken away, their homes were burned, their property was seized, many were herded into stockades, and thousands died. Such thinking on the part of white Americans also led to the passage of the Dawes General Allotment Act of 1887, which took two-thirds (90 million acres) of the tribal lands previously granted to Native Americans by treaty (Parillo, 2005).

HATE AND HATE CRIMES

The connection between hate and hate crimes is complex. Some perpetrators come to the crime scene with an intense dislike for their victims; others do not. Over the longer term, however, hate is the emotion that often keeps an intergroup conflict going by preventing peacemakers from intervening effectively. Before they can even confront the thorny political and economic issues that originally divided two groups of people, they must first address the hatred that has kept them separated and in what essentially can be considered a state of war.

Thrill-motivated hate crimes are frequently committed by groups of bored and idle teenagers who go out looking for a little excitement at the expense of their victims (J. Levin & McDevitt, 2002; McDevitt et al., 2005). Sadism plays a role in motivating some of the assailants—typically, the leader, but there is much more psychologically working to provoke the attack. For example, a white teenager may assault someone who is Latino because his friends expect him to comply, not because, initially, he harbors intense hatred toward his victim. If he views the target of his attack as a flesh-and-blood human being with feelings, friends, and a family, the offender may feel guilty. By accepting the dehumanized image of his victim, however, he may actually come to believe that his crime is justified. After all, the rules of civilized society apply only to human beings, not to demons or animals.

The youngsters who commit a thrill hate crime gain an advantage that they consider of supreme importance. They have perpetrated an offense that will put them in good standing with their friends. The perpetrators who attack in a group have proven their loyalty to one another. They gain bragging rights with their peers. It often takes only a sadistic leader who is filled with hate to catalyze the group. He depends on fellow travelers—his friends, who go along to get along (Watts, 1997).

Similarly, an individual who commits a *defensive* hate crime easily finds the justification in his or her own culture. The individual seeks to protect his or her job in a bad economy, his or her place in the college of his or her choice, his or her personal health from the presence of disease, and his or her neighborhood from the invasion of outsiders. Unlike youngsters who attack in a group, the perpetrator of a defensive hate crime more often operates alone. There is usually some precipitating episode that inspires him or her to take action—a gay rights rally, the first Asian family in a previously all-white neighborhood, or a terrorist attack. Seeking to defend his or her territory or turf, the perpetrator becomes totally convinced that all members of group X or Y or Z are rapists and murderers. Who would want a rapist living next door?

Since the early 1990s, when youth crime had spiked to an unprecedented level, the contribution of thrill hate attacks has declined, at least to some extent. In their place, we are seeing larger numbers of adults who seek to defend their territory, or at least what they believe to be their territory, at the expense of the civil rights of other groups.

CONCLUSION

Cultural hate has played an important role in justifying violence directed against victims who differ from the perpetrator in socially significant ways. While often ignored, this element is shared and enduring. Because these influences come from the mainstream, rather than the margins, of society, they only serve to enhance the accessibility of hate's justificatory powers. Hate crimes may find their individual motivation in such "benefits" as thrill, defense, and retaliation, but there is a more socially widespread aspect to such attacks. Historically, dehumanizing sentiment has spread to justify eliminating the competition for jobs and taking the lands belonging to outsiders. But it would be far less likely for conventional, otherwise ordinary members of society to carry out or lend support to hate offenses without dehumanizing their victims. Thus cultural hate identifies appropriate targets for violence, increases in the aftermath of an attack, and maintains intergroup conflict in the face of efforts at peace making.

REFERENCES

Allport, G. W. (1954). *The nature of prejudice.* Reading, MA: Addison-Wesley.

Barnett, V. J. (1999). Bystanders: Conscience and complicity during the holocaust. Westport, CT: Greenwood Press.

Blee, K. M. (2003). *Inside organized racism: Women in the hate movement.* Berkeley: University of California Press.

Browning, C. R. (1992). *Ordinary Men.* New York: Harper Perennial.

Ehrlich, H. (1972). *The social psychology of prejudice.* New York: John Wiley.

Feagin, J. & Vera, H. (1995). *White Racism.* New York: Rutledge.

Fein, H. (1979). *Accounting for genocide: National responses and Jewish victimization during the Holocaust.* New York: Free Press.

Gambino, R. (1977). *Vendetta.* New York: Doubleday.

Goldhagen, D. J. (1996). *Hitler's willing executioners: Ordinary Germans and the Holocaust.* New York: Basic Books.

Helm, T. (2001, February 8). Young Germans see "good side" to Nazis. *Daily Telegraph,* p. 17.

Hofstede, G. (1997). *Cultures and organizations: Software of the mind.* New York: McGraw-Hill.

Jacobs, J. B., & Potter, K. A. (1998). *Hate crimes: Criminal law and identity politics.* New York: Oxford University Press.

Jacobs, P. & Landau, S., with Pell, E. (1971). *To serve the devil* (Vol. 1). New York: Vintage.

Jenness, V., & Broad, K. (1997). *Hate crimes: New social movements and the politics of violence.* New York: Aldine de Gruyter.

Jenness, V., & Grattet, R. (2004). *Making hate a crime: From social movement to law enforcement.* New York: Russell Sage Foundation.

Katz, F. E. (1993). *Ordinary people and extraordinary evil.* Albany: State University of New York Press.

Keen, S. (1986). *Faces of the enemy.* New York: Harper and Row.

Kovel, J. (1971). *White racism: A psychohistory.* New York: Vintage Books.

La Gumina, S. J. (1973). *Wop!* San Francisco: Straight Arrow.

Lawrence. C. (1987). The id, the ego, and equal protection: Reckoning with unconscious racism. *Stanford Law Review. 39,* pp. 317–323.

Lawrence, F. M. (1999). *Punishing hate: Bias crimes under American law.* Cambridge, MA: Harvard University Press.

Levin, B. (1992–1993, Winter). Bias crimes: A theoretical and practical overview. *Stanford Law and Policy Review,* pp. 165–171.

Levin, J. (1997, July 14). N. Irish racialize the "Troubles." *Bergen County Record.* p. 5.

Levin, J. (2007). *The violence of hate: Confronting racism, anti-Semitism, and other forms of bigotry.* Boston: Allyn and Bacon.

Levin, J. & Arluke, A. (2007, September 18). Reducing the link's false positive problem: An exploratory study of animal abuse and serial murder. A paper presented at the Conference on Animal Abuse and Human Violence, Oxford University, Oxford, U.K.

Levin, J., & Levin, W. J. (1982). *The functions of discrimination and prejudice.* New York: Harper and Row.

Levin, J., & McDevitt, J. (1993). *Hate crimes: The rising tide of bigotry and bloodshed.* New York: Plenum.

Levin, J., & McDevitt, J. (2002). *Hate crimes revisited: America's war against those who are different.* Boulder, CO: Westview Press.

Levin, J., & Paulsen, M. (1999). Hate. *Encyclopedia of human emotions* (Vol. 1). New York: Macmillan Reference.

Levin, J., & Rabrenovic, G. (2004a). Preventing ethnic violence: The role of inter-dependence. In Y.-T. Lee (Ed.), *The psychology of ethnic conflict* (pp. 257–272). Westport, CT: Greenwood Press.

Levin, J., & Rabrenovic, G. (2004b). *Why we hate.* Amherst, NY: Prometheus Books.

McDevitt, J., Levin, J., & Bennett, S. (2005). An updated typology of hate crime motivations. *Journal of Social Issues, 58,* 303–317.

Michener, W. (2003). *Third-party revenge and evolution.* Unpublished manuscript, Cambridge, MA.

Opotow, S., & McClelland, S. I. (2007). The intensification of hating: A theory. Social Justice Research, 20(1), 68–97.

Parillo, V. N. (2005). *Strangers to these shores: Race and ethnic relations in the United States.* Boston: Allyn and Bacon.

Perry, B. (2003). Where do we go from here? Researching hate crime. *Internet Journal of Criminology.* Retrieved September 25, 2008, from http://www.internetjournalofcriminology.com/Where%20Do%20We%20Go%20From%20Here.%20Researching%20Hate%20Crime.pdf

Smith, R. C. (1995). *Racism in the post civil rights era.* Albany: State University of New York Press.

Sung, B. L. (1961). *The mountain of gold: The story of the Chinese in America.* New York: Macmillan.

Stylinski, A. (2001, March 16). Polish role is admitted in 1941 massacre. *Boston Globe,* p. 15.

Sykes, G., & Matza, D. (1957). Techniques of neutralization: A theory of delinquency. *American Sociological Review, 22,* pp. 664–670.

Watts, M. (1997). *Xenophobia in united Germany.* New York: St. Martin's Press.

Weiss, J. (1996). *Ideology of death: Why the Holocaust happened in Germany.* Chicago: Ivan R. Dee.

Westie, F. R. (1964). Race and ethnic relations. In R. E. L. Faris (ed.) *Handbook of Modern Sociology.* Skokie, IL: Rand McNally. pp. 32–49.

CHAPTER 4

THE SOCIOLOGY OF HATE: THEORETICAL APPROACHES

Barbara Perry

The role of theory in criminology and sociology is to identify and make sense of patterns in human behavior and experience. However, in the book *In the Name of Hate: Understanding Hate Crimes* (Perry, 2001), observation was made that the social sciences had failed us with respect to enhancing our theoretical understanding of hate crime. It is disturbing that, in a 2002 publication, Kellina Craig could still claim—quite accurately—that efforts to explain hate crime theoretically remain rare. In part, the limitations of definition and measurement that characterize the study of hate crime help to explain the limited attempts thus far to theorize hate crime. Berk, Boyd, and Hamner (1992) astutely observe that "much of the available data on hate motivated crime rests on unclear definitions; it is difficult to know what is being counted as hate motivated and what is not" (p. 125). As a result, while both academic and media reports make the claim that ethnoviolence represents a "rising tide," the truth is that we don't know whether, in fact, this is the case or not (Jacobs & Potter, 1998). For the most part, existing methodologies are both too new and too flawed to give us an accurate picture of changes over time. For example, because the hate crime data are collected in the same way as the other Uniform Crime Reports data, they are fraught with the same well-documented deficiencies (Bureau of Justice Assistance, 1997). A recent analysis of the first decade of data gathering under the Hate Crime Statistics Act of 1990 documents the many limitations that continue to inhibit accurate counting (McDevitt et al., 2000). Among the problems are a lack of law enforcement agency policies on investigating and recording hate crime, a lack of intensive training on hate crime, and police officers' lack of understanding of or sympathy for hate crime as an offense category.

In the absence of empirical information about bias-motivated violence, it is difficult to construct conceptual frameworks. Without the raw materials, there is no foundation for theorizing. Additionally, the relatively recent recognition of hate crime as a social problem (Jenness & Broad, 1998) also contributes to the lack of theoretical accounts. To be sure, racially, religiously, and gender-motivated violence have long been part of the history of all nations, yet such phenomena have not been readily acknowledged as problematic until recent decades.

It is curious that hate crime has not been an object of extensive theoretical inquiry. Conceptually, it lies at the intersection of several themes that are currently to the fore, for example, violence, victimization, race/ethnicity, gender, sexuality, and difference. In spite of the centrality of violence as a means of policing the relative boundaries of identity, few attempts have been made to understand theoretically the place of hate crime in the contemporary arsenal of oppression. It is not an area that has been seriously examined through a theoretical lens. Where social science, and especially criminology, touches on the experiences of marginalized populations, the emphasis has rarely been on victimization motivated by prejudice; rather, the focus has been on the criminality and criminalization of minority groups. The goal of hate crime theory, then, is to conceptualize this particular form of violence within the psychological, cultural, or political contexts that condition hostile perceptions of, and reactions to, the Other. In particular, it places perpetrators and their actions in context.

To date, the literature has been dominated by psychological and social-psychological accounts of hate crime; that is, the emphasis has been on individual-level analyses. According to Green, McFalls, and Smith (2001), such accounts "seek to understand the psychological causes that compel people to commit hate crimes. Sometimes these causes are sought in enduring psychological orientations or propensities; in other cases, hate crime is said to arise because individuals with certain kinds of beliefs and aversions find themselves in situations where these psychological attributes are brought to the fore" (p. 484). This is not to say that broader social or cultural conceptualizations are not available. In fact, Green and colleagues published an overview of hate crime literature in which they identified an additional five macro-level theories found in the hate crime literature: historical-cultural, sociological, economic, political, and synthetic accounts. In what follows, the author focuses primarily on the sociological and political accounts, which form the bulk of the theoretical work available to date.

PSYCHOLOGICAL/CULTURAL HETEROSEXISM

I begin with a hybrid perspective that spans both psychological and sociological disciplines. The twin notions of psychological and cultural heterosexism were among the first explanatory accounts rendered, in this case, to explain antigay/lesbian violence in particular. Gregory Herek's (1992) work, presented initially in *Hate Crimes: Confronting Violence against Lesbians and Gay Men* (Herek & Berrill, 1992), offers valuable insights into the psychological and contextual factors that make hate crime functional for perpetrators.

To begin, Herek (1992) defines heterosexism as "an ideological system that denies, denigrates, and stigmatizes any nonheterosexual form of behavior, identity, relationship or community" (p. 89). Thus it is a system of thought that both justifies and in fact encourages a broad array of inequitable treatment of gay men and lesbians, including hate crime. Moreover, in attempting to link social context with individual behaviors, Herek observes that heterosexism is "manifest both in societal customs and institutions such as religion and the legal system, and in individual attitudes and behavior" (p. 89).

On one hand, Herek writes of the sociological functions of hate crime. What is it in the perpetrator's environment that either shapes his or her attitudes toward gay men and lesbians or makes violence against them appear to be a legitimate reaction? Herek (1992) points to key institutions that perpetuate heterosexism by rendering homosexuality invisible and/or stigmatized: religion, law, mental health, and media. From the exclusion of gays from civil rights and hate crime protections, to biblical condemnations of homosexuality as "unnatural," to curricular constraints on positive presentations of homosexuality, heterosexism is transmitted through cultural institutions.

There is an extensive cultural mythology that facilitates antigay sentiment and activity. It is a mythology that constructs gay identities as dangerous and wicked. Contemporary imagery and stereotypes surrounding gay men, in particular, often resurrect the historical construction of homosexuality as sin and illness. The dominant Western perspective has been shaped by the social and moral agenda of the Euro-Christian majority. Drawing on the English common law, the colonial state determined that "what was sinful in the eyes of the church was illegal in the eyes of the state" (Biery, 1990, p. 10). So it was that sodomy and buggery came to be seen as immoral acts and as so-called crimes against nature. Varied (mis)interpretations of Christian scripture, in particular, have been used to justify societal exclusion and persecution of gay men and lesbians.

While there are still proponents of the "homosexuality as sin" perspective, this religiously grounded view has been supplemented, if not supplanted, by the more so-called scientific view of same-sex relations as illness. It was not until 1974 that homosexuality as a diagnosis was removed from the American Psychiatric Association's *Diagnostic and Statistical Manual of Mental Disorders*. Moreover, some international documents retain the notion of homosexuality as a mental disorder. This interpretation maintains that sexual acts are symptoms of a sickness. In contrast to the sin conception, the sickness view sees the desire to engage in homosexual activity inhering in the individual's identity.

Whether grounded in religion or science, an immutable stigma is applied to gay identity, which is perceived as a moral and physical threat to the public's well-being. By engaging in "unnatural" sexual behavior, gays are said to thwart God's law; they promote a "deviant lifestyle" to the young and pliable; they carry disease and degeneracy like rats carry the plague. Homosexuals of both sexes are perceived to be predatory and menacing. Moreover, the unspoken threat is that gay men, especially, are gender traitors because they have broken ranks with dominant males, thereby threatening to destabilize carefully scripted gender relationships. Long-standing gender boundaries are uncomfortably blurred by homosexuality.

Given such pervasive negative sentiments, it is perhaps not surprising that gay men (and lesbians) still suffer considerable legal discrimination and exclusion. The antigay mythology is embedded in the legal order. To an alarming extent, gay men and lesbians remain outside the law. Restrictions on their sexuality, relationships, and civil rights mean that gay men and women typically do not enjoy the same freedoms as their heterosexual counterparts. This interventionist stance is in contrast to the practices of many other Western democratic nations. In 1967, Canada's former prime minister Pierre Trudeau claimed that the state has "no place" in the bedrooms of the nation. (CBC, 1967). Additionally, compare the national backlash to Hawaii's legalization of same-sex marriages to the normalization of such relationships in the Netherlands or, more recently, in Canada.

Herek (1992) summarizes the marginal legal status of gay men and lesbians as follows:

> Except in four states . . . and several dozen municipalities, discrimination on the basis of sexual orientation is not prohibited in employment, housing, or services. Gay relationships generally have no legal status, and lesbian and gay male parents often lose legal custody of their children when their homosexuality becomes known. . . . Nearly one half of the states outlaw private consenting homosexual acts and their right to do so was upheld by the U.S. Supreme Court in 1986. (p. 91)

The Supreme Court decision to which Herek refers was *Bowers v. Hardwick* (1986) and, until recently, was the most significant contemporary statement of the status and rights of gays. In that case, the court upheld the constitutionality of Georgia's sodomy statute. In his majority opinion, Chief Justice Warren Burger concluded that "to uphold that the act of homosexual sodomy is somehow protected as a fundamental right would be to cast aside millennia of moral teaching." (Bowers v. Hardwick, 1986).With these words, he denied the legal right to private, consensual, same-sex sodomy. Moreover, he reaffirmed the moral prescriptions against homosexuality as defined by Christian canons.

Until 1961, all states outlawed homosexual sodomy—and most classed it as a felony. Twenty states continued to criminalize same-sex sexual relations until the end of the twentieth century, referring to them variously as "sodomy," "unnatural intercourse," "deviate sexual conduct," "sexual misconduct," "unnatural and lascivious acts," and "crimes against nature." Significantly, such restrictions were struck down nationally in 2003 by the Supreme Court in the case of *Lawrence v. Texas*.

While prosecutions under these various statutes were rare, their presence nonetheless has historically had a dramatic impact on gay men and lesbians. Symbolically, this legislation, and the terminology used, marginalizes and stigmatizes a whole community. They send the message that same-sex activity is "unnatural," "deviant," and not to be tolerated. At the practical level, these laws are "frequently invoked to justify other types of discrimination against lesbians and gay men on the ground that they are presumed to violate these statutes" (Editors of the *Harvard Law Review*, 1990, p. 11). So, for example, the "criminality" of gay men or lesbians has been used to refuse parental rights, or the right to adopt, or the right to marry. The legally ambiguous status of gay men and women can even be invoked as a means of denying them freedom from discrimination in employment and job benefits (e.g., domestic partner benefits).

In short, cultural heterosexism defines gay people as suitable targets, by virtue of their public image or legal status, for example. It is in such a context that psychological heterosexism takes over. At the individual level, antigay violence is functional for the perpetrator; that is, it serves some psychological or emotional purpose for the perpetrator, depending on his (usually) or her (rarely) psychological needs. In other words, perpetrators may engage in antigay violence depending on such factors as "the individual's past experiences with the victim (if any), her or his psychological needs and personality characteristics, and the demands created by the immediate situation" (Herek, 1992, p. 164). Importantly, Herek maintains that these needs interact with context and cultural climate to condition violence. It is the cultural forms of heterosexism that are the primary determinants of hate crime.

Finally, Herek (1992) draws a distinction between the functions that antigay violence may play for the perpetrator: *evaluative* or *expressive*. In the first case, hate crime may not be motivated by hostility toward gay victims generally; rather, these are akin to the *actuarial* offences noted by Berk and colleagues (1992). In such cases, the violence plays some pragmatic role for the offender and is unrelated to homophobia; rather, victims are targeted as individuals, not members of a group. At most, their identity as gay or lesbian might identify them as easy targets due to a perception that they are unwilling to report their victimization. Here the victim's identity is taken as a cue to the ease with which he or she might be robbed, for example.

In contrast, it is *expressive* violence that is best understood as hate crime. In these incidents, it is the perceived or real homosexual identity of the victim that precipitates the violence since the offender is expressing a value orientation with regard to homosexuality: "Expressing a particular attitude toward them helps the individual to affirm her or his self-concept in terms of important values, to feel accepted by significant others, or to reduce anxieties" (Herek, 1992, p. 159). Hate crime becomes a means by which offenders can reaffirm "appropriate" moral boundaries as well as affirming their own correspondence with social norms of masculinity and/or heterosexuality. The distinctions Herek draws between the two are crucial. Just as not all violence perpetrated against black people or Jews, for example, is not motivated by any sort of animus, so, too, is it the case that not all violence against gay people is necessarily bias motivated. Each case must be considered and examined for either its *evaluative* or *expressive* roles.

While focusing solely on antigay violence, Herek's (1992) insights provide some important themes that might also be applied to other forms of hate crime. Most significant is the emphasis on cultural and societal supports for hate crime. Just as key social institutions provide "permission to hate" gays, so, too, do they create motives and justifications for violence against religious minorities and women, for example. It is equally apt to say that cultural forms of misogyny shape the individual behaviors of men who sexually assault women, or that social structures, practices, and beliefs that institutionalize racism provide ample support for racially motivated violence. As so many sociological perspectives on hate crime would argue, such forms of violence can only emerge and flourish in enabling environments.

OPPRESSION AND VIOLENCE

Indeed, Iris Marion Young's (1990) account of the "five faces of oppression" is among those accounts that follow a similar logic. It takes as its frame the cultural, social, and political processes that underlie hate crime. From this perspective, hate crime is at once part of and symptomatic of larger patterns of intergroup conflict, and especially of subordination. Such racial violence is, in fact, a social practice embedded in broader patterns of oppression that systematically restrict the capacities and autonomy of its victims. Young operationalizes oppression in a way that provides a very useful framework for contextualizing bias-motivated violence. She articulates five interrelated faces of oppression by which we might characterize the experiences of common target groups: exploitation (e.g., employment segregation), marginalization (e.g., impoverishment), powerlessness (e.g., underrepresentation in political office), cultural imperialism (e.g., demeaning stereotypes), and violence (e.g., hate crime). Together, structural exclusions and cultural imaging leave minority members vulnerable to systemic violence, and especially ethnoviolence. The former makes them vulnerable targets; the latter makes them "legitimate" targets.

Exploitation, from Young's (1990) perspective, refers to processes that transfer energies from one group to another in such a way as to produce inequitable distributions of wealth, privilege, and benefits. While typically understood in class terms, the notion of exploitation can also be extended to racial and ethnic relations. Historically, people of color have been relegated to the category of menial laborers, or even servants. Such racialized job segregation persists to this day. People of color continue to be overrepresented in menial and low-paying jobs and dramatically underrepresented in the professions. Consequently, their share of the national income remains low enough to leave a significant minority in poverty.

Beyond the exploitation associated with underemployment, there is a lengthy history of resource exploitation, especially among Native Americans (Churchill, 1992; Osborne, 1995), who have lost over 95 percent of their land base. What is left is indeed resource-rich. However, consecutive abrogations of treaty rights with respect to mineral resources (Churchill & LaDuke, 1992), water (Guerrero, 1992), and fishing (Institute for Natural Progress, 1992) have all but ceded control of resources to governments and corporations, at the expense of Native economies.

Related to the exploitation of minority communities is their *marginalization:* the process of pushing them to the political and social edges of society. More so than other minority groups, American Indians have even been geographically marginalized, first through expulsion into the frontier and, subsequently, by relocation onto reservations or into fragmented urban communities (Bigfoot, 2000; Stiffarm & Lane, 1992). Beyond physical segregation have been a myriad of practices intended to expel minority groups from "useful participation" in the economic and political life of society. Economically, African Americans, Latinos, and Native Americans are among the most impoverished. They also experience elevated rates of unemployment.

The marginality of disadvantaged groups renders them powerless within the context of structural and institutional relationships. Most pressing among Native Americans, for example, is their ongoing loss of autonomy (Robbins, 1992; Snyder-Joy, 1996). By virtue of being a colonized people, American Indians were very early stripped of their right to control their own destinies. The attempt to eliminate Native sovereignty was exacerbated by the Major Crimes Act of 1885, for example, which extended federal jurisdiction over felonies to Indian territories. This was followed by over 5,000 additional statutes extending federal control to Native jurisdictions (Robbins, 1992). This political disempowerment, coupled with their economic marginalization, leaves American Indians with little strength with which to exercise the right to freely determine their own political, economic, and social directions. Many other racialized communities as well as people with disabilities and some religious communities face similar restrictions on their ability to engage in political processes. Consider, for example, the fact that

> nationally, an estimated 5.3 million Americans are denied the right to vote because of laws that prohibit voting by people with felony convictions. This fundamental obstacle to participation in democratic life is exacerbated by racial disparities in the criminal justice system, resulting in an estimated 13% of Black men unable to vote. (Sentencing Project, n.d., para. 1)

Here we see how an already vulnerable community is losing its political voice.

Many of the aforementioned patterns are legitimated under the aegis of *cultural imperialism*. Specifically, this dimension of oppression refers to the ways in which "the dominant meanings of society render the particular perspective of one's own group invisible at the same time as they stereotype one's group and mark it as the Other" (Young, 1990, pp. 58–59).

Cultural beliefs about the Other intersect with other structural patterns to give rise to relations of inequality. Speaking of the production of culture, Fiske (as cited in Apple, 1997) contends that

> all meanings of self, of social relations, all the discourses and texts that play such important cultural roles can circulate only in relation to the social system. . . . Culture . . . and meanings . . . are centrally involved in the distribution and possible redistribution of various forms of social power. (p. 124)

Culture is a vast complex that spans the breadth from political discourse, to ideological constructs, to media representations, to religious dogma. In the most coherent and perhaps authoritarian cultures, each of these would correspond exactly. However, in Western culture—presumed to be more "open" and "democratic"—the fit is much looser; there remains more autonomy among and between the various forms. Nonetheless, even in the United States, it is possible to detect a relatively consistent discursive formation, as described by Goldberg (1995):

> a totality of ordered relations and correlations—of subjects to each other and to objects; of economic production and reproduction, cultural symbolism, and signification; of laws and moral rules; of social, political, economic or legal inclusion and exclusion. The socio-discursive formation consists of a range of rules: "is's" and "oughts," "do's" and "dont's," "cans" and "cannots," "thou shalts" and "thou shalt nots." (p. 270)

Culture acts to define representations of groups independently and in relation to others—in ways that reinforce hierarchical structures. Thus those characteristics of groups, those "natural" predispositions, those rules of sexuality, find expression in cultural processes. They are institutionalized in ideologies and stereotypes of racial or gender inferiority, in laws that marginalize or exclude particular groups and individuals, in media depictions that demonize the Other. Culture takes up the content of those other structural supports and gives them tangible substance.

The structural constraints on minority communities, together with their construction as deviant Others, provide the context for *systemic violence*—what we are here referring to as hate crime. As noted previously, the restrictions suggested here make them vulnerable targets; stereotyping and disparaging imagery make them legitimate targets. Because of their relative powerlessness, and because they are represented in negative terms, subordinate groups are frequently subject to "mundane" everyday experiences of "random, unprovoked attacks on their person or property, which have no motive but to damage, humiliate or destroy the person" (Young, 1990, p. 61).

It is also apparent that retaliatory forms of hate crime may emerge during periods of activism on the part of subordinate groups. Rights claims have frequently been the motive force underlying racialized or homophobic mobilization and violence, for example. Such incidents of collective mobilization and empowerment are taken as an affront to carefully aligned hierarchies of identity and power. Rights claims have frequently been the only provocation for hate crimes intended to reaffirm the powerlessness of Native Americans (Ryser, 1992), as in the case of conflicts over natural resources. Similarly, states that have placed gay rights initiatives on the ballot have typically seen escalating rates of antigay violence in those contexts.

STRAIN THEORY

Another orientation that is grounded in the cultural context in which hate crime occurs is strain theory. At the heart of the general theory, as developed by Merton (1938), is the notion of anomie. According to Merton, deviant behavior emerges as a result of disequilibrium, or a lack of correspondence between culturally proscribed goals and the socially structured means by which to achieve them. A *deviant adjustment* is in fact a response to a situation in which "those institutionalized procedures which promise a measure of successful attainment of the goals are not available to the individuals" (Merton, 1938, p. 676). In short, frustration of one's efforts to achieve "success" (however defined by the culture in question) gives rise to aberrant behavior.

In U.S. culture, the so-called American dream prevails as the shared cultural goal. Success comes to be defined by the accumulation of wealth, material goods, and status. People are expected to strive for the ideal of a comfortable suburban lifestyle, replete with three-bedroom house, two-car garage, the weekday Buick and the weekend Bronco, savings in the bank, and an outing to the theater every Thursday night. And of course, it is agreed that the appropriate means for attaining such a state is by adherence to the Protestant work ethic: get an education, get a good job, work hard, work honestly.

Therein lies the rub. In a society as hierarchically structured by race, class, and gender as the United States, access to resources is unequally distributed. Not all members of society are readily able to succeed by legitimate means. There are those who are structurally unable to compete for scarce material and social resources. The resultant strain is most dramatically experienced among those in the lower class, for whom education and employment opportunities are limited.

This anomie, then, leads to one of five modes of adaptation. *Conformists* continue to subscribe to both the cultural goals and norms, regardless of their perceived level of success. *Innovators*, on the other hand, maintain an allegiance to culturally defined goals; however, faced with substantial obstacles to success, they resort to alternative illegitimate means (e.g., theft). *Ritualists* abandon any hope of ever achieving great wealth and status but nonetheless retain a formalistic adherence to the institutionalized norms of society and the workplace. *Retreatists* and *rebels* are both characterized by rejection of the prevailing ends and means. The former, unable to succeed by legitimate or illegitimate means, simply withdraws from the broader society into a world of his or her own. The latter explicitly denounces the prevailing order and seeks to impose an altogether different synthesis of goals and means.

It is possible to slot hate crime perpetrators into at least two of Merton's (1938) deviant modes of adaptation. Some might be considered innovators to the extent that they seek their thwarted status rewards through victimization and subjugation of others. Indeed, many variants of strain theory—such as those proposed by Miller (1958), Cohen (1955), or Cloward and Ohlin (1960)—explicitly argue that lower-class youths generally resort to crime and violence as an alternative means of achieving the status and prestige denied them in the broader culture. Hate crime perpetrated against minorities, then, is one means by which these young men can prove their toughness, their strength. In analyses like that of Levin and McDevitt (1993), the emphasis is generally on a youth subculture characterized by alienation, downward mobility, economic uncertainty, and loss of turf or privilege. Singly and in groups, young men attempt to adapt to their immediate environment by lashing out at the Other, by constructing and then victimizing the cause of their weakened position.

Alternatively, strain theorists might attribute a rebel identity to hate crime offenders. While this culture extols equality as a valued principle, hate-motivated offenders would seek to overturn this platform in favor of white supremacy or white domination. Consequently, they are willing to resort to whatever means necessary—harassment, violence, and so on—to eliminate the "inferior races." In place of diversity, they would enforce uniformity of race, creed, and color. This philosophy underlies many organized hate groups such as Aryan Nations or the Order. The preamble to the Aryan Nations Oath of Allegiance makes this explicit (Ridgeway, 1995):

> I, as a free Aryan man, hereby swear an unrelenting oath upon the green graves of our sires, upon the children in the wombs of our wives, upon the throne of God almighty, sacred is His name, to join together in holy union with those brothers in this circle and to declare forthright that from this moment on I have no fear of death, no fear of foe; that I have a sacred duty to do whatever is necessary to deliver our people from the Jew and bring total victory to the Aryan race. (p. 107)

The majority of scholarly (and journalistic) accounts of hate crime and hate groups to have emerged in recent years are at least implicitly driven by strain theory. There is a tendency to argue that hate crime is symptomatic of the general malaise, the sense of threat felt by those who see themselves as "victims of affirmative action." From this perspective, hate crime (illegitimate means) is an outgrowth of enhanced economic competition for jobs (legitimate means). Hate offenders are said to blame their economic instability or lack of job security on the immigration of "foreigners" or the global financial conspiracy of the Jews, for example. Levin and McDevitt (1993) draw attention to such resentment as a possible motive in hate crime. Kelly, Maghan, and Tennant (1993) introduce their collected edition on hate crime with the assertion that hate crimes are "occasioned by systematic unemployment and poverty that lives side by side with colossal affluence" (p. 4).

CRITICAL CRIMINOLOGY

Like strain theory, critical criminology represents a set of general perspectives on crime, not just hate crime. One might expect this orientation to provide important insights into bias-motivated violence since it is explicitly concerned with the importance of power in the context of crime and social control. However, while Marxist-inspired analyses of gender have been prevalent for at least two decades, similar attention to other nonclass divisions, such as race, ethnicity, or sexual orientation, has been lacking. Cornel West has asserted, not infrequently, that the stuff of hate crime—racism, nationalism, homophobia, sexism, xenophobia—has been undertheorized by Marxists. This is overwhelmingly the case in criminology, where the most neglected field of inquiry has been "the relationship of crime and minority groups within society" (Flowers, 1990, p. xiii).

This is especially disturbing given that radical or critical criminology emerged out of the civil rights movements of the 1960s. Marxist criminology aligned itself not with the "establishment," as had traditional mainstream criminology; rather, it assumed an oppositional stance, more in sync with the liberationist struggles of the day. That is, critical analyses were rooted in the experiences and perceptions of the oppressed. In spite of this, there has been little scholarly consideration of the relationship between minority status and crime. Feminist criminology has recently begun to gain influence within the discipline; the same cannot be said for "racial criminology" or "gay criminology." Moreover, with respect to race and ethnicity, at least, criminologists are most likely to examine patterns of offending and criminal justice processing of minority offenders, rather than their victimization. And they are unlikely to examine victimization based on the victim's status. Nonetheless, some efforts have been made to account for hate crime. The strongest such effort is undoubtedly Mark Hamm's (1994) exploration of U.S. skinheads. This is an explicit attempt not only to expose the skinhead culture, but also to theorize its motives and structure. Hamm is unafraid to approach the issue in an innovative and eclectic manner, both methodologically and theoretically. The very nature of the skinhead subculture required an unorthodox style of research. Hamm was faced with the task of overcoming the paranoia, resistance, and violence of this movement. What emerged, then, was a rich ethnography that drew its sample from a diverse range of sources. For 10 interviews, Hamm approaches skinheads on the streets of U.S. cities. Seventeen telephone interviews resulted from letters sent to known skinheads as identified by Metzger's White Aryan Resistance (WAR) mailing list (two of these subjects were interviewed twice). He was also able to conduct three bonus interviews, which resulted from unsolicited contact from skinhead leaders who apparently learned of the research. Two subjects were solicited through Metzger's WAR electronic bulletin board. Finally, two skinheads serving time for alleged hate crimes joined the sample. Ultimately, then, Hamm's creative subject search yielded 36 interviews.

The structured interview was constructed so as to glean data that could be linked theoretically to elements of functionalist, differential reinforcement and neo-Marxist cultural theories. To that end, Hamm (1994) solicited information on "class, goals, school, family, politics, style, music, television, literature, computers, religion, drugs, guns, group dynamics and hate crime" (p. 103).

A complex and surprising picture of the skinhead subculture emerges from Hamm's (1994) interviews. Correspondingly, Hamm's theoretical interpretation is equally complex since it integrates elements of the three perspectives noted previously. While skinhead culture appears to be a working-class phenomenon (subcultural), it is also characterized by *synanomie*, rather than *anomie*; that is, skinheads appear to be "hyperactively bonded to the dominant social order" (Hamm, 1994, p. 212). This is apparent in their commitment to school and to blue-collar employment.

It is via the mechanisms of differential reinforcement that these working-class youths enter the terrorist subculture. In particular, exposure to white power music and to WAR media (zines, electronic bulletin boards, etc.) seems to be the dominant factor in explaining the conversion to neo-Nazism. The bonding within skinhead groups is completed by the adoption of a shared, readily identifiable countercultural style. However, unlike their European counterparts, in the United States, "most terrorist skinheads do not look like skinheads at all" (Hamm, 1994, p. 130). U.S. skinheads have adopted a style of their own, which is more indebted to Levi Strauss than Doc Marten. Two cultural objects complete the style and prepare the skinheads for terrorism: the Smith & Wesson .357, and beer. The latter, while unanticipated, plays a central role as a trigger to the "berserking" that can include minority victimization. No cases of violence uncovered by Hamm (1994) were committed in the absence of massive quantities of beer.

Hamm's (1994) analysis was the first of its kind. It is worthy of praise on this basis alone. However, it is also outstanding in terms of the novel and unexpected insights it allows into the skinhead subculture. These are not the alienated, disenfranchised misfits of the media stereotypes; rather, they are relatively successful hyperconformists who use beer as a catalyst for violence. This in itself forces us to reevaluate popular conceptions of who hate crime offenders are.

THE GEOGRAPHY OF HATE/DEFENDED NEIGHBORHOODS

A very recent approach to hate crime is one that is grounded in the "geography of hate." This is a perspective that pays particular attention to the ways in which hate crime may serve to protect carefully crafted social and physical space. It becomes a resource by which to keep the in-group in and the out-group out of defended territories. Such analyses are generally grounded first in the notion of the social construction of difference.

Throughout the history of the United States, whiteness has been conceived as the norm, thus supporting racialized boundaries that assume whiteness as the standard against which all others are judged. It divides white from nonwhite, unraced from raced. There is an ideological presumption of innate, biological differences between races, which is then extrapolated to cultural and ethical differences. One's biological race is understood to determine one's "essence," to the extent that physical characteristics are linked to all other elements of one's identity. This construction of racial difference subsequently justifies the full array of practices associated with racial exclusion and marginalization. Since difference has been understood negatively in the United States, it has come to signify deficiency or deviance. Consequently, nonwhite is equivalent to difference and inferiority. Nonwhite is the antithesis of white and must necessarily remain subordinate to white. Moreover, whiteness is generally (and paradoxically) defined more precisely by who is excluded than who is included. Whites are those who are not nonwhite, those who are not racially marked, those who are not clustered together to form a category or racial minority. (Blee, 2004, p. 52)

As this suggests, race also implies insides and outsides, places of belonging and not-belonging, such that certain people may be seen to be in or out of their *places*. Such race-based juxtapositions are central to legitimating and rationalizing the marginalization of the Other who stands outside the boundaries of whiteness: "The ability to create and enforce these boundaries is related to societal power, as different formations of power rely on territorial rules about 'what is in or out of place' for their existence" (Sumartojo, 2004, p. 89). Our place thus becomes racialized, thereby shaping our lived experiences and related life chances. The connection between race and place is much more than a merely symbolic metaphor. It has dramatic material consequences as well. Consider Razack's (2002) assessment:

When police drop Aboriginal people outside the town limits leaving them to freeze to death, or stop young Black men on the streets or in malls, when the eyes of shop clerks follow bodies of colour, presuming them to be illicit, when workplaces remain relentlessly white in the better paid jobs and fully "coloured" at the lower levels, when affluent areas of the city are all white and poorer areas are mostly of colour, we experience the spatiality of the racial order in which we live. (p. 6)

This talk about inside and outside, about border crossing and other spatial metaphors, implies the centrality of geographical understandings of racial formations. In short,

geography is relevant to the social construction of race and ethnicity because identities are created not only by the labels that are borne but through the spaces and places within which they exist . . . geography, the spaces and places that we exist in and create simultaneously shapes and records the way life unfolds, including the lived experience of ethnicity and race. (Berry & Henderson, 2002, p. 6)

As the preceding quotation implies, central to our understanding of the "geography of race" is one particular element of the spatial as it relates to racial construction: boundaries, or borders. Borders are especially important as markers of the distinct boundedness of racialized groups, setting the limits as to who belongs where. They symbolically (and often physically) determine and reinforce ethnic separation and segregation. Whiteness, in particular, is a closely guarded fortress, which is, by and large,

defined by its boundaries. . . . In determining whiteness, borders are more significant than internal commonality. Over time whiteness has been constructed, in the words of the legal theorist Cheryl Harris, as "an exclusive club whose membership was closely and grudgingly guarded." (Blee, 2004, p. 52)

Significantly, boundaries signify both the social and spatial margins of race. They can take the symbolic form of cultural difference, of legislative control, or popular imaging. Yet they are likely to assume a spatial dimension such as walls, fences, or railroad tracks. Native American reservation boundaries, for example, represent something in between. They are invisible geopolitical borders, which nonetheless assume—in the imaginations of both Native and non-Native—a very real presence and impediment between residents and nonresidents (Sumartojo, 2004).

As important as they are for separating "us" from "them," boundaries are nonetheless not fixed. In both symbolic and material terms, they are permeable and subject to ongoing tendencies to transgression (Webster, 2003). Native Americans leave the reservation for job opportunities; black Americans move into predominantly white neighborhoods to gain access to better schools and other infrastructural supports; immigrants come to the United States to pursue the American dream; people of color generally demand the right to inclusion and participation in the machineries of economics and politics. As such, they represent threats; they have violated the carefully crafted barriers intended to keep them in their respective boxes. It is in these contexts—at the "symbolic boundaries"—that racialized violence is likely to occur (Webster, 2003, p. 99). It thus becomes a territorial defense of cultural, often national, space. It is a means to reassert the marginality of the Other who dares to transgress (Sumartojo, 2004):

> Hate crimes are exclusionary acts motivated in part by offenders' desires to assert power over a given space, whether it be a neighborhood or public street. The effect of such acts is to send a "message" to members of the targeted group that they are unwelcome. In addition, hate crimes and responses to them contribute to the meaning of a place, representing a struggle between the meanings informing offenders and those informing other groups. (p. 105)

Barnor Hesse and his colleagues were among the first to explicitly address the spatiality of hate (Hesse, 1993; Hesse, Rai, Bennett, & McGilchrist, 1992). In a chapter featuring an experiential analysis of racial violence, Hesse and colleagues (1992) devote a section explicitly to the "geography of victimization." What is especially intriguing here is their discussion of white territorialism as a precursor to racial violence specifically. In their analysis, white racial violence perpetrated against a threatening Other is conditioned by a "sense of proprietorial relation to social space," such that perpetrators come to see themselves as *defending their space against change and transformation*" (Hesse et al., 1992, p. 173).

Taking the notion of defense a little further, Green, Strolovitch, and Wong (1998) have turned their attention to the notion of defended neighborhoods as a means for understanding the spatial distribution of crime, especially in urban areas. Looking at the distribution of hate crime in New York City, for example, they found "antiminority crime to be powerfully influenced by the interaction between in-migration and the long-standing predominance of the white population" (Green et al., 1998, p. 387). This held true for antiblack, anti-Asian, and anti-Latino violence. Significantly, for approaches guided by a geographical analysis, this trend "hinges on the spatial arrangement of population growth, in particular, the extent to which newcomers cross into areas where whites have traditionally been numerically dominant" (Green et al., 1998, p. 391). In other words, racial violence in this context appears to be an attempt to stem the flow of racialized newcomers into formerly white strongholds.

More recently, Colin Flint (2004b) has made an even more explicit foray into the field with the publication of an innovative collection of essays specifically devoted to the geography of hatred and intolerance. Here contributors offer varied explorations of the ways in which organized and informal groups assert their territorial claims in efforts to purge their neighborhoods, cities, regions, or nations of the encroaching threats represented by people of color, and gay men and lesbians, in particular. The authors share the recognition that "imperatives of the territorial defense of places and spaces result in the adoption of exclusionary visions and practices" (Flint, 2004a, p. 9). Blee (2004), for example, examines the "geography of racial activism." Interviews with white supremacists suggested to Blee that the ways in which these actors perceive social and territorial space condition the racial violence in which they are willing to engage. Similarly, Sumartojo (2004) makes the point that antigay hate crimes constitute "acts of exclusion based on perpetrators' interpretations of place meaning" (p. 87). It is when victims are perceived to be out of place in social as well as spatial terms that they become vulnerable to victimization. Interestingly, it is this notion of being out of place that is also reflected in the final framework discussed in this chapter.

DOING DIFFERENCE, DOING HATE CRIME

When we engage in the process of identity formation, we do so within the confines of structural and institutional norms. In so doing—to the extent that we conform to normative conceptions of identity—we reinforce the structural order. However, not everyone always performs "appropriately." Frequently, we construct our gender, or race, or sexuality in ways that in fact challenge or threaten sociocultural arrangements. We step out of line, cross sacred boundaries, or forget our place. As argued at length in *In the Name of Hate* (Perry, 2001), it is in such a context that hate crime often emerges as a means of responding to the threats. The tensions between dominant and subordinate actors may culminate in violent efforts to reassert the dominance of the former and realign the position of the latter.

Moreover, it is important to keep in mind that identity is shaped relationally. Both the perpetrator and the victim of hate are continually engaged in the process of constructing their identities (Rothenberg, 1992):

> it is not only the racist or sexist who constructs difference, but the victim of each or both who seeks to create difference as well. At times, the "victim" has done so in response to the racism and/or sexism in the society in order to survive, but at other times movements made up of these "victims" have sought to redefine difference as part of a struggle for power and personhood. (p. 48)

Such alternative constructions of difference challenge the carefully molded perceptions about how the world should be, and what each person's or each group's place is in that world. When confronted with such novelties, one means by which to "put things right" is through violence. Consequently, hate crime provides a context in which the perpetrator can reassert his or her hegemonic identity and, at the same time, punish the victim for the individual or collective performance of his or her identity. In other words, hate-motivated violence is used to sustain the privilege of the dominant group and to police the boundaries between groups by reminding the Other of his or her place. Perpetrators thus recreate their own masculinity, or whiteness, for example, while punishing the victims for their deviant identity performance.

A paradox is apparent here. On one hand, hate crime perpetrators are said to be punishing victims for inappropriate performances of sexuality or race, for example. So a black man engaged in a relationship with a white woman is victimized for having transcended both the boundaries of sexuality and race. On the other hand, he is also being punished for engaging in what is *perceived* to be race-appropriate behavior: he is living the stereotype of "black-man-as-predator," which has long been used to justify the inferior position of black males. What this suggests is a lose-lose situation. Victims may be punished for *transcending* normative conceptions of relevant categories of difference, but they may also be sanctioned for *conforming* to relevant categories of difference.

Where the popular image of the Other is constructed in negative terms—as it frequently is—group members may be victimized on the basis of those perceptions. Hate crime is thus "bolstered by belief systems which (attempt to) legitimate such violence" so as to "limit the rights and privileges of individuals/groups and to maintain the superiority of one group" (Sheffield, 1995, pp. 438–439). We saw a similar logic in the work of Herek (1992), referred to earlier. Members of subordinate groups are potential victims *because of* their subordinate status. They are already deemed inferior, deviant, and therefore deserving of whatever hostility and persecution comes their way. In sum, they are damned if they do, and damned if they don't. If they perform their identities on the basis of what is expected of them, they are vulnerable. If they perform in ways that challenge those expectations, they are equally vulnerable.

Hate crime, then, is a forceful illustration of what it is to engage in situated conduct. The interactions between subordinate and dominant groups provide a context in which both compete for the privilege to define difference in ways that either perpetuate or reconfigure hierarchies of social power. Simultaneous and oppositional efforts to do difference set up tensions, in which the act of victimization co-constructs the victim and perpetrator. This confrontation is informed by the broader cultural and political arrangements, which "allocate rights, privilege and prestige according to biological or social characteristics" (Sheffield, 1995, p. 438). Perpetrators attempt to reaffirm their dominant identity, their access to resources and privilege, while at the same time limiting the opportunities of the victims to express their own needs. The performance of hate violence, then, confirms the "natural" relations of superiority/inferiority. It is a form of interpersonal and intercultural expression that signifies boundaries. And significantly, the boundary is "capable of organizing personal interactions in sometimes lethal ways" (Cornell & Hartmann, 1998, p. 185).

CONCLUSION: COMMON THREADS

There are identifiable themes running through many of these sociological accounts of hate crime. First and foremost is the general tendency to regard hate crime as nested within broader social patterns of oppression and disadvantage. Several accounts recognize that bias-motivated violence is but one strategy in the arsenal by which subordinate groups are kept in their place. Such violence, then, can be seen as both enabled by and enabling of the disempowerment of minority communities.

Related to this, particular attention is devoted to the ways in which cultural imaging gives rise to hate crime. When we dehumanize, or demonize, or stigmatize a whole community, it becomes very easy to then justify their victimization. Often, the distorted images of the Other engender intense hostility, anger, or fear, such that hate crime becomes a viable option. So, for example, if gay men are constructed as diseased or as pedophiles, or if African American men are portrayed as sexual predators, then it becomes quite "appropriate" to neutralize such threats through violence.

Additionally, hate crime is often theorized to be an important means by which perpetrators attempt to police boundaries between "us" and "them." It is seen as a mechanism for minimizing "border crossings." It is intended to discourage transgressors from crossing gendered or racialized lines and punish those who fail to heed the warning. Culturally, we create binaries around white/nonwhite, heterosexual/nonheterosexual, and so on. In each of these cases, either side of the border is significant to the extent that each is posted with exclusionary signs that keep whites or heterosexuals on one side of the fence and blacks or homosexuals on the other. Should the signs not discourage crossings, then violence may emerge in an attempt to defend one's cultural, and even geographical, territory.

This raises perhaps the final common thread: that racial violence is very likely to occur when relatively powerless communities seek to enhance their position. Retaliatory violence is a particular form of hate crime that emerges in contexts wherein the formerly disadvantaged challenge the other bases of oppression, as when they seek to empower themselves economically or socially through rights claims. Efforts directed toward empowerment are commonly met with equally steadfast reactionary mobilizations, some of which are relatively isolated, but many of which constitute organized opposition.

This chapter offers but a cursory overview of a select range of sociological accounts of hate crime. It is by no means meant to be exhaustive, but to give the flavor of contemporary theorizing in this field.

REFERENCES

Apple, M. (1997). Consuming the other: Whiteness, education and cheap French fries. In M. Fine, L. Weis, L. Powell, & L. Mun Wong (Eds.), *Off white: Readings on race, power and society* (pp. 121–128). New York: Routledge.

Berk, R., Boyd, E., & Hamner, K. (1992). Thinking more clearly about hate-motivated crimes. In G. Herek & K. Berrill (Eds.), *Hate crimes: Confronting violence against lesbians and gay men* (pp. 123–143). Newbury Park, CA: Sage.

Berry, K., & Henderson, M. (2002). Introduction: Envisioning the nexus between geography and ethnic and racial identity. In K. Berry & M. Henderson (Eds.), *Geographical identities of ethnic America* (pp. 1–14). Reno: University of Nevada Press.

Biery, R. (1990) *Understanding homosexuality.* Austin, TX: Edward-William Publishing. Bigfoot, D. S. (2000). *History of victimization in native communities.* Oklahoma City, OK: Center on Child Abuse and Neglect.

Blee, K. (2004). The geography of racial activism: Defining whiteness at multiple scales. In C. Flint (Ed.), *Spaces of hate: Geographies of discrimination and intolerance in the U.S.A.* (pp. 49–68). New York: Routledge.

Bowers v. Hardwick, 478 U.S. 186 (1986).

Bureau of Justice Assistance. (1997). *A policy maker's guide to hate crimes.* Washington, DC: Author.

CBC (1967). There's no place for the state in the bedrooms of the nation. Broadcast date, December 21, 1967. Available at http://archives.cbc.ca/politics/rights_freedoms/dossier/538.

Churchill, W. (1992). The earth is our mother: Struggle for American Indian land and liberation in the contemporary United States. In A. Jaimes (Ed.), *The state of Native America: Genocide, colonization, and resistance* (pp. 217–240). Boston: South End Press.

Churchill, W., & LaDuke, W. (1992). Native North America: The political economy of radioactive colonialism. In A. Jaimes (Ed.), *The state of Native America: Genocide, colonization, and resistance* (pp. 241–266). Boston: South End Press.

Cloward, R. A., & Ohlin, L. E. (1960). *Delinquency and opportunity: A theory of delinquent gangs.* New York: Free Press.

Cohen, A. K. (1955). *Delinquent boys: The culture of the gang.* New York: Free Press.

Cornell, S., & Hartmann, D. (1998). *Ethnicity and race: Making identities in a changing world.* Thousand Oaks, CA: Pine Forge Press.

Craig, K. (2002). Examining hate-motivated aggression: A review of the social psychological literature on hate crimes as a distinct form of aggression. *Aggression and Violent Behavior, 7,* 85–101.

Editors of the *Harvard Law Review* (1990). *Sexual Orientation and the Law.* Cambridge MA: Harvard University Press.

Flint, C. (2004a). Introduction. In C. Flint (Ed.), *Spaces of hate: Geographies of discrimination and intolerance in the U.S.A.* (pp. 1–20). New York: Routledge.

Flint, C. (2004b). *Spaces of hate: Geographies of discrimination and intolerance in the U.S.A.* New York: Routledge.

Flowers, B. (1990). *Minorities and criminality.* Westport CT: Greenwood Press.

Goldberg, D. T. (1995). Afterword: Hate or power? In R. Whillock & D. Slayden (Eds.), *Hate speech* (pp. 267–276). Thousand Oaks, CA: Sage.

Green, D., McFalls, L., & Smith, J. (2001). Hate crime: An emergent research agenda. *Annual Review of Sociology, 27,* 479–504.

Green, D., Strolovitch, D., & Wong, J. (1998). Defended neighborhoods, integration, and racially motivated crime. *American Journal of Sociology, 104,* 372–403.

Guerrero, M. (1992). American Indian water rights: The blood of life in native North America. In A. Jaimes (Ed.), *The state of Native America: Genocide, colonization, and resistance* (pp. 189–216). Boston: South End Press.

Hamm, M. (1994). Conceptualizing hate crime in a global context. In M. Hamm (Ed.), *Hate crime: International perspectives on causes and control* (pp. 173–194). Cincinnati, OH: Anderson.

Herek, G. (1992). The social context of hate crimes: Notes on cultural heterosexism. In G. Herek & K. Berrill (Eds.), *Hate crimes: Confronting violence against lesbians and gay men* (pp. 89–104). Newbury Park, CA: Sage.

Herek, G., & Berrill, K. (eds.) (1992). *Hate crimes: Confronting violence against lesbians and gay men.* Newbury Park, CA: Sage.

Hesse, B. (1993). Black to front and black again: Racialization through contested times and spaces. In M. Keith & S. Pile (Eds.), *Place and the politics of identity* (pp. 162–182). London: Routledge.

Hesse, B., Rai, D., Bennett, C., & McGilchrist, P. (1992). *Beneath the surface: Racial harassment.* Aldershot, UK: Avebury.

Institute for Natural Progress. (1992). In usual and accustomed places: Contemporary American Indian fishing rights struggles. In A. Jaimes (Ed.), *The state of Native America: Genocide, colonization, and resistance* (pp. 217–240). Boston: South End Press.

Jacobs, J., & Potter, K. (1998). *Hate crimes: Criminal law and identity politics.* New York: Oxford University Press.

Jenness, V., & Broad, K. (1998). *Hate crimes: New social movements and the politics of violence*. New York: Aldine de Gruyter.

Kelly, R., Maghan, J., & Tennant, W. (1993). Hate crimes: Victimizing the stigmatized. In R. Kelly (Ed.), *Bias crime: American law enforcement and legal responses* (pp. 23–47). Chicago: Office of International Criminal Justice.

Lawrence v. Texas, 539 U.S. 558 (2003).

Levin, J., & McDevitt, J. (1993). *Hate crimes: The rising tide of bigotry and bloodshed*. New York: Plenum.

McDevitt, J., Balboni, J., Bennett, S., Weiss, J., Orschowsky, S., & Walbot, L. (2000). *Improving the quality and accuracy of bias crime statistics nationally: An assessment of the first ten years of bias crime data collection*. Washington, DC: Bureau of Justice Statistics.

Merton, R. (1938). Social structure and anomie. *American Sociological Review, 3*, 672–682.

Miller, W. B. (1958). Lower class culture as a generalizing milieu of gang delinquency, *Journal of Social Issues, 14*, 5–19.

Osborne, S. (1995). The voice of the law: John Marshall and Indian land rights. In M. Green (Ed.), *Issues in Native American cultural identity* (pp. 57–74). New York: P. Lang.

Perry, B. (2001). *In the name of hate: Understanding hate crimes*. New York: Routledge.

Razack, S. (2002). When place becomes race. In S. Razack (Ed.), *Race, space and the law: Unmapping a white settler society* (pp. 1–20). Toronto: Between the Lines.

Ridgeway, J. (1995). *Blood in the face*. New York: Thunder's Mouth Press.

Robbins, R. (1992). Self-determination and subordination: The past, present and future of American Indian governance. In A. Jaimes (Ed.), *The state of Native America: Genocide, colonization, and resistance* (pp. 87–122). Boston: South End Press.

Rothenberg, P. (1992). The construction, deconstruction and reconstruction of difference. In R. Baird & S. Rosenbaum (Eds.), *Bigotry, prejudice and hatred* (pp. 47–64). Buffalo, NY: Prometheus.

Rÿser, R. (1992). *Anti-Indian movement on the tribal frontier*. Kenmore, WA: Center for World Indigenous Studies.

Sentencing Project. (n.d.). *Felony disenfranchisement*. Retrieved December 18, 2007 from http://www.sentencingproject.org/IssueAreaHome.aspx?IssueID=4

Sheffield, C. (1995). Hate violence. In P. Rothenberg (Ed.), *Race, class and gender in the United States* (3rd ed., pp. 432–441). New York: St. Martin's Press.

Snyder-Joy, Z. (1996). Self-determination and American Indian justice: Tribal versus federal jurisdiction on Indian lands. In M. Nielsen & R. Silverman (Eds.), *Native Americans, crime and justice* (pp. 38–45). Boulder, CO: Westview Press.

Stiffarm, L., & Lane, P. (1992). The demography of Native North America. In A. Jaimes (Ed.), *The state of Native America: Genocide, colonization, and resistance* (pp. 23–54). Boston: South End Press.

Sumartojo, R. (2004). Contesting place: Anti-gay and -lesbian hate crime in Columbus, Ohio. In C. Flint (Ed.), *Spaces of hate: Geographies of discrimination and intolerance in the U.S.A.* (pp. 87–108). New York: Routledge.

Webster, C. (2003). Race, space and fear: Imagined geographies of racism, crime, violence and disorder in northern England. *Capital and Class, 80*, 95–122.

Young, I. M. (1990). *Justice and the politics of difference*. Princeton, NJ: Princeton University Press.

CHAPTER 5

POSING THE "WHY" QUESTION: UNDERSTANDING THE PERPETRATION OF RACIALLY MOTIVATED VIOLENCE AND HARASSMENT

David Gadd and Bill Dixon

"MY HEART IS BROKEN"

The devastated mother of racist murder victim Anthony Walker said she would forgive his killers—but only when they showed genuine remorse. Special needs teacher Gee Walker, 49 . . . described Anthony as "the man of the house" . . . who could defuse a family row by pointing out the humour in most situations. . . . She wept as she explained the void his death created. . . . Despite her obvious pain, Mrs Walker's strong Christian faith means she cannot hate Barton and Taylor . . . "Hatred is a life sentence. . . . It eats you up inside like a cancer". . .

The fact that Anthony's killers grew up in the same area—Taylor attended the same junior school—is particularly hard for Mrs. Walker to accept. "They played together, they stood in the same dinner queue. . . . I believe that all kids are innocent and something went wrong along the way. Someone planted a seed of hate in their minds . . . it's down to all of us to find out where and why." . . . Mrs. Walker was keen to stress the comfort she had taken from the huge outpouring of public sympathy . . . "We wouldn't have survived without that." ("My heart is broken" *The Sun*, November 30, 2005)

The mushrooming literature on hate crime testifies powerfully to the harms caused by racially motivated forms of violence and harassment. Ehrlich, Larcom, and Purvis (2003) observe that victims of *ethnoviolence* are more likely to suffer a range of psychosomatic symptoms than victims of other crimes, including "nervousness, trouble concentrating or working, anger and a desire to retaliate . . . fear . . . and feeling exhausted or weak for no reason" (p. 158). Bowling and Phillips (2002) describe how "serious and mundane incidents are interwoven to create a threatening environment which undermines" the "personal safety and freedom of movement" (p. 114) of people from black and minority ethnic communities. Racially motivated murders may be relatively rare in relation to other forms of homicide, but the horror these evoke is associated in the minds of many people from black and minority ethnic groups with the more commonplace phenomena of racially motivated assaults, racial harassment, racist graffiti, racist joking, and discrimination on the bases of skin color, religion, and nationality. While the practice is not without its critics (Jacobs, 2003), the harsher sentences handed down to those convicted of racially aggravated offences have been welcomed by practitioners and academics on the grounds that "hate crimes hurt more," "are more likely to involve excessive violence," and "send out a terroristic message to members of the victim's group" (Iganski, 2003, p. 135).

Yet, as the news story at the beginning of this chapter testifies, better and harsher justice is not the only thing those who suffer the hurts caused by racially motivated crime want and need. Gee Walker, the mother of a black schoolboy killed when two white men wearing ski masks bludgeoned him to death with an ice axe, has talked repeatedly to the media about her desire to understand and forgive her son's killers. Knowing what to make of such news coverage, particularly the claim that the nation's sympathy enabled the grieving family to "survive," is not easy. Such sentiments mitigate the public's sense of culpability and obscure from view the many racist attacks, including some racist murders, that pass without media comment (Institute of Race Relations, 2008). Gee Walker's oft-repeated expressions of bewilderment at the killers' actions, however, merit further consideration. In asking what had planted "the seed of hate" in their minds, the parameters of Gee Walker's own experience, as both a single mother of six and a special needs teacher, who successfully raised a young man emotionally adept enough to "defuse" many a family conflict, come into play. Given that her son's killers were brought up in the same neighborhood, played with Anthony, and that one of them went to his school, Gee Walker is understandably perplexed as to how they turned out so differently from her own son. From this perspective, her conclusion that something must have "gone wrong" for Barton and Taylor seems plausible, and her insistence that we all have a duty to "find out where and why" they became so hateful seems entirely justified.

Walker is not alone in taking this stand. As Pumla Gobodo-Madikizela's (2003) moving account of her interviews with Eugene de Kock, the South African police colonel who oversaw the murder and torture of many of apartheid's opponents, testifies, coming to terms with the humanity of perpetrators can be part of the process of overcoming the dehumanizing impact of racism and the atrocities it facilitates. In South Africa, the desire to come to terms with loss, trauma, and brutalization was so great that during the

Truth and Reconciliation Commission's hearings, some victims offered to forgive perpetrators before they apologized. Gobodo-Madikizela witnessed the wife of a man murdered in a bombing orchestrated by the security forces shed tears of forgiveness for Eugene de Kock. She further notes that while many people find it hard to contemplate having anything to do with perpetrators, some victims need to be given the opportunity to engage with them, despite the emotionally disturbing consequences of doing so. For these victims, identifying with the perpetrators' pain is one way of ridding themselves of the poisonous self-loathing instilled in them by victimization and oppression instilled. Consequently, to

> dismiss perpetrators simply as evildoers and monsters shuts the door to the kind of dialogue that leads to an enduring peace. Daring, on the other hand, to look the enemy in the eye and allow oneself to read signs of pain and cues to contrition or regret where one might almost have preferred to continue seeing only hatred is the one possibility we have for steering individuals and societies towards replacing longstanding stalemates out of a nation's past with genuine engagement. (Gobodo-Madikizela, 2003, p. 126)

Of course, it is not necessarily the task of academics to facilitate dialogues between perpetrators and victims. But if criminologists are to make a contribution to alleviating the problem of racially motivated violence and harassment, and/or helping people overcome the many hurts it causes, then we cannot afford to shy away from the challenge of rendering perpetrators' motives comprehensible; to search for signs of pain and cues of contrition beneath the hatred; to tease explanations out of excuses; to find the human within the dehumanizing. In sum, it is the job of academics to find a language capable of helping victims, perpetrators, and their wider communities make sense of the phenomenon of racially motivated forms of harassment and hate crime, its most serious and apparently "mundane" manifestations included.

CRIMINOLOGICAL PERSPECTIVES

Criminological writing about perpetrators has largely shied away from this challenge. The most cited works tend to be typological or otherwise loosely descriptive profiles derived from secondary analyses of police incident data. These have enabled distinctions to be drawn between "thrill-," "defensive-," "retaliatory-," and "mission-" motivated offenders (McDevitt, Levin, & Bennett, 2003); "expressive and instrumental motives" (Berk, Boyd, & Hamner, 2003); "premeditated and unpremeditated attacks" (Berk et al., 2003); and "versatile" (generalist) offenders tinged with "bias" and "specialist" hate crime offenders (Messner, McHugh, & Felson, 2004). These typologies show that not all racially motivated offenders are the same, that motives and rationales vary, and that offenses aggravated by the use of racist terms are not always initiated because of hateful feelings. But in failing to grapple with how offenders' motives resonate with the contradictory mixture of popular prejudices; historically ingrained ideas about race and belonging; and contemporary concerns about nationality, entitlement, and migration, typological approaches tend to oversimplify the distinctions between perpetrators and nonperpetrators.

From this base, Barbara Perry's (2002) attempt to apply structured action theory to the perpetration of hate crime was a radical move forward. Within Western culture, Perry argues, difference is often constructed in negative relational terms as "deficiency" so that those who deviate from the hegemonic position in social relations—currently occupied by white, economically successful, heterosexual men—are constructed as inadequate, inferior, bad, or evil. From Perry's perspective,

> hate crime . . . connects the structural meanings and organization of race with the cultural construction of racialized identity. On the one hand, it allows perpetrators to reenact their whiteness, thereby establishing their dominance. On the other hand, it coconstructs the nonwhiteness of the victims, who are perceived to be worthy of violent repression either because they correspond to a demonized identity, or, paradoxically, because they threaten the racialized boundaries that are meant to separate "us" from "them." (p. 58)

Perry (2002) claims that the perpetration of hate crime serves multiple objectives. It reinforces the normality of white sexuality, while punishing those who transgress, or who are imagined to have transgressed, the norm. Victims are often harassed for *transcending* normative conceptions of difference—for doing things white men think black and ethnic minority men are not entitled to do—but they may also be punished for *conforming* to relevant categories of difference, for behaving in ways whites consider to be stereotypical of nonwhites. Although the process of victimizing others instills a positive sense of identity in those perpetrators who feel marginalized in terms of their class, knowledge of this victimization among the victim's community reinstates the racialized injustices of the wider society. Grounding her work in the histories of slavery, segregation, and exploitation, which initially defined white Americans' relationships with African and Native American people, Perry's thesis avoids the profilers' tendency to pathologize, while also attending to the way in which so many racist attacks appear to be as much about gender, age, and sexuality as they are about "race." But in accounting for "hate" in terms of class and gender-related marginalization, Perry's analyses, like much of the structured action theory on which she draws, has a rather "deterministic feel," which makes it harder, rather than easier, to get to grips in any meaningful way with the inner worlds of the offenders in question (Gadd & Jefferson, 2007).

In exposing the feelings of inadequacy contemporary racism so often conceals, some United Kingdom–based researchers have offered a more humanizing perspective on the etiology, or origins, of hate crime. Rae Sibbitt (1997) attempted as much in her British Home Office–funded study of racist victimization cases when she argued,

> For perpetrators, potential perpetrators and other individuals within the perpetrator community, expressions of racism often serve the function of distracting their own—and others'—attention away from real, underlying concerns which they feel impotent to deal with. (p. viii)

Likewise, Ray, Smith, and Wastell's (2004) study of those convicted of racially aggravated offenses in greater Manchester has drawn attention to the prevalence of racist crime in areas where white residents perceive themselves as under threat from an expanding south Asian population, even though this population is similarly affected by the decline of Britain's manufacturing industries. Ray and colleagues' interviews with those on probation for racially aggravated offenses suggested that most (white) racially motivated offenders tended to share the values and prejudices of the communities from which they came. Deploying a framework developed by Thomas Scheff (1994), Ray and colleagues (2004) detected unacknowledged shame in the verbal disclosures and body language of around two-thirds of their 36 respondents. These racist offenders

> saw themselves as weak, disregarded, overlooked, unfairly treated, victimized without being recognised as victims, made to feel small; meanwhile, the other—their Asian victims . . . was experienced as powerful, in control, laughing, successful, "arrogant." (pp. 355–356)

But while Ray and colleagues (2004) published many accounts of what offenders think about ethnic minorities, they published few of their interviewees' explanations of their offending behavior. This made it hard to gauge whether "shame" was always the "master emotion" behind racist crime; whether unacknowledged shame was more acute for those who committed acts of racist violence than for those who simply held racist views; and what caused the more acute shame supposedly felt by hate crime perpetrators.

WHAT WE DID AND WHY WE DID IT

Our own research, conducted in North Staffordshire, England, set out to address these shortcomings. The overall aim of our project was to tease out the connections and tensions among pervasive forms of racism and xenophobia, the expression of antiracist sentiments, and the motivations of the minority of the population who perpetrate a range of racially motivated offences.

Focus group discussions were conducted with 13 naturally occurring groups of local people. These included people from a residents' association, a neighborhood watch, a working men's club, a day center, and two antiracist groups as well as young offenders, asylum seekers, and white and minority ethnic users of two youth centers. Free-Association Narrative Interviews were conducted with 15 people implicated in acts of racial harassment (Hollway & Jefferson, 2000). Twelve of these were accessed via probation services and youth offending teams, although only five of these had ever been charged with racially aggravated crimes. Three participants, all of whom were politically involved in racist political groups, were recruited through more direct approaches. Recordings of the focus groups and in-depth interviews were fully transcribed. Analytic attention was given to fragments of words, overlapping speech, changes of tone, and other nonverbal cues as well as to emerging themes and intersubjective dynamics.

RACIST CRIME IN NORTH STAFFORDSHIRE

Stoke-on-Trent is a predominantly white city about 160 miles north of London with a population of about 240,000. In 2005 one in every three minority ethnic residents of Stoke-on-Trent had experienced some form of racial harassment in the previous three years: one in four had been verbally abused; one in 20 had suffered a violent racist attack. These rates of victimization were higher than those found by the British Crime Survey (Salisbury & Upson, 2004) for England and Wales as a whole. Local racist incident data for Stoke-on-Trent suggested that by 2003, refugees and asylum seekers from Afghanistan, Iraq, and Iraqi Kurdistan experienced even higher rates of victimization than the (heavily victimized) Pakistani and Bangladeshi populations. These high rates persisted despite the fact that the perpetrators of racially aggravated offences in Staffordshire were less likely to be cautioned and more likely to be referred for prosecution than in other parts of the country. Most racist incidents, however, never come to the attention of the police, let alone the courts. The police in Stoke-on-Trent recorded only 468 such incidents in 2002–2003. In November 2003 only one person in North Staffordshire was in custody for racially aggravated offences, and only 13 racially motivated offenders were listed in probation caseloads.

DEINDUSTRIALIZATION AND THE RISE
OF THE BRITISH NATIONAL PARTY

At the time of our research, Stoke-on-Trent had endured at least three decades of economic decline. By the end of the 1990s, the area's three major industries—ceramics, coal mining, and steel production—had almost disappeared. While other similar cities had offset losses in manufacturing jobs with an expanding service sector, in Stoke-on-Trent, employment in financial services dwindled, forcing unemployment rates up and disposable incomes down far below the national average (Parkinson et al., 2006). With a population experiencing greater out-migration than in-migration, these factors combined to reduce the city council's fiscal base, thus diminishing its capacity to sustain adequate public services (Parker, 2000). This, in turn, enabled a succession of independent councilors to blame asylum seekers and travelers for consuming scarce resources that "belonged" to local people. As the local electorate's long-standing support for the Labour Party ebbed away, the far-right British National Party (BNP) began to benefit from the racialization of social deprivation and local rivalries. In the 2004 Stoke city council elections, the BNP secured between a quarter and a third of the vote in the wards it contested, a level of support it maintains at the time of writing, notwithstanding reversals in its fortunes elsewhere in the Midlands and north of England in 2007.

THE WHITE COMMUNITY SPEAKS

Perhaps predictably, given the decline of the city, white participants in our focus groups offered an overwhelmingly negative assessment of life in Stoke-on-Trent. Younger people dismissed it as a "shithole," a "dump," or "crap." Their elders compared Stoke-on-Trent today unfavorably with the city they had grown up in, though many paid tribute to the enduring friendliness of its people and could not contemplate living anywhere else. Call centers, distribution hubs, and retail outlets had replaced major industries. Skilled, relatively well paid jobs had been lost and stable, self-sustaining communities broken up. Mining villages and vibrant commercial centers full of hardworking, respectable people had been reduced to wastelands. At the mercy of absentee landlords and uncaring housing providers, respectable neighborhoods had become "dumping grounds" for "foreigners" and "riff-raff." According to them, parts of the city had come to resemble a "war zone," "Beirut," "Africa," or "Bombay." Older people saw evidence of a decline in social discipline everywhere. Children respected nobody. Parents and police alike seemed to lack the will to do anything to control them. Drugs were ubiquitous and binge drinking and violence the apparently inevitable by-products of the burgeoning nighttime economy. By turns self-serving, uncaring, and incapable of delivering adequate and affordable public services, national and local politicians were distrusted by people of all ages and accused of favoritism, being out of touch, and allowing Stoke-on-Trent to fall far behind nearby cities such as Birmingham and Manchester.

Identity: "Us" and "Them"

Young and old alike associated industrial decline and social change with the presence of people they saw as outsiders, sometimes from elsewhere in the city or other parts of Britain, but most frequently from southern and eastern Europe, the Middle East, south Asia, and Africa. People described as "foreigners" or "immigrants" were widely perceived as both symptom and cause of Stoke-on-Trent's current malaise: evidence of the decline of "community" in previously homogenous working-class neighborhoods and responsible for much of the crime, disorder, and drug abuse that affected the quality of local people's lives. Although most participants made exceptions for particular individuals or groups, discussions generally proceeded on the basis of a straightforward distinction between "us" (people who belong in England, Stoke, and/or "our" community) and "them" (people who do not). Who "they" were, and what made "them" different, had little to do with participants' very imperfect knowledge of the law on immigration, asylum, and nationality. Birthplace, length of residence, and skin color were much less significant in people's judgments than ethnicity, attitude, and behavior. Londoners, "gypsies," and "riff-raff" from other parts of Stoke could find themselves condemned along with "foreigners" and "immigrants," while "niggers," "half-castes," and "Chinks" (despite the offensive language used to describe them) were accepted as "safe" and "sound": hardworking, respectful, and appreciative. For many younger people, "they," those who did not belong "here," who had a "bad attitude" and did not behave appropriately, were simply "Pakis." There was no necessary connection between "Pakis" and Pakistan: people of Indian, Iraqi, and Afghan origin could be "Pakis" too. Only "Kosovans" formed a distinct, but equally distrusted, alien group.

Immigration and Asylum: Who Deserves What?

Asked for their views about the way in which immigration and asylum were being dealt with by the government, focus group participants rarely paused to distinguish between asylum seekers, refugees, and other newcomers to Britain. People in the younger groups often competed with each other to suggest the most lethal and fantastical solutions to immigration (Dixon & Gadd, 2006). On reflection, many of them expressed similar views to their elders: the government should come clean about the scale of "the problem" (no one doubted that immigration was a problem); claims of persecution by those seeking asylum should be more thoroughly investigated; many more migrants should be "sent back" to where they came from; and access to benefits, housing, and health care should be restricted to dispel Britain's "soft touch" image. The crucial question for most participants was, Who deserves what? "Genuine" asylum seekers fleeing persecution; well-qualified, English-speaking professionals with valuable skills; and people prepared to live by "our" rules, speak "our" language, and work hard to make new lives for themselves all deserved to be allowed into Britain; illegal entrants, "srroungers," terrorists, disease carriers, people who refuse to "integrate," and "bogus" asylum seekers did not.

Victimization, Entitlement, and Disrespect

Participants' attitudes toward Stoke-on-Trent as a multiethnic community were often informed by quite limited personal experience of interacting with people from different backgrounds. Some participants gave firsthand accounts of adversarial and violent encounters with people from ethnic minority groups. The tellers were inclined to see themselves as the innocent victims of abusive and aggressive "Pakis" and "Asians," although the details of their accounts often left scope for interpretations of events contrary to their own. Common to all of these stories was the feeling that the police and the criminal justice system were biased against white people, indifferent to "our" victimization and obsessed with uncovering and punishing "our" racism. The health service, the benefits system, and local agencies responsible for providing social housing had also been coerced into favoring "them" as the only means of avoiding accusations of racism. While pensioners, ex-servicemen, and hardworking mothers providing for their children on meager salaries struggled to survive, lazy, good-for-nothing "Asians" and "asylum seekers" were given new homes and money for cars, driving lessons, designer clothes, and cell phones.

White people's feelings of relative disadvantage led us to conclude that part of the appeal of racism lay in its capacity to act as a receptacle for many unacknowledged emotions: shame about their inability to secure decent lives for themselves and their families; anxieties about ill health and the risk of criminal victimization; humiliation as their investments in the locality were exposed as unsophisticated or imprudent. It was as if the people we spoke to were aware that others perceived them as cultural and economic failures—as losers—and that, try as they might, there was little they could do counter this evaluation. In what were often quite paranoid-sounding polemics, migrants and ethnic minorities were frequently accused of lacking respect for "us," "our" country, "our" rules, and "our" way of life. Britain and Stoke-on-Trent were being "swamped" by the combined effects of mass immigration and unrestrained reproduction. Immigrants and their children were experienced as a constant, insubordinate, and intimidating presence on the streets, while a terrorist minority of "them" presented a profound threat to the nation's security. Instead of integrating and adapting to "our" way of life, "theirs" was being forced on "us": "our" children were "taught Muslim in school"; "they" thought they could treat women, including "white girls," as "second-class citizens"; "they" chose not to adhere to "our" standards of public hygiene; "they" maintained "their" own impenetrable cultural traditions and could speak in their own incomprehensible languages, while "our" culture and "our" language was there for everyone to understand but none to celebrate. Worse still, by working or being trained as doctors, some young people were afraid that immigrants could rapidly become better educated, wealthier, and more respected than they were—fears expressed even as they spoke highly of minority ethnic doctors who had treated them and their families in times of need. Rather than confront this discomforting contradiction, many participants fell back on the binary logic of racial politics. A vote for the BNP was equated with a vote for "us" whites against the intrusive presence, and potential one-upmanship, of a foreign "them."

Reading Racist Violence: "Brothers Jailed for Race Attacks"

Nevertheless, when asked to review a newspaper story about three local white brothers who had been sent to prison for attacking a "black student" and a "50-year-old Turkish man" after a night out, nearly all participants condemned what were presented as unprovoked, racially motivated attacks. Insofar as the story could be taken at face value, the majority of participants thought that the three brothers—two of whom had been sentenced to four years, the other to 18 months—had got no more than they deserved. Indeed, some older participants thought that the brothers had got off too lightly and saw the sentences as further evidence of the malign influence of politically correct "do-gooders" on the criminal justice system. However, having condemned the attacks as reported, some participants went on to reinterpret them either as having been provoked in some way or as having little or nothing to do with "race." The most streetwise group of young people thought that the victims must have said or done something to provoke the violence—even a look from the Turkish man would have sufficed, if, as they suspected, the brothers had been drinking. They and others also wondered whether the brothers might have objected to the student having a white girlfriend. For many older people, the incidents were unexceptional evidence of the worrying effects of alcoholic excess and the impulsivity of youth, rather than of any deep-seated racial antagonism. That the brothers had been convicted and punished at all, and the story reported so prominently in the local newspaper, was interpreted by some as yet another example of institutionalized bias against white people on the part of the criminal justice system and the media.

PERPETRATORS IN PERSPECTIVE: MULTIPLE PROBLEMS AND MIXED MOTIVATIONS

We describe here the 15 people implicated in acts of racial harassment in Stoke-on-Trent who took part in in-depth biographical interviews as "perpetrators," although many of them would not have recognized themselves as such. Although 7 or more of our 15 interviewees had, at some point in their lives, been routinely involved in violent crime, none could justifiably be characterized as a specialist racially motivated offender. Drunkenness, illicit drug consumption, drug dealing, and territorial and school-based loyalties were more typical features of the violence in which members of this sample were implicated. Five had been diagnosed with some kind of mental illness—including chronic or manic forms of depression. At least three had suffered paranoid delusions. Predictably, many of our respondents had experienced unhappy childhoods, been excluded from school, or were regular truants. Eight out of 15 of them disclosed childhood experiences of abuse, neglect, and/or domestic violence. Nine members of the sample were from homes "broken" by divorce, separation, and/or death.

RACIST ATTITUDES, HATE, AND DENIAL

Our research found that criminal justice outcomes were often a poor indicator of racist attitudes. Some of the least racist interviewees we met had convictions for racially aggravated crimes; some of the more prejudiced had none. In fact, the stories most of our interviewees told suggested that racism was rarely, if ever, the sole factor motivating their offending behavior and/or political activism. This was not simply because our perpetrators were "in denial" about their racism. Only two of our interviewees, Marcus and Shahid (given pseudonyms here, like all our respondents), provided accounts that suggested that they were denying the racism evident at the time the incidents in question occurred. Moreover, one of our respondents, Alan, appeared to have been convicted in circumstances where either the evidence of racial aggravation had been fabricated by the victim or where a psychotic bout Alan was suffering led him to use racist language to which he was self-consciously opposed. Conversely, a number of the younger white males (e.g., Greg, Paul, Steve, Stan) in our sample were relatively open about what they had done and unguarded in their often (but by no means universally) negative evaluations of different ethnic groups.

Stan was probably the only offender in our sample who could justifiably be accused of deploying race as a primary justification for violence; but even his behavior could only be understood when contextualized in terms of his experiences of injustice and victimization. Stan was a 19-year-old prisoner who conceded that he was a "proper little racist back in school," who "hate[d] Pakis" and wished that he was still involved with the far-right National Front. When Stan recounted the brutal attack he had made on a worker in a Turkish takeout restaurant, the breaching of standards of sexual and racial propriety were implicated. The story that unfolded was about Stan's desire to punish a "Paki bastard" who made suggestive remarks to a younger (white) woman with whom Stan had had a sexual relationship. Stan's story also revealed a life scarred by domestic violence, sexual abuse, drug taking, and involvement in organized crime.

Gender, Heterosexism, and Racial Propriety

Typically, the meaning of what appeared to be racially motivated offending or racist political activism only made sense when placed in the context of the alleged perpetrator's wider experiences of social interaction. Issues of gender and sexuality featured in many of the stories we heard. Belinda, an 18-year-old probationer, complained about refugees "gawping" at her as well as black and Asian men who have "no respect for women." She also pointed to examples of friends of hers who had been sexually harassed or physically beaten by men from ethnic minority groups. Conversely, Greg complained about a Turkish man who had chased his younger sister because their brother had stolen from him (Gadd & Jefferson, 2007). When he saw a white woman in the Turkish man's window, Greg threw a glass bottle at her. Recalling his thoughts at the time of the incident, Greg had the following to say:

> The cheeky twat . . . taking my white woman . . . my race. . . . I don't mind about black men . . . they can have as many white women as they want. It's just Asians, Turks, Albanians, whatever you want to call them. . . . I don't like seeing them with white women.

Conversely, Emma, a 28-year-old street robber of mixed ethnicity, had, on many occasions, been called "a dirty lesbian" by black and Asian men in her neighborhood. When she was younger, Emma had sent a letter purporting to be from the National Front to one of the black men who had harassed her, saying that he was "going to get slaughtered." Ten years later, the racially aggravated assault for which Emma was currently on probation had taken place after an exchange of similar racial and sexual slurs between her and four Pakistani men, none of whom had been arrested or prosecuted.

Injustice, Deprivation, and Paranoia

The themes of less eligibility and unequal treatment surfaced in many of our interviews. Paul, a 15-year-old aspiring member of the Young BNP, was particularly aggrieved by Asian youth ("dirty little things") who denied him access to play areas in a local park. However, Paul also got on well with the Asian shopkeepers who gave him credit. He was most concerned with immigrants who were "claiming taxes" and "not working," unlike his parents, who had "worked all their lives." This discourse about the "burden" imposed by immigrants on public services was a frequent feature of interviewees' recycling of common myths about the benefits nonwhites were assumed to be receiving. Darren, a disqualified driver and errant father, fantasized about putting a "bomb" to the "Pakis" he believed claim "for everything" for their "90,000 children" and was outraged by rumors that asylum seekers were getting free driving lessons, from which he, too, could have benefited. Others complained of unequal treatment by criminal justice practitioners. Marcus, a 22-year-old prisoner, explained that he had been a victim of racial harassment by a group of immigrant men who had told him to stay away from the "half-Asian" woman his friend was dating. Marcus claimed that these men, with whom he and a friend had fought, had benefited from a system loaded in their favor: "If they say you are being racist, you can't get out of it." Marcus claimed that his experiences of a biased criminal justice system had destroyed his sympathy for the Asian people he had grown up alongside.

Both the Asian men in our sample of perpetrators had similar complaints. Kamron, a 17-year-old British Bangladeshi and one-time cocaine dealer, had been remanded in custody for eight months for a racially aggravated assault on a boy who had daubed racist graffiti on their school walls, even though the boy conceded that Kamron had never said anything racist to him. Similarly, Shahid, a 22-year-old man of Pakistani descent who had been disqualified for drunk driving, complained that when the police approached the scene of an altercation in which he was not involved, they had singled him out for questioning because he was the "only Asian there." Shahid had been prosecuted for calling the arresting officers "white bastards" and for threatening to "kill their wives" but felt that these were "defensive" responses to the overzealous and demeaning treatment to which the police had subjected him.

Two of those with alcohol problems indicated that paranoia sometimes fuelled their racism. Steve, a 16-year-old in trouble for a range of antisocial behaviors, had "filled in" three "Kosovans" who had looked at him while he was drunk. He also claimed that they had muttered incomprehensibly in their own language before he started behaving in a threatening way toward them. Likewise, Carl, a 25-year-old recovering alcoholic, complained about the asylum seekers living in a nearby hostel who walked around in groups for their own protection and whose presence made him feel nervous when he had not drunk enough to boost his confidence. Carl was on probation for calling the female police officer who arrested him for drunk and disorderly behavior a "black bitch." Having previously been arrested and imprisoned for crimes he claimed not to have committed, Carl felt aggrieved with the police but insisted that he did not feel hostile toward established minority groups. Indeed, he expressed envious admiration for a group of Asian children who had thrown milk bottles at him because their mothers, unlike his own (a "dark-skinned" woman whom he had not seen since infancy), disciplined their children. Steve's views on established minorities were also broadly positive. He had "always" got along with "black" people, "black" being a term he used broadly to include Asians. His "best mate" was black, and he enjoyed going "rabbiting" with local gypsies. It was only "Kosovans" that Steve did not like because they "come over here to get benefits." But even here, Steve made an exception: a Kosovan lad was the only person at work with whom Steve felt he could "have a laugh."

Safety, Respect, and "Blatant" Racism

This kind of qualified racism ran through most of the accounts our interviewees provided and was often contrasted with what one of the BNP candidates (Frank, aged 44) described as the "blatant racism" inherent in discriminating against all nonwhite people, including those born in Stoke (Gadd, 2006). Frank himself had parted company with the BNP when he discovered that the party excluded "black and half-caste" people from membership. Likewise, Belinda, who complained about the threat posed to women by ethnic minority men, was just as critical of "wiggas," white boys "who talk as if they're black and wear all the big gold." Notwithstanding his qualms about "asylum seekers" stealing "his white women" and his involvement in numerous fights with Asians laying claim to "his" school and "his" town, Greg also said that he was not racist because he had "sound" "Asian mates" to whom he sold skunk marijuana. Meanwhile, Kamron, despite his experiences of racism, felt sorry for those poor white people whose communities had been blighted by drugs. Kamron was also the most critical of "Kosovans," whom he branded, somewhat contradictorily, as "tramps," affluent tax-evaders, "rapists," and "desperados." Kosovans had, in Kamron's view, given the local Asian community a bad name, something he felt justified his burglary of a Kosovan's flat.

It is these qualifiers that explain why themes such as respect and safety were as prominent as hate in many of the life stories we elicited. Among our sample of perpetrators, feelings of hatred were often inspired by what was perceived to be disrespectful or threatening behavior on the part of others. From the perspective of most of our perpetrators, the violence in which they were implicated had been provoked by threats to their own safety or reputations. Most of those within our sample who were routinely violent were young people who were generally not "well respected" by their teachers, parents, the police, or other adults in authority. Most of those respondents who engaged in racist violence could also recall earlier periods in their lives when older people had compromised their safety, while those in positions of authority had not acted appropriately in response. For Terry, the antiasylum activist, and Nigel, the BNP campaigner, the perceived disrespect shown by both the city council and young Asian people for local war memorials and graveyards was a source of considerable anger and frustration.

CONCLUSION

At a time when globalization processes routinely restructure ethnonationalist sentiments so that they assume a peculiarly localized form, bearing little relation to the state of the nations in question or their place in the world, it is difficult to know whether the findings of locally based studies like ours can be generalized to shed any light on the phenomenon of racial harassment elsewhere. Our view is that racist violence can rarely be fully understood without also understanding the histories of the places in which it is perpetrated and the people implicated in perpetrating it. That said, and to the extent that working-class people in many regions of the Western world have witnessed an upsurge of in-migration at a time when the security provided by traditional industries has waned, we believe our study of racism in Stoke-on-Trent has some wider purchase. Our research found racist attitudes to be widespread among the white, working-class population of Stoke-on-Trent. Thinking and talking in terms of "us" and "them," of people who belong and people who do not, was something that perpetrators shared with people of all ages from across the region. Older focus group participants felt an obvious sense of loss: industries, jobs, communities, a whole way of life had gone, never to return. Though they had never known the good times (real or imagined), younger people were living with the consequences of deindustrialization. They identified with their elders' sense of themselves as victims of discrimination imposed by a distant, "politically correct" elite that consistently expected the worst of people like them.

This context, coupled with the extent to which anti-immigrant sentiment appears to have gained global respectability, makes it all the more difficult to delineate clear differences between perpetrators and nonperpetrators. Meanwhile, the abhorrence of racial harassment expressed by most of the ordinary people we spoke to, like the public sympathy for Gee Walker, renders the concept of a "perpetrator community" (Sibbitt, 1997) too simplistic, and the notion that hate crime reproduces preexisting structures of domination (Perry, 2002) overly general. In Stoke-on-Trent, the vast majority of ordinary white people we interviewed associated immigration with everything that was wrong with their lives: crime, unemployment, inadequate health care, and substandard housing. Increasingly diverse migrant and minority ethnic populations were perceived by many members of the local white population as both a cause of the city's decline and as an indicator of their own inability to "have a nice home and a nice life," as one young mother expressed it—in other words, evidence of the extent to which they, working-class whites, appeared to be "losers" or cultural and economic failures. It is tempting, therefore, to conceptualize their racism as a defense against the shame of redundancy, as Ray and colleagues (2004) do. We agree, but we wish to emphasize two further things about this racism: its sadistic quality and its infusion with envy. Many of the ordinary white people we spoke to in focus groups took pleasure in imagining the suffering of ethnic others, particularly when encouraged to do so by fellow participants. This pleasure was often connected to their own feelings of powerlessness. Contemplating the humiliation of ethnic minority individuals who appeared to have achieved success in the face of adversity was one way in which some white people imagined they might win back their own sense of self-respect.

Among people who worked, relaxed, or studied together, shame, sadism, powerlessness, envy, and humiliation coalesced, turning minor and specific grievances into a generalized fear of a menacing ethnic other about to destroy everything good in the world. It is this coming together of a range of racializable grievances—rather than an underlying and common racist mindset—that the Far Right in Britain has successfully exploited as immigration has moved up the political agenda. That many white, working-class people feel themselves to be under attack by a political elite that blames the poor for their own poverty, and the many for the "antisocial" behavior of a few, feeds into the feelings of persecution that render the politics of blame superficially soothing. That many of these same people can also identify with the pain of bullying and physical victimization and freely acknowledge debts of gratitude to black and minority ethnic people who have helped them as professionals or befriended them and their families may provide enough of a reality check on paranoid thinking to stop the spiraling of racial hatred. Such checks, however, are much less effective when the demonized other takes the form either of the newly arrived "asylum seeker" or the densely mythologized "Paki" and is thus construed as so completely unknowable that no familiar individual or identifiable ethnic group can be related to it.

Paradoxically, the perpetrators we met, at least when interviewed on a one-to-one basis, tended to appear much less totalizing in their animosities than the nonperpetrators we interviewed in groups, the former tending to locate their grievances in specific conflicts with identifiable individuals on particular occasions, rather than in terms of negative feelings toward all-embracing stereotypes. When it came to recalling disputes that had culminated in the perpetration of acts of racial harassment or violence, however, it usually became evident that similar spiraling dynamics had come into play, with specific grievances and insecurities rapidly giving way to more general racialized fears and hatreds, fuelled, on occasion, by like-minded accomplices, friends, and family members. Considered in the context of their own biographies, we found that it was possible to identify with the anger and hurt associated with many perpetrators' feelings of aggression without also condoning their racist attitudes and behavior. At least some measure of pain and contrition could be detected behind most perpetrators' expressions of hatred, if only we, as researchers, were prepared to be receptive to it.

The defensive processes that help some "ordinary" white people cope with unsettling and uncertain circumstances, their fears of loss, inferiority, and insignificance, are very similar to those employed by the perpetrators of racial harassment in coming to terms with their experiences. But the perpetrators we met often had particularly acute reasons for feeling ashamed, worthless, humiliated, and fearful—and for feeling very much alone in these sorrowful states. While a few of them had gained a modicum of respectability among similarly criminalized peers, they were, by and large, some of the least respected people from their communities: excluded from school, deserted by their parents, unjustly treated, neglected and abused by those who owed them a duty of care. White and nonwhite perpetrators alike had upbringings that seemed brutal and devoid of the kind of containing care young people generally need to help them cope with experiences of threat and anxiety in later life. Predictably, they suffered more than their fair share of the alcohol, drug, and mental health problems that are features of the lives of the poor and the criminalized. For all their tough talk, almost all had been vulnerable, lonely, and troubled individuals when they racially abused others.

That racist individuals, especially when prone to violence, tend be complex and contradictory characters has been the main message of psychoanalytic engagements with the subject since Adorno, Frenkel-Brunswik, Levinson, and Sanford (1950). Unfortunately, this message has too often been obscured by Adorno and colleagues' misguided attempt to chart a single and unitary path from poor parenting to authoritarian personality. Those who follow this path overlook the many sources of trauma and shame that render prejudice *simultaneously alluring and repulsive* to so many people. Certainly there are crimes of *hate* in which perpetrators either satisfy some thrill-seeking, retaliatory, defensive, or missionary goals, as the profilers have documented, or physically project onto their victims parts of themselves they wish to counter or disown, thus enabling them—as the doing difference approach predicts—to accomplish a form of racialized identity by attacking someone else. The investment of many of the perpetrators we interviewed—Greg, Stan, Darren—in the idea that migrants were guilty of things they themselves had done—committing petty crime, carrying concealed weapons, harassing women, driving dangerously, and hanging around in menacing groups—is testimony to the role played by these kinds of projective processes and the extent to which they remain outside the conscious awareness of those most caught up in them. But the many acts of racial harassment that occur when vulnerable people—like Shahid, Emma, and Carl—suddenly feel under attack and lash out suggest a rather different etiology. In these instances, racial harassment is not simply motivated by "hate"; rather, racist epithets are used by those whose prejudices are not ordinarily strong to defend against the humiliation of having lost control. Such conceptual distinctions make no difference to the administration of justice in most jurisdictions. Nor do they usually count for much from the victim's perspective since, in both cases, the offender compounds the hurt caused by disowning his or her feelings of worthlessness by projecting them onto another. But to the extent that it is not possible to change either perpetrators or the communities from which they come without first recognizing the complex mix of hard-to-admit feelings on which racism and violence thrive, it is important to find ways of engaging with the specificities of particular offenders' motives. If there is to be any prospect of securing lasting change among those who cause pain by carrying out acts of racist violence and harassment, we must take care not to give the impression that we think that they, too, are all the same.

REFERENCES

Adorno, T. W., Frenkel-Brunswik, E., Levinson, D. J., & Sanford, R. N. (1950). *The authoritarian personality*. New York: Harper and Row.

Berk, R. A., Boyde, E. A., & Hamner, K. (2003). Thinking more clearly about hate-motivated crimes. In B. Perry (Ed.), *Hate and bias crime* (pp. 49–60). New York: Routledge.

Bowling, B., & Phillips, C. (2002). *Racism, crime and justice*. Harlow, Essex: Longman.

Dixon, W. J., & Gadd, D. (2006). Getting the message? "New" Labour and the criminalization of "hate." *Criminology and Criminal Justice, 6*, 309–328.

Ehrlich, H., Larcom, B. E., & Purvis, R. D. (2003). The traumatic effects of ethnoviolence. In B. Perry (Ed.), *Hate and bias crime* (pp. 153–217). New York: Routledge.

Gadd, D. (2006). The role of recognition in the desistance process: A case study of a far-right activist. *Theoretical Criminology, 10*, 179–202.

Gadd, D., & Jefferson, T. (2007). *Psychosocial criminology*. London: Sage.

Gobodo-Madikizela, P. (2003). *A human being died that night*. Claremont, Western Cape: David Philip.

Hollway, W., & Jefferson, T. (2000). *Doing qualitative research differently*. London: Sage.

Iganski, P. (2003). Hate crimes hurt more. In B. Perry (Ed.), *Hate and bias crime* (pp. 131–138). New York: Routledge.

Institute of Race Relations. (2008). "Factfile: Racially Motivated Murders (Known or Suspected) 2000 onwards http://www.irr.org.uk/2002/november/ak000008. html, last retrieved 08 December 2008.

McDevitt, J., Levin, J., & Bennett, S. (2003). Hate crime offenders: An expanded typology. In B. Perry (Ed.), *Hate and bias crime* (pp. 109–116). New York: Routledge.

Messner, D., McHugh, S., & Felson, B. (2004). Distinctive characteristics of assaults motivated by bias. *Criminology, 42*, 585–618.

Parker, M. (2000). Identifying in Stoke. In T. Edensor (Ed.), *Reclaiming Stoke-on-Trent* (pp. 255–270). Stoke-on-Trent, England: Staffordshire University Press.

Parkinson, M., Champion, T., Evans, R., Simmie, J., Turok, I., Crookston, M., et al. (2006). *State of the English cities*. London: Office of the Deputy Prime Minister.

Perry, B. (2002). *In the name of hate*. London: Routledge.

Ray, L., Smith, D., & Wastell, L. (2004). Shame, rage and racist violence. *British Journal of Criminology, 44*, 350–368.

Salisbury, H., & Upson, A. (2004). *Ethnicity, victimisation and worry about crime*. London: Home Office.

Sibbitt, R. (1997). *The perpetrators of racial harassment and racial violence*. London: Home Office.

Sun. (2005, November 30). Retrieved October 29, 2007, from http://www.thesun. co.uk/article/0,,2–2005550542,00.html

CHAPTER 6

FROM THE KLAN TO SKINHEADS: A CRITICAL HISTORY OF AMERICAN HATE GROUPS

Mark S. Hamm

Scholars have traditionally lumped hate groups together under the rubric of "right-wing extremists," suggesting that one group is no different than another. In this way, neo-Nazi groups like the Order are linked to tax resisters and bankrupt farmers of the Posse Comitatus, who are linked to the Aryan Brotherhood prison gang, who are in turn linked to the skinheads. All of these groups, so goes the argument, have in one way or another carried on the violent legacy of the Ku Klux Klan.

However, a careful analysis of the historical record reveals that hate groups, like the dominant cultures from which they come, are shaped by the historical context in which they emerge. Each hate group is therefore inflected by a specific ideological force field transmitted from the past. This historical transmission then gives each hate group its own unique life and meaning. "Moreover," writes hate crime scholar Barbara Perry (2006), "the understanding of hate crime requires consideration of the specific socio-historical context in which it emerges—an approach which is also a hallmark of recent critical theorizing" (pp. 156–157). Indeed, American hate groups are best understood in terms of seven waves of history.

THE FIRST WAVE: THE RECONSTRUCTION-ERA KU KLUX KLAN

Hate groups have existed in the United States since the Ku Klux Klan first appeared in Pulaski, Tennessee, in 1865. This earliest incarnation of the Klan was a secret, loosely knit vigilante network whose violence grew out of white rage over the South's defeat in the Civil War. From 1867 until its "official" disbandment by the authority of President Ulysses S. Grant's Ku Klux Klan Act of 1871, the Klan thundered across the war-torn South and former Confederate border states, sabotaging Reconstruction governments and imposing a reign of terror that included an untold number of murders, hangings, shootings, whippings, tar and featherings, acid brandings, rapes, castrations, and other forms of human mutilation (Wade, 1987). African Americans were the Klan's primary enemy because blacks posed a threat to southern white male hegemony. Freedom for the slaves led to recession in the southern economy; thus class concerns became intertwined with race and masculinity issues. For the Klan, white males were in a class above all nonwhites, women, and homosexuals. This established a trend that would last for generations: the purpose of the white supremacy movement was to maintain not only the status quo of white power, but also white male power. The Klan's most violent members—the notorious night riders—remained anonymous, however, shrouded in secret ceremonies, rituals, and costumes that bonded men to each other and to the cause itself.

THE SECOND WAVE: THE KU KLUX KLAN OF THE 1920s

The Ku Klux Klan resurfaced in the early twentieth century as a result of two developments: massive immigration and America's entry into World War I. For many Americans, these events led to widespread fear of foreigners and foreign powers. While no less violent than its predecessor, the second Klan—which, at its peak in 1925, boasted some 5 million members—stressed its role as a "benevolent" brotherhood and set out to convince nonbelievers that it was dedicated to defending the American way of life. During these years, the Klan drew its members mainly from the rural middle class: landowning farmers, merchants, small business owners, professionals, and skilled laborers. Sympathy for the Klan's nativism began to expand westward, first to rural Indiana and then to Kansas, Oklahoma, Texas, Colorado, and Oregon (Schlatter, 2006). The spectacular growth of the Klan was due largely to the fact that these rural areas of America had an entrenched history of racism and an equally long tradition of collective local action and vigilante justice (Davidson, 1996). The Klan's targets were expanded to include not only blacks, but Asians, immigrants, and bootleggers as well nightclubs, roadhouses, and all manner of scandalous behavior. With its newfound mission of social vigilance, the Klan identified its newest enemy: the Jew. Spurred on by a series of anti-Semitic articles published in the early 1920s by automobile tycoon Henry Ford, the Klan forged an argument that all of America's problems could be traced to an international Jewish conspiracy. Although women were allowed to join Klan auxiliaries, the heavy political lifting was still left to men, who were expected to be the propagators and protectors of the Anglo Saxon race.

THE THIRD WAVE: NAZISM AND THE APOCALYPTIC

Following a series of criminal scandals, Klan membership plummeted in the 1930s and 1940s, along with public support for its racist ideology. But political extremism did not disappear from the American landscape; rather, it found other outlets brought on by the Great Depression and the rise of Nazi Germany. These calamitous world affairs helped to shift the focus of prejudice from blacks to Jews and Communists, thereby leading to the creation of numerous organizations that thrived on native or imported versions of anti-Semitism, anti-Communism, and opposition to the New Deal policies of Franklin Delano Roosevelt—including fascist, pro-German, and Nazi movements (Toy, 1989).

The third wave of American hate groups emerged from these movements. Most significantly was the activism of Gerald L. K. Smith, who would provide the vital link between American Nazism of the 1930s and the rural radicalism of the white paramilitary hate groups that would appear in the American West 50 years later. In 1933 Smith was among the first to join William Dudley Pelly's Silver Shirts, a pro-Hitler group that copied the military dress, rhetorical style, and ideology of the German dictator. Predominantly native-born Protestants from the West and Midwest, the Silver Shirts attempted to emulate the violent tactics of Hitler's storm troopers. Equally important, due to Smith's influence, the Silver Shirts became the first American hate group to espouse the peculiar religious tenets of Christian Identity—a theology that gives the blessing of God to the racist cause. Identity proceeds from the notion that Jews are the children of Satan, while white "Aryans" are the descendants of the biblical tribes of ancient Israel and thus are God's chosen people. Identity holds that the world is on the verge of a final, apocalyptic struggle between good and evil, and that Aryans must do battle with the Jewish conspiracy so that the world can be saved (Barkun, 1997). By the late 1940s, Smith was the most prominent anti-Semite in America. His focus was on mobilizing Christian Identity figures in the American West on behalf of a militant right-wing political agenda.

THE FOURTH WAVE: THE CIVIL RIGHTS–ERA KU KLUX KLAN

Between 1956 and 1966, a new generation of southern Klansmen unleashed the most violent reign of hate crime terror witnessed in the American twentieth century. In response to John F. Kennedy's commitment to bringing racial equality to all Americans—a commitment that would not have been possible without the activism of Martin Luther King Jr. and the southern civil rights movement—Klansmen and their supporters were responsible for more than 130 bombings and were implicated in dozens of shootings, hangings, and mutilations (Toy, 1989). The Klan firebombed the homes of African Americans involved in the civil rights campaign. They firebombed black churches, in one instance killing four young girls in Birmingham, Alabama. Hundreds of civil rights volunteers were beaten by the Klan, including women and children. Dozens were kidnapped and murdered.

Historians attribute the sharp increase in racial violence to the Klan's evolving organizational capabilities. Membership in the southern Klan steadily rose, from roughly 20,000 in the late 1950s to an estimated 60,000 by the mid-1960s. Most of their violence was planned and executed by an inner circle of Klansmen and their allies, whose identities were often kept secret from rank-and-file members, thereby providing a built-in firewall of protection against law enforcement (Abanes, 1996; Toy, 1989). Not that a firewall was always necessary. When Freedom Riders arrived in Birmingham in 1961, police commissioner William "Bull" Connor gave Klansmen 15 minutes to attack the riders before sending in the police. During a 1964 Klan counterdemonstration against civil rights workers, police turned their backs as Klansmen drove through the Birmingham streets in a sound truck blaring the Klan theme song, "Move Them Niggers North" (Branch, 2006)—presaging the widespread use of music as a weapon of intimidation that would become a trademark of the skinhead subculture 20 years later. These were just two of many examples of an alliance between law enforcement and the Ku Klux Klan to carry out violent resistance to desegregation efforts.

THE FIFTH WAVE: PARAMILITARY SURVIVALISTS OF THE REAGAN ERA

Klan violence of the civil rights era led President Lyndon Johnson to enact federal policies that would effectively curtail crimes committed by American extremists. Urban race riots, political assassinations, and the war in Vietnam did little to rekindle public sympathy for white supremacists, and by the early 1970s, Klan membership had dwindled to less than 4,000 members nationwide (Toy, 1989). Yet the recession-prone late 1970s and early 1980s brought about a resurgence of American hate groups, energized by mythologies of the American West. As Louis Beam (1983), a militant Texas Klansman and ambassador at large of the Aryan Nations, warned at the time, "Out of the west . . . the wind of revolution. It is the time of the radical now."

Like the early Klan, white racists of the 1980s were influenced by a militarized vision of their own masculinity. Many of these men had come of age during the Vietnam War: their participation in that lost cause, or their failure to make a personal appearance on the battlefield, became a turning point in their lives (Gibson, 1994). As adults, they saw that the white man's world they had taken to be permanent was gone. Dark forces of chaos had overtaken America—immigration, drugs, crime, abortion, and the trickle-down economics of the Reagan administration. Since these hot-button issues were often seeded with race and gender considerations, white supremacists exploited them to their advantage in the 1980s, much as the Klan had done in the 1920s. It therefore became not only permissible, but morally imperative, for some powerless white men to transform their personal rage into a political cause (Berry, 1999). Masculinity and whiteness became entwined as never before—to be a "real" white man was to be hypermasculine. Paramilitary mythology came to be seen as the path to redemption. In secret camps across rural America, white extremists of all descriptions began training in the use of assault weapons, grenades, rocket launchers, and explosives—all in preparation for a coming war against Jewish-inspired race-mixing policies designed to mongrelize, and thus weaken, the Aryan race. Many extremists traded in their robes for combat boots and were reborn as Aryan warriors.

Robert J. Mathews was the definitive Aryan warrior of this era. Alongside six other white men from the American West, Mathews founded the Order at his home in Metaline Falls, Washington, in 1983. Integrating long-standing threads of American neo-Nazism with Christian Identity and the fantastic possibilities of William Pierce's science fiction novel, *The Turner Diaries* (1978), Mathews's gang hit on a formulation of how warriors could achieve a sacred order. They began acting out the plot of the *Diaries*. They armed themselves, studied guerilla warfare, conducted assassinations, became involved in counterfeiting, and planned large-scale sabotage of public utilities—all as part of what the Order believed was a struggle for white survival within the context of a frontier heritage embedded in ideas about the American "character" (Schlatter, 2006).

The federal government was Mathews's primary stated enemy because it represented a Jewish-inspired program bent on extending equal rights to minorities, women, and homosexuals. Yet the Order's top priority was stealing money—lots of it. And they did, robbing banks and armored trucks to the tune of millions of dollars, which were incrementally funneled into the white racist underground in support of more deadly attacks against the U.S. government.

The Order's terrorism ended on December 8, 1984, when Mathews was killed by Federal Bureau of Investigation (FBI) agents in a legendary shoot-out on Whidbey Island, Washington. The surviving Order members were arrested and given extended prison sentences. And with that, the Order became a revolutionary role model for white supremacists around the world. That others would attempt to emulate their violence was inevitable.

THE SIXTH WAVE: NEO-NAZI SKINHEADS OF THE THATCHER/REAGAN ERA

In many ways, contemporary hate groups are emblematic of late modernity's defining trait: a world always in flux, awash in marginality and exclusion. As we have seen, the eccentric beliefs and cultures of American hate groups are sewn together from the threads of previous movements. Essentially, the skinheads cut those threads and began from scratch. American hate groups have traditionally emerged from Protestant agrarianism and Western mythology; xenophobia and the apocalyptic; white male hegemony and overstated masculinities. The skinheads would forge their ideology from the blazing fires of youth subculture. For them, violence had less to do with the nativistic impulses to preserve the American way of life than it did with subcultural *style*. The skinheads emerged not from rural areas, but from urban landscapes swaying under the weight of globalization. And while American hate groups have long shaped their cultural and racial identities from the rugged individualism of the archetypical white frontiersman, "pushing ever westward, seeking new homelands and new beginnings," as Schlatter (2006, p. 83) contends, the skinheads drew their inspiration from Great Britain.

The Early Years

The skinheads were born in London sometime around 1969. The skinhead subculture was based on two seemingly incompatible sources: the style of a flashy but tough black Jamaican street gang called the "rude boys," and a mythical image of the traditional British working-class community (Hebdidge, 1979). Skinhead values included a pride in neighborhood territory; a rough machismo demeanor; obsessions with soccer and beer drinking; and a stripped-down, regressive approach to consumer capital. The early skins (also referred to as suede heads or bone heads) cut their hair in a short rude boy crop, wore work jeans, and polished dockworker boots called Dr. Martens (Frith, 1978). But the original skinheads were not ostensibly racist (to the contrary, early skins included black Jamaicans known as two-toners). Nor did they believe in Nazism. All of that would come later.

Skinhead violence surfaced in the East London dance halls around 1971 with what was then called "idiot dancing" (slam dancing, as it is known today)—a wild and aggressive boogie intended to draw blood, or at least render some serious pain. Idiot dancing led to fights between skinheads and hippies; these fights spilled onto the streets, and in time, the skinheads identified a second victim: the Pakistani immigrant. Thus was born the style of "Paki-bashing." And shortly thereafter came "queer bashing."

In the mid-1970s, the British economy plummeted to its lowest point since World War II, bringing the nation a host of new social ills. With massive unemployment and daily power outages affecting nearly every London working-class neighborhood, the ominous specter of racial violence became an all-too-frequent feature of British society. It was within this context that the punk music scene was born. Invigorated by such classic punk bands as the Sex Pistols, the Clash, and the Damned, the punk movement defined its subcultural space through symbols of nihilism, sexism, anarchy, and violence—violence expressed abstractly against anyone, including each other and themselves (Dancis, 1978).

In 1976 glam rockers David Bowie, Lou Reed, and Iggy Pop entered what they called their Berlin phase. Owing to their fascination with these rock icons, punks developed an interest in the decadence of Nazi Germany. Hence the swastika was adopted as a new punk symbol. Like the abstract way in which they expressed their violence, however, the punks themselves did not adopt the ideology of Nazism denoted by this symbol (Laing, 1985). "The signifier (swastika) had been willfully detached from the concept (Nazism)," wrote sociologist Dick Hebdidge (1979), "and although it had been re-positioned (as "Berlin") within an alternative subcultural context, its primary value and appeal derived precisely from its lack of meaning" (p. 117).

Nazi symbolism became fashionable across the youth subcultural scene. London youths began wearing swastikas and jewelry emblazoned with the Iron Cross and the SS insignia. Even heavy metal bands got in on the act, as rock God Jimmy Page of Led Zeppelin, on at least one occasion, performed in concert wearing the uniform of a Nazi storm trooper (Davis, 1985). Offending all sensibilities about the Holocaust, the Sex Pistols released a single titled "Belsen Was a Gas." An early skinhead band, the Exploited, dropped one called "Hitler's in the Charts Again." These were the days when a band appeared on the streets of London with the name Elvis Hitler (Hamm, 1993).

Neo-Nazi Skinheads

A second generation of London skinheads came to the fore around 1982 against the backdrop of two key policy initiatives of the Margaret Thatcher administration. The first dealt with immigration. Thatcher inaugurated her tenure as prime minister by declaring that she understood "the feelings of those who fear that the British culture may be swamped by an alien one" (as quoted in Bowling, 1990, n. 2). Such nationalistic rhetoric led a number of analysts to conclude that Thatcherism had facilitated the incorporation of a common-sense form of racist logic into mainstream political discourse. The second policy initiative involved economic reforms intended to ameliorate Britain's financial woes through the creation of thousands of new, low-paying jobs designed to provide goods and services to the affluent upper class. In concert with her most influential global ally, U.S. president Ronald Reagan, Thatcher therefore made important strides in facilitating the pursuit of self-interest in British society. Social historian Neil Nehring (1993) aptly describes the effects of these policies:

> Thatcherism and Reaganism . . . robbed the word *public* of any positive reso- nances. . . . The two leaders damned long-established efforts at social reme- diation as inherently repressive. When the people of the United States and England allowed common sense to be defined in this way early on, by Reagan- ism and Thatcherism, those demagogic, populist appeals could then be accom- panied by the imposition of authority and order—the actual expansion of state power—against the supposed drags on the economy. . . . The ruling economic interests broke more expansive labor and curtailed spending on social relief, while fueling the immensely profitable military industry. (pp. 97–98)

These crucial historical developments—the introduction into public life of a rhetoric of nationalism, and with it, a legacy of racism; the rise of self-interest in British society, coupled with an increase in militarism; and the punk move- ment, with its rage and Nazi fetishism among working-class youth—created the basis for what Stuart Hall (1988) has referred to as Britain's "new authori- tarianism." The stage was set for the appearance of the neo-Nazi skinheads. Yet their emergence would not have been possible without a deliberate, well- orchestrated recruitment and indoctrination campaign to bring thousands of youth into the ranks of right-wing extremism.

At the center of that campaign was Ian Stuart Donaldson (widely known by his stage name, Ian Stuart), front man for the definitive racist skinhead band Skrewdriver. Stuart encapsulated the political mood of the times into a form of protest music intended to appeal to legions of English teenagers who had been shoved into a near-lumpen status by the British economy. Yet Skrewdriver's music was altogether void of English parochialisms; instead, it was designed as world music. Moreover, Stuart appropriated the new au- thoritarianism and transformed it into a seductive style of lowbrow enter- tainment that eventually captured the imagination of millions of alienated white kids from London to Berlin, from Stockholm to New York.

This trajectory is traced to 1982 with the release of Skrewdriver's semi- nal white power album *Hail the New Dawn*, containing Stuart's anthems of human survival for white youth of the 1980s: "White Power," "Race and Na- tion," and "Rudolf Hess (Prisoner of Peace)." The intention of these songs was to produce a sort of mystical, "bully boy" appeal for a "clean white Brit- ain" in which the Viking—that barbarous Celtic warrior of Led Zeppelin lore—returns once again to rule the British Isles. A music critic wrote at the time, "Skrewdriver turned the clock back hundreds of years and glori- fied the age where life was a day to day battle for survival, disease was rife, war ever present, and the mass of people lived as virtual slaves" (as quoted in Hamm, 1993, p. 34). *Hail the New Dawn* was not an artistic rebellion *against* Thatcherism and Reaganism; rather, it was a full-throttled endorse- ment of everything those regimes stood for. Assisted by the National Front (a neo-fascist organization with offices in London, Paris, Berlin, and Rome), in 1983, Skrewdriver became the world's leading white power rock band.

This occurred by dint of the fact that a number of hard-core London punks were still flirting with the violent, reactionary symbols of Nazism. Ian Stuart was suddenly in the right place at the right time. Breathing intendment into the otherwise meaningless punk symbols of Nazism, Stuart and his associates created a homologous paramilitary youth subculture dedicated to intimidation and violence against persons because of their race, religion, or sexual preference. Doc Marten boots were transformed into weapons of street combat. Gluttonous amounts of beer became the elixir. The Viking was converted to a symbol of British nationalism and masculinity. Violence became subcultural *style* expressed in "Paki- bashing," "beserking," and "sidewalk cracking."

By 1990 the number of racial attacks provoked by skinheads was estimated by the British Home Office at roughly 70,000 per year, including a total of 74 murders of Afro-Caribbean and Pakistani men between 1985 and 1989. Skinheads were also implicated in the bombing of some 20 mosques in London (Hamm, 1993). With the collapse of Communism, skinhead violence spread to Western Europe and then into former eastern bloc countries. German skinheads reportedly injured more than 80,000 foreigners and asylum seekers during the early 1990s. Other European skinheads adopted a more global posture by joining mercenary movements in Croatia; supporting the policy of ethnic cleansing against Muslims; and, in Iraq, supporting Saddam Hussein's campaign of genocide against the nation's Kurdish population (Schmidt, 1993). Meanwhile, the international marketing of Nazi memorabilia became a $100 million-a-year commercial enterprise. Record companies in Germany, France, and the United States created a stable of racist skinhead bands and a thriving market for white power rock music, fictionalizing violent nationalism. Hate crime was now an international commodity.

American Skinheads

The American skinheads took root in popular culture during the latter half of the 1980s, as the mainstream culture of the United States became anchored in conservatism, Republicanism, patriotism, militarism, and the traditional "family values" that were at the heart of both Reaganism and a growing religious revival waged by the Fundamentalist Christian Right. Over the years, the tally of skinhead hate crimes has run the gamut from homicide and attempted mass murder to cross burnings and desecrations of Jewish memorials. The skinhead movement is not monolithic, however. It comprises numerous subcultural entities with wide-ranging values, beliefs, and criminal tendencies. Some skinheads are hard-core racists; some are not. For example, Skin Heads against Racial Prejudice (SHARP) is an organization of antiracist youth who embrace first-generation skinhead principles of multi-culturalism and tolerance. These young people became skinheads strictly for cultural reasons: they liked the look and the music, but not the politics. In fact, SHARP considers itself an enemy of the neo-Nazi skinheads.

THE SEVENTH WAVE: PATRIOTS, SKINHEADS, KLANSMEN, AND CRIMINALS

American hate groups underwent a dramatic change in the mid-1990s. Inspired by the martyrdom of Robert J. Mathews, their primary goal was to complete the Order's unfinished business. This offered white supremacists an unprecedented point of unity. Skinhead, traditional Klan, and neo-Nazi groups all absorbed the revolutionary and religious beliefs popularized by the Order and kept the force of their rage turned toward the federal government—especially the paramilitary arm of the Justice Department responsible for the 1992 attack on the family of white separatist Randy Weaver at Ruby Ridge, Idaho, and the 1993 raid on David Koresh and the Branch Davidians in Waco, Texas. Their enemy list also included those whom they saw as receiving special treatment by the government: nonwhites and homosexuals.

From 1987 through the mid-1990s, the United States experienced a remarkable surge of hate crime violence, due in large part to the criminal activity of neo-Nazi skinheads. Once older white supremacists saw that the new generation was willing to carry out their own violent ideals, they rushed to enlist the loyalty of skinheads everywhere. This coalition produced an unintended consequence for the white power movement.

American skinheads are not a hate group per se; rather, they are part of an international youth subculture that owes allegiance more to the values, style, and music of British youth subcultures than it does to the politics of the American Far Right. Because of this global orientation, skinheads in the United States became more inclusive of women than were old-school Klan and neo-Nazi groups. After alliances were forged between skinheads and traditional white extremists, women began to play a role in constructing the white power agenda. Kathleen Blee (1996) has shown that while men still made up the bulk of the movement's membership, women would eventually comprise nearly half of the new recruits in many Klan, neo-Nazi, and skinhead organizations. Women seldom held positions of power within these groups, yet they contributed significantly to group solidarity and recruitment efforts. This participation allowed them to selectively disregard aspects of white supremacy ideology that varied from their personal beliefs and experiences. Accordingly, white power women began to support legal abortion and interracial relationships, despite the movement's strong prohibitions against those behaviors. But more to the point of this essay, women introduced into the movement a relatively broad-minded view of homosexuality.

The Aryan Republican Army

The archetypical hate group of this period was the Aryan Republican Army (ARA). The ARA was a six-member "cell" responsible for a string of professionally executed bank robberies in the Midwest between 1992 and 1996—the purpose of which was to support a series of terrorist attacks that included armored truck heists, sabotaging public utilities, derailing trains, assassinations, and bombings. As incredible as it may sound, the ARA's goal was to overthrow the federal government.

The ARA was composed of ex-convicts and skinhead musicians from the East Coast who were drawn to the American West on the strength of its mythology. The ARA drew its consciousness from three divergent sources: far-right German totalitarianism (Hitler's Third Reich), far-left Irish insurgency (the Irish Republican Army), and the "social banditry" of the Jesse James gang. They did so by dint of the odd religion known as the Phineas Priesthood, an offshoot of Christian Identity which holds that Anglo Saxons are the true Israelites depicted in the Old Testament, while Jews are actually the children of Satan. Phineas sermons teach that God's law prohibits race mixing, taxation, abortion, and the participation of Jews in government. Phineas actions are intended to rid society of these evils through robbing banks and armored trucks, assassinating political leaders, and bombing federal buildings. Among its heroes, the Phineas Priesthood counts such infamous criminals as Robin Hood, Jesse James, John Wilkes Booth, and Robert J. Mathews (Hoskins, 1990).

The ARA was founded in 1993 by Peter Langan, a 35-year-old career criminal once described by a veteran FBI agent as "one nasty dude" (as quoted in Hamm, 2004). Langan defied all the rules of the white supremacy movement. By day, he was known as Commander Pedro (a code name patterned after Robert Mathews's alias, "Carlos"), the hypermasculine ARA leader who robbed banks with paramilitary precision. By night, he was known as Donna McClure—a Kansas City drag queen dressed in a wig, makeup, jewelry, and an evening gown. Langan's involvement in the white supremacy movement was all about rectifying the crisis over his masculinity. It was all about gaining the respect of other men by employing terrorist imagery, style, and symbolic meaning to act out a warrior dream based on the movement's long-standing obsession with hegemonic masculinity.

Hegemonic masculinity (or the preponderant influence of white males over others) is defined by what it opposes—the feminine, the weak, the passive, the nonwhite. It is characterized by such traits as competitiveness, aggressiveness, and heterosexuality. Hegemonic masculinity has been the cornerstone of the American white supremacy movement since its inception. Without it, the movement is doomed. Movement leaders are acutely aware of this and have identified the influence of feminist thinking as their primary culprit on the grounds that it emasculates white men. Rampant feminism, argued *Turner Diaries* author William Pierce, had created a generation of activists who were "sissies and weaklings . . . flabby, limp-wristed, non-aggressive, non-physical, indecisive, slack-jawed, fearful" men who were heterosexual in theory only, with "not a vestige of the old Macho spirit . . . left in them" (as quoted in Hamm, 2002, p. 286). With some of these words, he could have been describing Langan and the ARA.

Feminism derives its appeal from the fact that hegemonic masculinity has been an extremely difficult goal to achieve for many males in the white power movement. They have been unable to achieve that goal for a number of reasons. Among them is the undisputable fact that the movement's various campaigns of ideological violence have all been monumental failures. To recount the history of hate groups in America is to recall a legacy of lost causes. Warrior dreams turn out to be little more than that: grand delusions. Shortly after he was sentenced to life in prison for his role in the ARA's bank robbery campaign, Langan told the author,

> I wish I hadn't done it. I'd rather be in one of your classes at the university, arguing with you over gun control. . . . I can say with no exaggeration that my gender dysphoria and not being able to deal with it in a positive way has put me where I am today.

Of course, the history of American hate groups does not end there. Around the country, new hard-core racist and anti-Semitic groups appear with astonishing regularity. It is from this fringe that tomorrow's radicals will come—alienated young white men trying to live out the warrior dreams of their generation. Then, in time, like those who have come before, they will drift off into the desolation and monotony of prison life, where nothing but regret and loss awaits them.

REFERENCES

Abanes, R. (1996). *American militias: Rebellion, racism and religion.* Downers Grove, IL: InterVarsity Press.

Barkun, M. (1997). *Religion and the racist Right: The origins of Christian identity.* Chapel Hill: University of North Carolina Press.

Beam, L. (Speaker). (1983). *We have a nation* Audiotape.

Berry, B. (1999). *Social rage: Emotion and cultural conflict.* New York: Garland.

Blee, K. (1996). Becoming a racist: Women in contemporary Ku Klux Klan and neo-Nazi groups. *Gender and Society, 10,* 680–702.

Bowling, B. (1990). *Racist harassment and the process of victimization: Conceptual and methodological implications for crime surveys.* Paper presented at the Realist Criminology Conference, Vancouver, BC, Canada.

Branch, T. (2006). *At Canaan's edge: America in the King years 1965–68.* New York: Simon & Schuster.

Dancis, B. (1978). Safety-pins and class struggle: Punk rock and the Left. *Socialist Review, 8*, 58–83.

Davidson, O. G. (1996). *Broken heartland: The rise of America's rural ghetto.* Iowa City: University of Iowa Press.

Davis, S. (1985). *Hammer of the gods: The Led Zeppelin saga.* New York: Ballantine.

Frith, S. (1985). Britbeat. In D. Marsh et al. (Eds.), *Rock and roll confidential.* New York: Pantheon.

Frith, S. (1978) *The sociology of rock.* London: Constable.

Gibson, W. J. (1994). *Warrior dreams: Violence and manhood in post-Vietnam America.* New York: Hill and Wang.

Hall, S. (1988). *The hard road to renewal: Thatcherism and the crisis of the Left.* New York: Verso.

Hamm, M. S. (1993). *American skinheads: The criminology and control of hate crime.* Westport, CT: Praeger.

Hamm, M. S. (2002). *In bad company: America's terrorist underground.* Boston: Northeastern University Press.

Hamm, M. S. (2004). Apocalyptic violence: The seduction of terrorist subcultures. *Theoretical Criminology, 8*, 323–339.

Hebdidge, D. (1979). *Subculture: The meaning of style.* London: Methuen.

Hoskins, R. K. (1990) *Vigilantes of Christendom: The history of the Phineas Priesthood.* Lynchburg, VA: Virginia Publishing.

Laing, D. (1985). *One cord wonders: Power and meaning in punk rock.* Milton Keynes, England: Open University Press.

Nehring, N. (1993). *Flowers in the dustbin: Culture, anarchy, and postwar England.* Ann Arbor: University of Michigan Press.

Perry, B. (2006). Missing pieces: The paucity of hate crime scholarship. In W. DeKeseredy & B. Perry (Eds.), *Advancing critical criminology: Theory and application* (pp. 155–178). Lanham, MD: Rowman & Littlefield.

Schlatter, E. A. (2006). *Aryan cowboys: White supremacists and the search for a new frontier, 1970–2000.* Austin: University of Texas Press.

Schmidt, M. (1993). *The New Reich: Violent extremism in unified Germany and beyond.* New York: Pantheon.

Toy, E. V. (1989). Right-wing extremism from the Ku Klux Klan to the Order, 1915–1988. In T. R. Gurr (Ed.), *Violence in America: Protest, rebellion, reform* (pp. 131–152). Newbury Park, CA: Sage.

Wade, C. W. (1987). *The fiery cross: The Ku Klux Klan in America.* New York: Simon & Schuster.

CHAPTER 7

WHITE NATIONALISM IN AMERICA

Heidi Beirich and Kevin Hicks

As scholar Michael Barkun (1994) has pointed out, white nationalists are "not simply younger than their predecessors but better educated, more polished, more adroit in shaping their message to a skeptical audience, having learned from David Duke's example how effectiveness, appearance, and manner can deflect hostility" (p. 253). White nationalism is a variegated movement, but most groups see the future of white America as threatened by the liberalizing forces of *cultural Marxism* and the devastating impact of third world immigration.

HISTORY OF THE WHITE NATIONALIST MOVEMENT

The history of American white nationalism as a political movement is rooted in the creation of the White Citizens Councils, on one hand, which arose to fight desegregation in the South, and in the ideas propagated by George Lincoln Rockwell, founder of the American Nazi Party (McMillan, 1971). The first chapter of the White Citizens Council was founded in 1954 by 14 whites under the leadership of Robert "Tut" Paterson in Indianola, Mississippi, in response to the U.S. Supreme Court ruling in *Brown v. Board of Education*, which determined segregated schools to be unconstitutional. Within a few months, the councils had spread into the rest of the Deep South. Hodding Carter, a newspaper owner in the Mississippi Delta, described the Citizens Councils at the time as an "uptown Klan." They didn't wear robes, met openly, and were seen by many as being "reputable"; in most communities, there was little or no stigma associated with being a member of the councils.

White nationalism was also influenced by the ideas of George Lincoln Rockwell, founder of the American Nazi Party. Though an explicit neo-Nazi and Hitler partisan, Rockwell is credited with developing a more expansive definition of the white race. Up until Rockwell, Adolf Hitler's views of race were considered sacrosanct in white supremacist circles. According to Frederick J. Simonelli (1999), Hitler "posited a systematic grouping of the earth's 'races' within a hierarchical structure in which the Germans—the 'master race'—together with their ethnic cousins—northern European Anglo-Saxons and Scandinavians—stood above the less-blessed 'races,' in descending order: the Mediterranean peoples, the Slavs, the Asiatics, and the blacks" (p. 101). Rockwell's epiphany was that a white racial movement in America would need to include all European ethnic groups to be politically viable. As Simonelli (1999) has noted, Rockwell came to see Hitler's hierarchy as "a fatal impediment to his political ambition" (p. 101)—so he included Americans of southern and eastern European ethnicity and those from the Mediterranean, most surprisingly, Turks, in his definition of white people. Consequently, the American Nazi Party ruptured in 1965, leading Rockwell to change its name to the National Socialist White People's Party.

For white nationalists, Rockwell's redefinition of the white race helped to advance their racial agenda. Seeing themselves as a more mainstream movement, they typically reject the ideological trappings of neo-Nazis and other racist groups, such as skinheads, whom they view as not being of their class or more ganglike than political. For Trask (2002), writing in the academic racist newsletter *American Renaissance*, the "white" category today includes "1) Nordic (English, Celtic, German, Scandinavian), 2) Slavic (Russian, Baltic, Polish, Czech, Serbian, Croatian), 3) Mediterranean (Spanish, Italian, Greek, Hungarian, Jewish)" (p. 5). Although some white nationalists would object to the inclusion of Jews, the notion of creating a movement with such broad potential appeal is just as attractive to white nationalists as it was to Rockwell in his day.

By the 1980s, the Whites Citizens Councils were all but defunct, having lost the battle against desegregation. But in 1985, using the original mailing lists of the White Citizens Councils, and with the help of Patterson, Gordon Lee Baum, a white nationalist and personal injury lawyer from St. Louis, Missouri, sought to revive the institution (Southern Poverty Law Center [SPLC], 1999). Baum created the Council of Conservative Citizens, which, in 2006, had 42 chapters in 19 states, not all of them southern (SPLC, 2007b, p. 55). Baum has claimed that the council has had as many as 15,000 members, making it one of the largest racist organizations in America (Beirich & Moser, 2004). The group is specifically antiblack, having described blacks as "a retrograde species of humanity," and anti-immigrant (Stuebner, 2002).

For years, the group attracted high-level politicians to speak at its meetings, which are similar to Rotary Club events, but decorated with Confederate flags and marked by racist speeches. Senate majority leader Trent Lott (R-Miss.) spoke to the group several times, once telling its members they "stand for the right principles and the right philosophy," then later claiming he had "no firsthand knowledge" of it (as cited in Beirich & Moser, 2004, p. 11). In 1998, after Lott's relationship with the council was exposed, the Grand Old Party (GOP) head, Jim Nicholson, took the unusual step of asking party members to resign from the group because of its "racist views" (Pitcavage, 1999).

During the 1990s, another explicitly southern variant of white nationalism emerged, usually referred to as the neo-Confederate movement, an amalgam of groups that celebrate the antebellum era, glorify confederate society, and discount the evils of slavery. The most important of such groups, the League of the South, argues for southern secession and the creation of a new southern society that would be hierarchical and patriarchal, with white men at the top and blacks at the bottom. Founded in 1994 by a group of academics with PhDs, mostly from southern universities, many of whom would eventually quit as the league became more explicitly racist, the group would adopt a theocratic idea of southern nationalism in which white Christian males would rule and people other than white Christians would be allowed to live in the South, but only if they bowed to "the cultural dominance of the Anglo-Celtic people and their institutions" (as cited in SPLC, 2000, p. 15). At its height, the league's head, J. Michael Hill, who holds a PhD in Celtic history from the University of Alabama, claimed to have some 9,000 members (SPLC, 2000).

The council and the league represent the southern strand of the white nationalist movement, but arguably the most important single figure in the development of modern white nationalism is David Duke. In 1980, he founded the National Association for the Advancement of White People, a white nationalist organization whose name was a riff on the civil rights organization called the National Association for the Advancement of Colored People (NAACP). Though he was photographed as a young man in Klan robes, Duke had a semisuccessful political career in Louisiana in the 1980s and early 1990s, in which he used coded racist appeals against affirmative action and busing to build up white support. In 1989, Duke ran as a Republican for a seat representing his hometown, Metairie, in the Louisiana House of Representatives. He defeated fellow Republican John Treen in a victory that came despite appeals in favor of Treen's candidacy by then president George H. W. Bush and other GOP notables ("GOP Condemns," 1989). In a losing run for the governorship in 1991, Duke received 671,009 votes, which was 38.8 percent of the total vote, something he considered an unqualified success. "I won my constituency. I won 55 percent of the white vote" said Duke (as quoted in Bridges, 1995, p. 236), which a number of exit polls confirmed.

By the late 1990s, Duke became deeply ensconced in the neo-Nazi movement, and his books and Web sites began spewing vitriol against Jews. In 1998, Duke published his autobiography *My Awakening: A Path to Racial Understanding*. The book details Duke's life and his social philosophies, especially his reasoning behind the need for racial separation. While personal scandal and a criminal conviction forced Duke into the political wilderness by the turn of the century,[1] his racial appeals remain popular in white nationalist circles, and his concerted effort to build a viable political movement is seen as groundbreaking. And his imprint on Louisiana politics remains. During the 2003 gubernatorial elections, Duke voters, according to an academic analysis, overwhelmingly chose the white Democratic candidate, Kathleen Blanco, over the Indian American Republican candidate, Bobby Jindal, securing the Democratic win (Skinner & Klinker, 2004).

Today, the most significant sector of the white nationalist movement is made up of academic racists who specialize in "proving" the inferiority of those with dark skin.[2] The most important entity pushing the idea that race and IQ are linked is *American Renaissance* (officially, the organization is called the New Century Foundation, which is a 501(c)3 nonprofit, but it is better know by the name of its monthly publication, *American Renaissance*). The group's head, Jared Taylor, has long been a leader in the Council of Conservative Citizens as well. What marks Taylor's group from more extreme white supremacists is an attempt to feign the academic life. At his conferences, coats and ties are required and impolite talk banned. For years, Jews were courted and active in the group's conferences and newsletter, something unacceptable in other sectors of the white nationalist movement.

Taylor's work, and that of many other academic racists, is bankrolled by the Pioneer Fund, which was established in 1937 to "improve the character of the American people" by promoting the study of eugenics and the procreation of descendants of the original white colonial stock (Mehler, 1999). Today largely restricted to providing funds to racists since mainstream researchers shun the organization, at one time, the fund backed well-known American eugenicists, including William Shockley.[3] The Pioneer Fund has been headed since 2002 by J. Philippe Rushton, an academic racist at the University of Western Ontario, Canada, who is perhaps most well known for his "scientific" finding that there is an inverse relationship between brain and genital size. Rushton has used the fund's money to line the pockets of his own Charles Darwin Research Institute in Port Huron, Michigan, which sells his books in the United States (many are banned in Canada), and to financially support his board members and followers, including Taylor (SPLC, 2002a).

The work of some academic racists actually found its way into the mainstream media in the early 1990s. At that time, Sam Francis, who would later be a dominant force in the council, was a columnist and editor for the conservative newspaper *The Washington Times*. In 1994, the publication of Charles Murray

and Richard Herrnstein's *The Bell Curve,* which argued that blacks were genetically predisposed to have a lower IQ than whites, propelled the work of others,
including Taylor, who held his first *American Renaissance* conference the year
of the book's publication. At that time, *National Review* was also publishing
Taylor and other white nationalists, including Francis and Lawrence Auster,
under the editorship of John O'Sullivan.[4] Taylor's (1992) racist book, *Paved
with Good Intentions,* even received glowing reviews in the conservative press
and from *The Bell Curve's* Herrnstein after its publication in 1992. Picking up
on Duke's ideas, Taylor's book attacked affirmative action and quotas and put
forward the notion that such programs taint black achievements.

By the late 1990s, however, white nationalist voices, such as Taylor's and
Francis's, had been purged from the establishment Right. Francis was fired for
racist comments he made during the 1995 *American Renaissance* conference. By
that time, white nationalist materials no longer appeared in *National Review.*
White nationalist Kevin Lamb worked for *Human Events* and the *Evans-Novak
Political Report* until 2005, but when his racist publishing activities were exposed that year by the Southern Poverty Law Center, he was promptly fired
(Beirich & Potok, 2005). Even so, Francis still has allies at *The Washington
Times.* When he died in 2005, the *Times* wrote a glowing obituary that failed
to mention Francis's racism or his firing ("Sam Francis," 2005, p. A6). And the
paper's managing editor, Fran Coombs (2006), wrote approvingly of a posthu-
mous compilation of Francis's writings, *Shots Fired* (Francis, 2006).

The most recent additions to this academic racist panoply are several
organizations created and funded by William H. Regnery, a descendant of
the family that established the well-known conservative book powerhouse,
Regnery Publishing. With white nationalist ideas no longer acceptable in
far-right circles, Regnery has set about creating a parallel universe of men in
suits and ties discussing the inferiority of blacks and Latinos. In 2001, Regnery founded the Charles Martel Society, named for a French king who halted
the advance of Muslims into Europe in the 700s. The society publishes *The
Occidental Quarterly,* an academic-looking journal that is filled with articles by
America's top white nationalists and notable anti-Semite Kevin MacDonald,
who was awarded $10,000 by the group in 2005 for his "research" on how
Jews have an evolutionary drive that compels them to undermine America's
white majority (Beirich, 2007b). In 2005, Regnery founded the then Arling-
ton, Virginia, based National Policy Institute (now in Augusta, Georgia),
which "educates the public on trends and policies that affect the interests
of the United States' founding people and historic majority population"
(National Policy Institute [NPI], 2005, para. 5). In an August 2005 speech
to the Chicagoland Friends of *American Renaissance,* Regnery warned that
"within the first or secondhand memories of people in this room, the white
race may go from master of the universe to an anthropological curiosity" (as
cited by SPLC, 2006, p. 28). The group issues "reports" on what it considers

threats to white America, including its 2007 "The State of White America" and "NPI Analysis: Abolish Affirmative Action.

BASIC WHITE NATIONALIST TENETS

At its core, the white nationalist movement is defined by its fundamental belief in a biological conception of race. Here's how Jared Taylor (2004), a noted white nationalist, put it in a speech to his *American Renaissance* group's 2004 biannual gathering:

> We just want to be left alone. We are the heirs to the magnificent traditions of Europe, we are a biologically distinct group known as white people, we want to be left alone to carry forward our traditions and to pursue our own destiny. It is as simple as that. We wish other groups well, but we cannot welcome them in our midst because they are not us. We have a deep, healthy loyalty to our own kind, and we know populations are not replaceable or interchangeable. We have the right to be us, and only we can be us. (para. 2)

For white nationalists, humankind is made up of a number of naturally occurring racial divisions; each race possesses traits that are the product of genetic inheritance and that serve to characterize it as a distinct human type. Culture is the partner of this inheritance and that which binds together members of the same race in a community of common interests, habits, and characteristics. When members of the same race create political organizations, like the nation-state, these institutions are necessarily an expression of both the race and the culture of their creators. In the case of America, white nationalists see it as an intrinsically white nation, the result of a superior Western European racial and cultural inheritance.

The White Race

In 2005, William Regnery argued in a speech that the existence of the white race has been genetically proven:

> Using new DNA evidence, Ryk Ward of Oxford University's Institute of Biological Anthropology believes that about 1,000 individuals, and possibly as few as 50, gave rise to the modern northern European gene pool. It's theorized that this remnant population retreated to the Balkans or Spain to escape the spread of the glaciers. Support for this "Choke Point Theory" comes from recent DNA studies in England. (p. 3)

Several academic racist works address specifically this issue and purport, regardless of much scientific work to the contrary, to prove the genetic basis of distinct races.[5]

The white race—biologically defined—is also responsible, according to white nationalists, for the creation of the highest level of human civilization: Western civilization. In their eyes, culture and race are coterminus—you can't have one without the other—and they are jointly responsible for the rise of the West. White nationalists proclaim that the majority of all culture has been created by white people. Charles Murray, who produced the hotly contested work *The Bell Curve*, which argued that black people are not as smart as whites, put out a book in 2003 titled *Human Accomplishment: The Pursuit of Excellence in the Arts and Sciences, 800 BC to 1950*. Both works are well liked in white nationalist circles, and the latter has been cited for showing, in Taylor's (2004) view, that "just about everything significant ever done by human beings was done by white people" (para. 16).

Taking a page from their racial adversaries, white nationalists argue that whites need to get politically organized to fight for their own rights, in the same manner as they allege blacks and other minorities do. Taylor (2004) has addressed this point:

> We are the only people who are not supposed to want to preserve our way of life for our children. Only white people have no rights to pride in people-hood. Our movement, of course, is to take back that right and to ensure for our descendents a continued existence as a distinct people with a glorious heritage and a promising destiny. (para. 4)

To achieve this goal, some white nationalist groups have advocated for the establishment of a separate white homeland in the North American continent. As Harold Covington (as cited in "A Brief History," 2007), a longtime supporter of such an idea, noted, the goal of the movement is to "level the present order and substitute something new which will restore the white man to his rightful place in the world" (para. 5). In Covington's case, that "something new" is an ethnic state in the American Northwest that could serve as a refuge for white people and a place to protect and preserve Western civilization.

Many white nationalists feel strongly that the white race is currently engaged in a bitter struggle for its very survival. At times, their rhetoric can be nearly apocalyptic about the future of whites. Jared Taylor engaged in this type of hyperbole in his 2004 speech to his *American Renaissance* conference:

> I will say only this: that as men of the West, our duty is clear. . . . Our cause is the central challenge of our age, the number one responsibility of our generation. . . . We have on our side every law of nature and morality. History, biology, human nature, and the accumulated wisdom of our ancestors all clearly show us the path we must take. (Taylor, 2004, para. 75)

For white nationalists like Taylor, the greatest threat to the white race is inaction. Given their natural superiority, white people should dominate the world; however, the problem is that they do not recognize the threats posed by other races and consequently have not worked to protect their interests. White nationalists' fear is that by the time they realize their survival is at stake, it might be too late.

Though Taylor (2004) claims to "wish other groups well," at its base, white nationalism contends that minorities are inherently, genetically flawed. For example, in a recent essay for the anti-immigrant Web site vdare.com, Taylor pontificated on the impossibility of blacks ever rising above what he considers their inherent IQ limitations. Taylor (2007) concludes that because of a genetic tendency to regress toward an IQ mean in all populations, and given that black IQ is demonstrably lower than white IQ, "it is just plain harder for middle-class blacks than for whites to pass on their intelligence—and therefore their social status—to their children" (para. 23). Taylor (2007) also argues that blacks face other genetic disadvantages such as their inability to think long term or avoid criminality:

> This probably has to do with greater impulsiveness, or a lower willingness to sacrifice in the present for gains in the future. . . . [British race scientist] Richard Lynn has written that blacks consistently score higher than whites on tests of psychopathic personality, again, even when they are matched for the same IQ. . . . Psychopathic personality—and the misbehavior that goes with it—is just the kind of thing that contributes to bad grades, and drags middle-class black children into the underclass. (para. 28–29)[6]

For Taylor, African Americans are clearly inferior to white people.

Many ills are ascribed by white nationalists to Latinos as well. The National Policy Institute (NPI) has posted dozens of articles to its blog on the evils of Latino immigrants. Edwin S. Rubenstein (2005) wrote a report for NPI, *The Economics of Immigration Enforcement: Assessing the Costs and Benefits of Mass Deportation*, arguing that "no matter how high the costs of deporting illegal aliens may seem, the costs of *not* deporting them are larger still" (NPI, 2005, p. 2) due to their deleterious effect on American society. Among the costs cited by Rubenstein (2005) are allegedly massive social spending and the importation of deadly diseases. Taylor's organization has issued a report, *Hispanics: A Statistical Portrait*, that purports to prove that Hispanics are more criminal, less educated, and more promiscuous than white Americans. Taylor's report also paints Latino immigrants as welfare mooches who don't assimilate into American society because they remain perennially attached to their home countries. For *American Renaissance*, that factor poses a threat to American society: "It is legitimate to wonder whether it is wise for the United States to welcome large numbers of a potentially irredentist population within its borders, especially when that population is concentrated in those parts of the United States to which Mexicans have an emotional claim" (New Century Foundation, 2006, p. 10).

America as a White Ethnic State

Because they view the world through a racial lens, white nationalists do not agree with the notion that America is a creedal or proposition nation, meaning one whose societal and cultural norms are based on acceptance of the Declaration of Independence and the other founding documents. The concept of a creedal nation, a fundamental tenet of egalitarian democracy, argues that the racial identity of newcomers is irrelevant to their ability to assimilate into America's "melting pot." White nationalists do not believe that anyone can become a good American, regardless of race or nationality, by accepting the democratic values laid out in these documents. Instead of this vision of American democracy, white nationalists believe that America is the way it is (or more accurately, has been the way it has been) due to the culture that was established by its white settlers and their descendants, including Europeans who arrived during prior periods of immigration. With the recent influx of nonwhites into the country, America's culture is fundamentally threatened because, for white nationalists, culture and race are intimately linked. America will not stay the same—meaning that such things as representative government, the rule of law, and freedom of speech will disappear—if nonwhites continue to come here and gain greater political power.

The idea that America is at its core a white nation has served as a rallying cry for one nationally know political figure, Patrick Buchanan. Three-time presidential candidate and white nationalist, Buchanan has written several tracts attacking the proposition nation idea. In *State of Emergency*, he argues that America, despite what its founders wrote, was a nation formed not on the basis of creed, but rather on a homogenous ethnic culture. A white nationalist tome, the book's thesis is that America must retain a white majority to survive as a nation. *State of Emergency* unapologetically reflects Buchanan's insistence on the centrality of race to the United States and its culture. According to Buchanan (2006), "this idea of America as a creedal nation bound together not by 'blood or birth or soil' but by 'ideals' that must be taught and learned . . . is demonstrably false" (pp. 145–146). Simply put, America is not a nation of ideas; it is a nation of people—white people. Buchanan is especially overt in making this case when he endorses the view of his late mentor and former Council of Conservative Citizens editor, Sam Francis, that American and European civilizations could never have been created without the "genetic endowments" of whites (Buchanan, 2006, p. 164).

HOW WHITES LOST POWER

White nationalists spend far more of their time theorizing about what went wrong for whites than trying to build a political movement. They have basically identified two main threats that have undermined white power: the rise of cultural Marxism (also called *political correctness*) and rising levels of immigration. However, among the ranks of academic racists, there are serious differences of opinion over the danger posed by Jews in American society and the legitimacy of anti-Semitism. Some of the major academic racist organizations have gone on record that they consider Jews to be white; that has led to a schism over the "Jewish question," which has roiled academic racist organizations over the last few years.

Cultural Marxism

Many white nationalists see the changes in American society, particularly since the hated decade of the 1960s, as the result of an orchestrated plan—called cultural Marxism—by leftist intellectuals to destroy the American way of life as established by whites. In a nutshell, the theory posits that the ideas and actions of a tiny group of philosophers—mainly Jews who taught at the Institute for Social Research in Frankfurt, Germany, and who fled Germany in the 1930s—dramatically changed American society. These men set up shop at Columbia University in New York City and founded the Frankfurt School of philosophy. White nationalists allege they devised an unorthodox form of Marxism that took aim at American culture, rather than its economic system, and worked to undermine the culture by introducing leftist ideas, particularly by extending civil rights to groups such as gays and women.

For the Council of Conservative Citizens, the Frankfurt School philosophers drove every negative change in American society, and combating their influence is a priority. James Owens (2000) explained cultural Marxism in an occasional paper for the Conservative Citizens Foundation, which is run by the Council of Conservative Citizens:

> "Cultural Marxism" is the social and political version of Marx's revolution in the economic order. Its goal is a cultural revolution, dismantling the traditional culture of Western civilization and its values, then replacing it with a new egalitarian world order. It has its origins in the neo-Marxist Frankfurt School of Social Research in the 1930s and its leading theoretician, Herbert Marcuse. . . . During the social upheavals of the 1960s, his writings galvanized protesters, driven by his concept of "critical theory" (systematic criticism and tearing down of the established order, such as meritocracy, the "dead white men" and most American traditions; that there is "no such thing as truth, the things we think are true are only the constructs of dominant [white] groups"). His influence today still pervades most public schools, universities and media as they "deconstruct" Western civilization, replacing it with the "truths" and values of egalitarian multiculturalism. (p. 34)

The theory holds that these self-interested Jews—the so-called Frankfurt School of philosophers—planned to convince mainstream Americans that white ethnic pride is bad, that sexual liberation is good, and that supposedly traditional American values—Christianity, "family values," and so on—are reactionary and bigoted. With their core values thus subverted, the theory holds, Americans would be quick to sign on to the ideas of the Far Left.

But it may be William Lind, who has long worked at the far-right Free Congress Foundation, run by his colleague Paul Weyrich, cofounder of the Moral Majority, who have done the most to define the enemies who make up the so-called cultural Marxists. Ultimately, this enemy has come to embody a whole host of Lind's bêtes noires: feminists, homosexuals, secular humanists, multiculturalists, sex educators, environmentalists, immigrants, and black nationalists. And, of course, the hated Frankfurt School philosophers are behind all of these things. In July 1998, Lind told a conference of the right-wing Accuracy in Academia that political correctness and cultural Marxism were "totalitarian ideologies" that were turning American campuses into "small ivy-covered North Koreas, where the student or faculty member who dares to cross any of the lines set up by the gender feminist or the homosexual-rights activists, or the local black or Hispanic group, or any of the other sainted 'victims' groups that political correctness revolves around, quickly find themselves in judicial trouble" (para. 5).

Cultural Marxism has had another, extremely deleterious effect: these assaults on American culture have made whites unable to form a coherent identity for themselves, something white nationalists argue has been encouraged to happen among minority groups, who have created their own identities, such as African American and Latino, and their own lobbying groups. White nationalists allege that a double standard has been put into place, where minorities can celebrate their culture and create institutions to further their interests, but whites cannot.[7] As Jared Taylor (2004) explains, "racial pride is fine for blacks and everyone else, but verboten . . . for whites. Not just American whites, mind you, but all whites everywhere" (para. 14). Because of this, one of the primary political goals of white nationalism is to forge a white identity, which they believe will be the first step to reestablishing white political power. In Taylor's (2004) words, "No group can survive without group identity. This is a law of nature. Deny to whites their identity as a group and you condemn them to obliteration and oblivion. And that, of course, is precisely what we refuse! We are not going quietly" (para. 18).

There is another rather popular explanation proffered by white nationalists for the failure of whites to secure the dominant position in American society. They suggest that whites have a highly evolved sense of altruism, something that developed over years of tribal life in northern Europe. Following is how William Regnery (2005) has explained this historical development:

So until the Age of Discovery the heartland of Europe was an insular peninsula inhabited for 10,000 years by an extended tribe. This "Volk" inherited

from a small founding population proclivities for social parity and gender
equality and altruism. These characteristics would have been essential for
the survival of a remnant cohort eking out a barely sustainable existence
in an inhospitable environment. (p. 6)

Thus altruistic and egalitarian behavior led to group success for whites as
long as they were isolated but has hampered them in the current environment. In Regnery's (2005) view,

I suggest to a greater or lesser extent whites been [*sic*] hard-wired to be
more concerned about others and more accepting of notions of universal
equality. Such instincts fathered the philosophical arguments and social arrangements that have been codified into an increasingly tyrannical agenda
that goes by the innocent sounding name of "political correctness." We
forged our own chains and willingly shuffle about in shackles. (p. 2)

In other words, whites are so given to helping their intellectual inferiors that
that they can't protect their own interests.

Furthermore, Regnery (2005) argues that whites suffer from *competitive
altruism*, a term coined by Ian Jobling, a former staffer at *American Renaissance*. Jobling (2003) explains,

What I will call "competitive altruism" is one of the key forces that shape
white societies. This form of competition emerges because altruism is
linked to social status. People who act altruistically gain the trust and
respect of others, which tends to increase their prestige and wealth. It follows that those who convince others they are altruistic reap greater status
rewards than those who do not. (para. 7)

Jobling notes that a key aspect to this form of altruism is *racial altruism*,
where high-status whites "express benevolence for non-whites" (para. 8), a
trend that emerged in the 1960s. Jobling blames these changes on the "New
Left," cultural Marxism's cousin, which made minorities the beneficiaries of
white benevolence:

In the 19th century, people climbed the social ladder by giving to chari-
ties that distributed Bibles to orphans and sent missionaries to Africa.
Today, elite commitment to specifically Christian philanthropy has been
replaced by competition among whites who make donations to the United
Negro College Fund or programs to promote diversity in higher education. (para. 22)

In the end, Jobling claims that this impulse puts whites at a disadvantage:
"An America run by non-whites will be a very different place; competitive
racial altruism is not a game non-whites play" (para. 36).

Regardless of Jobling's (2003) and other white nationalists' "theories," psychological research on altruism does not back them up. This research has found that all types of people, white or not, find satisfaction and status in assisting others. As psychologists Charlie L. Hardy and Mark Van Vugt (2006) have reported, nice guys actually do finish first—that's why they behave altruistically, not because they are white.

Immigration

For white nationalists, immigration also is something to be feared; in fact, to many, it is the greatest current threat to the white race because it is changing the demography of the United States, endangering its white majority. The Immigration and Nationality Act of 1965, which opened up the immigration system to people from the third world, is seen as a distressing partner to the civil rights movement in that the result was more nonwhites in America. White nationalists are acutely aware of the fact that Census predictions estimate that whites will be a minority by 2050. From their perspective, these immigrants will fundamentally alter American society because they come from a different genetic stock—which means they will create a vastly different culture.

Harvard Professor Samuel P. Huntington (2004), whose work on the impact of immigration into the United States is celebrated by white nationalists, has captured this sentiment well:

> The persistent inflow of Hispanic immigrants threatens to divide the United States into two peoples, two cultures, and two languages. Unlike past immigrant groups, Mexicans and Latinos have not assimilated into mainstream U.S. culture, forming instead their own political and linguistic enclaves—from Los Angeles to Miami—and rejecting the Anglo-Protestant values that built the American dream. The United States ignores this challenge at its peril. (p. 1)

Though Huntington's thesis has been heavily disputed and his assimilation data challenged,[8] he does express well the Balkanization thesis, which purports that immigration is rending the country apart. White nationalists believe that because today's immigrants come from a different genetic stock, their chances of assimilating are slim to none. They deny the idea that today's immigrants can join mainstream society in the same manner as the previously ghettoized Irish and Italian immigrants did—because those immigrants were white, unlike today's immigrants.

Television commentator and white nationalist Pat Buchanan (2002) addressed this issue in his anti-immigrant screed *The Death of the West*.[9] The thesis of the book is fundamentally alarmist: white people (i.e., Europeans and their U.S. descendants) are not reproducing fast enough to replace themselves, while non-Westerners are multiplying at a terrifying pace. As a result, Buchanan says, the "greatest civilization in history" is headed for an early grave: "America has undergone a cultural and social revolution. We are not the same country that we were in 1970 or even 1980. We are not the same people" (pp. 1–2). The three-time presidential candidate predicts that America will be a much impoverished and diminished third world nation by 2050, when whites will officially become a minority. Buchanan's book, which cites several white nationalist sources, bemoans the rise in nonwhite, non-Christian immigrants and uses information from the racist *American Renaissance* to back claims that blacks have an inherently more criminal nature than whites (SPLC, 2002b).

In white nationalist circles, one of the most influential and well-read books on immigration is a novel by the Frenchman Jean Raspail, *The Camp of the Saints*. Published for the first time in 1973, the book imaginatively recounts the events surrounding the future invasion of France by a huge fleet of third world refugees. At stake is nothing less than the fate of the Western world. Described as a "one swarming, miserable mass" (p. 154), the Hindi refugees from India are hungry, dirty, lazy, and determined to bring what Raspail (1995) describes as their oversexualized, diseased culture to Europe. Instead of denying them entry, many Frenchmen are motivated to offer assistance by their sense of Christian charity and guilt and self-loathing over their higher standard of living. But as the author notes, such a response amounts to cultural suicide:

> We gave way to one huge masochistic frenzy, dragged from nightmare to nightmare. We never said no. We wanted to show how permissive we could be, despite the foolish risk that, one day, we would have to face everything, all at once, and all alone. . . . It just means another kind of genocide. That's all. Our own. (p. 190)

Despite the warnings of some of their more patriotic countrymen, the French ultimately allow the refugees to land, who, as the novel's narrator notes, quickly transform from refugees into an invading army:

> Stretching as far as the eye could see, a lush, rich, land stood ready to greet them. . . . Indeed, it seemed to enfold and embrace them, and their very numbers made the refugees feel at home. . . . Quite simply the mob had developed a morale. A spirit of steel. A conquering spirit. The result was that more than three-quarters of the horde—the strongest and most adventurous—decided not to stop, but to push on still further. Later, historians would turn this spontaneous migration into an epic, dubbed "The Winning of the North." (p. 273)

In the end, even Switzerland had to succumb to the third world hordes, its passing marking the last gasp of European civilization.

The most extreme sectors of the modern anti-immigrant movement agree with white nationalist ideas regarding immigration, particularly the dystopian future laid out in *The Camp of the Saints*. This is especially true for those organizations founded and funded by John Tanton, the racist mastermind and chief ideologue for the modern nativist movement. Tanton publishes *The Camp of the Saints*, which is his favorite book (SPLC, 2002c): "*The Camp of the Saints* is coming our way," is the way that the editor of Tanton's *The Social Contract*, Wayne Lutton (as cited by SPLC, 2001a, p. 18), put it during a 1997 national Council of Conservative Citizens conference. Lutton added, "[Immigrants] have declared racial demographic war against us. It's up to us to respond" (SPLC, 2001a, p. 18). All white nationalists find impending doom in what Tanton referred to in 1986 in the "WITAN Memos"—a series of memos filled with racist commentary that were circulated among members of the Federation for American Immigration Reform's (FAIR) leadership, another group Tanton founded—as the "Latin onslaught" (the memos were leaked to the press in 1988 and led to Tanton being forced out as executive director of another group, U.S. English; Tanton, 1986).

Unlike most other white nationalists, Tanton and his colleagues in groups such as FAIR are also concerned with the impact of Roman Catholic immigrants on the United States. In this respect, they echo their forebears in the Know-Nothing Party and the 1920s-era Ku Klux Klan (KKK), whose major objection to Irish and Italian immigrants, which the KKK didn't think were white in any event, was their Roman Catholicism. The feeling then was that the new immigrants would ultimately be beholden to the Vatican. For Tanton and others, Vatican control is not the main concern; rather, it is the belief that Roman Catholic immigrants from places like Mexico will have large families that will outbreed whites. Tanton (1986) put it this way in the "WITAN Memos": "On the demographic point: perhaps this is the first instance in which those with their pants up are going to get caught by those with their pants down!" (para. 35).

This fear of takeover by Latinos has led to wild-eyed conspiracy mongering in racist anti-immigrant circles. A favorite is the Aztlán conspiracy, which portends that Latinos are invading the United States to reclaim the Southwest for Mexico; hence immigrants are really a secret fifth column coming here to take over America and oppress its white inhabitants. In a video put out by the anti-immigrant group American Patrol, a voice-over says, "Some scoff at the idea of a Mexican plan of conquest" (Voice of Citizens Together/American Patrol, 2000). The group's leader, Glenn Spencer, warns that Mexico is working in league with communist Chicano activists and their allies in America to bring about a little-known but highly effective plan—the Plan de Aztlán, a scheme already successful in "seizing power" in California—"to defeat America." A "hostile force on our border," the narrator of Spencer's video warns, is engaging in "demographic war" against the United States: "Mexico is moving to capture the American Southwest" (Voice of Citizens Together/American Patrol, 2000).

Variations on this Aztlán conspiracy theory are now widespread on the American radical Right. Columnists like Francis and Joseph E. Fallon, who has written on the subject for journals including *American Renaissance* and *Mankind Quarterly*, a publication specializing in "race science," have helped to publicize variations of the theory (SPLC, 2001b). Even Michael Hill, president of the League of the South since its founding in 1994, warns of plots by forces "overtly hostile to our civilization": "Already," Hill says, "radical Latinos have launched a Reconquista of our southern borders, especially from Texas to California" (as cited in SPLC, 2001b, p. 12). And recently, FAIR (2005) has also taken up the Aztlán conspiracy: "It is clear that there is a 'fifth column' movement in the United States that professes greater allegiance to a greater Mexico or a breakaway, separatist movement based on a Latino homeland, despite the efforts of Latino politicians to dismiss it as a quixotic idea of rambunctious Latino youth, largely on university campuses" (para. 11).

ANTI-SEMITISM AND WHITE NATIONALISM

All white nationalists agree on the threat posed by nonwhite immigration and politically correct culture—but what they don't agree on is what is often referred to in these circles as the "Jewish question." The neo-Nazi and racist skinhead movements consider Jews to be the main threat to white power, as does David Duke, but such surety is not found in all sectors of the white nationalist movement, where a major debate has raged in the last few years over whether or not Jews have an inordinate amount of power in American society and are using that power to weaken whites. During the 2006 *American Renaissance* conference held in Herndon, Virginia, and attended by about 200 white nationalists of varying stripes, this dispute erupted in a nasty exchange between David Duke and Michael Hart, which caused a rift in white nationalist circles that has not been closed between those who view Jews as a threat and those who don't (many of whom consider Jews to be white).

While in the past, Taylor had managed to bridge the divide over the "Jewish question" mainly by ignoring it, in 2006, he was forced to be more up front about the issue. Taylor put out a statement that tried to finesse the divide but that did not placate several critics. In his statement, Taylor (2006) wrote that he had avoided "taking positions on questions about which racially-conscious whites are likely to disagree. . . By taking no position, [*American*

Renaissance] has served readers who may be sharply opposed on these questions but who agree on the central importance of race, and are committed
to our survival" (para. 1). Several high-profile Jewish supporters demanded
that Taylor ban anti-Semites from his gatherings, but the furthest Taylor
(2006) would go was to ask his supporters to "bear in mind that Jews have a
valuable role in the work of *American Renaissance*, and are welcome participants and speakers" (para. 6). This was not enough for Taylor's Jewish supporters, one of whom, writing under the pseudonym Sam Raymond (2007),
dismissed the statement, saying that "Taylor is uncomfortable with the idea
of reading [*sic*] extremists and Nazis out of the organization" (para. 33).
This dispute led to a split among *American Renaissance*'s supporters, with
certain prominent racist Jews breaking off to form another organization,
inverted-world.com. There, Jewish racists lament the failure of Taylor to
take a hard line against anti-Semitism: "Through his refusal to denounce
the blatant anti-Semitism of many of his followers, Taylor has proved that
he either never understood what it would take to build a mass movement
or never wanted to. Taylor appears at last to have thrown in his lot with
the cranks, and the task of building a mass movement must fall to others"
(Raymond, 2007, para. 2). Ultimately, for Taylor and white nationalists
in general, the issue of anti-Semitism is a real dilemma. To try to build a
larger movement with electoral possibilities, like those increasingly seen
in Britain and Germany, would mean taking a stand against anti-Semitism.
Yet, to do so would mean rejecting the very energetic neo-Nazis whose
financial support is so critical to Taylor's organization.

For California State University, Long Beach, psychology professor Kevin
MacDonald, an alleged white nationalist of the anti-Semitic stripe, Jews are
a fundamental threat to white Americans. In MacDonald's view, Jews are essential to explaining the lack of an organized white movement. In a recent
piece for the white nationalist journal *The Occidental Quarterly*, for which he
serves as an editorial advisor, MacDonald (2006–2007) argued that whites
"are better able to inhibit their relatively positive attitudes about their own
group" (p. 17), causing them not to forge strong racial bonds with their fellow kinsmen. In effect, whites have the self-control to supersede their genetically driven biases for their own kind. However, according to MacDonald,
this positive quality has left white people vulnerable. Taking advantage of
this lack of strong racial bias, liberal activists in league with "a Jewish elite
hostile to the traditional peoples and culture of Europe" (p. 23) have created what MacDonald (2006–2007) calls a *culture of critique* that demonizes
any expression of white identity and favors leftist, egalitarian ideas about
race and ethnicity. This strategy has effectively permeated "intellectual and
political discourse among both liberals and conservatives and define[d] a
mainstream consensus among elites in academia, the media, business and
government" (p. 23). The result is that white people have been prevented

from developing a true consciousness of their own race. Hence, for MacDonald, the Jews are primarily responsible for impeding the healthy development of white nationalism.

WHITE NATIONALISM ABROAD

So what are the prospects of the white nationalist movement? Some alarmists, particularly Carol Swain (2002), believe that nonwhite immigration and programs that assist minorities must be scrapped to staunch the flow of white Americans into the white nationalist ranks. But the white nationalist movement is so marked by jealousies and infighting, as is obvious in the debate over anti-Semitism, that is it unlikely to find a political toehold in mainstream American society. Only the issue of immigration has raised the ire of conservative white Americans in the manner that Swain describes, with the anti-immigration movement sprouting nearly 150 "nativist extremist" groups between April 2006 and early 2007 (Buchanan & Holthouse, 2007).[10] The debate over immigration was also central to the GOP presidential primaries, where candidates were forced to take a harder and harder line against undocumented immigrants.

The future for white nationalists is much brighter in Europe, where political parties pushing racist ideas are having success at the ballot box.[11] In fact, Europe has several political parties that are organized around either racist or xenophobic, anti-immigrant views that would be appealing to American white nationalists. This is especially true of the whites-only British National Party, whose leader, Nick Griffin, has spoken more than once to *American Renaissance*, and which at one time had its own fundraising arm in the United States called the American Friends of the British National Party.[12] The British National Party has yet to win any parliamentary seats, but the group has won several local council elections. Perhaps the most successful anti-immigrant party in Europe is the Swiss People's Party, which, in October 2007, took 29 percent of the votes for that nation's lower house, the best result for any Swiss party since 1919, which translated into 62 seats in the nation's 200-seat National Council. The party's campaign was simple and would find favor with white nationalists: expulsion of foreign criminals and other immigrants, a continued refusal to join the European Union, and tax cuts. During the campaign, the party used racist anti-immigrant advertising depicting three white sheep standing on the Swiss flag and kicking one black sheep off it (SPLC, 2007a). Other extremist parties in Europe that have connections to the American radical Right include the French National Front; the German neo-Nazi National Democratic Party, which has seats in a few state legislatures; and the racist and xenophobic Belgian political party Vlaams Belang, which is anti-immigrant and pushes Flemish separatism. Its predecessor, the Vlaams Blok, which had several parliamentarians elected to national government, was disbanded in 2004 by the Belgian Supreme Court for "racism and xenophobia."

American white nationalist leaders seek out the advice of European extremist parties. Leaders of the British National Party and the French National Front have come to the United States to fundraise and speak at extremist events—both parties have sent apparatchiks to speak at *American Renaissance* conferences. And in 2007, leaders of the Vlaams Belang came to the United States to speak to the Robert Taft Club, whose leader attends *American Renaissance* events, and the Federation for American Immigration Reform (Beirich, 2007a, 2007c). And the electoral successes of European extremist parties inspire American white nationalists, who have found much less political support for their ideas. This is how Jared Taylor (2004), who has hosted several leaders of European extremist parties, has assessed the situation: "In just about every white country there is a nationalist political party that stands explicitly for national preservation—sometimes even for nothing less than ethnic or racial preservation—and gets voters because of this" (para. 33). For Taylor, this "proves" that American white nationalists may one day also have a viable political movement.

NOTES

1. In 2000, Duke fled to Europe after an investigation into the use of his supporters' money began. He pleaded guilty in December 2002 to federal charges related to his ripping off his supporters, which hurt his stature significantly (Lee, 2003). In 2004, the charter for his most recent organization, the European-American Unity and Rights Organization, was revoked after he failed to submit an annual report to the state of Louisiana. Since leaving prison, he has spent most of his time on an international speaking tour and attending Holocaust denial events such as the major conference held in Iran in 2007. Duke's prison time and his increasing anti-Semitism have effectively consigned him to the political margins.

2. Two classics of this genre put out by the New Century Foundation are *The Color of Crime: Race, Crime and Justice in America* (2005) and *Hispanics: A Statistical Portrait* (2006).

3. For more on the Pioneer Fund, see Mehler (1999) and Tucker (2002).

4. O'Sullivan's work now occasionally shows up on white nationalist Web sites, particularly vdare.com.

5. See, for example, Lynn (2006) and Levin (2005).

6. For Richard Lynn's work, see Lynn (2002).

7. White nationalists often point to the NAACP or the National Council of La Raza as examples of "racist" organizing by minorities, even though both groups are multiracial.

8. See, for example, Wolf (2004).

9. His book was edited by the Council of Conservative Citizens's Sam Francis, who wanted to call it *The Death of Whitey*.

10. The groups identified by the Southern Poverty Law Center as "nativist extremist" groups target people, rather than policy. They do not limit themselves to advocating, even in forceful terms, for stricter border security, tighter population control, or tougher enforcement of laws against hiring illegal immigrants.

11.   For more on European white nationalist parties, see Norris (2005), Mudde (2003), and Givens (2005).

12.   The group's leader was deported to the United Kingdom in 2002 after the Southern Poverty Law Center exposed his involvement in illegal activities related to British National Party fundraising efforts (SPLC, 2001c).

REFERENCES

A brief history of the white nationalist movement (part one). (2007, October 10). Message posted to http://groups.yahoo.com/group/AmRen_DiscussionGroup/

Barkun, M. (1994). *Religion and the racist right: The origins of the Christian Identity movement.* Chapel Hill: University of North Carolina Press.

Beirich, H. (2007a, October 8). *Extremist group announces speech by congressman.* Retrieved December, 15, 2007, from http://www.splcenter.org/blog/2007/10/08/extremist-group-announces-speech-by-congressman/

Beirich, H. (2007b, Spring). Promoting hate. *Intelligence Report,* pp. 28–37.

Beirich, H. (2007c, Winter). The Teflon nativists. *Intelligence Report,* pp. 40–45.

Beirich, H., & Moser, B. (2004, Fall). Communing with the council. *Intelligence Report,* pp. 10–18.

Beirich, H., & Potok, M. (2005, Spring). The news that fits. *Intelligence Report,* pp. 6–7.

Bridges, T. (1995). *The rise of David Duke.* Oxford: University of Mississippi Press.

Brown v. Board of Education, 347 U.S. 483 (1954).

Buchanan, P. (2002). *The death of the West.* New York: St. Martin's Press.

Buchanan, P. (2006). *State of emergency: The third world invasion and conquest of America.* New York: St. Martin's Press.

Buchanan, S., & Holthouse, D. (2007, Spring). Shoot, shovel, shut up. *Intelligence Report,* pp. 44–47.

Coombs, F. (2006). *Comments.* Retrieved January, 2, 2008, from http://www.shots fired.us/praise.html

Duke, D. (1998). *My awakening: A path to racial understanding.* Metairie, LA: Free Speech Press.

Federation for American Immigration Reform. (2005, January). *Chicano nationalism, revanchism and the Aztlán myth.* Retrieved December 14, 2007, from http://www.fairus.org/site/PageServer?pagename=iic_immigrationissuecenters861a

Francis, S. (2006). *Shots fired: Sam Francis on America's culture war.* Vienna, VA: FGF Books.

Givens, T. E. (2005). *Voting radical right in Western Europe.* Cambridge: Cambridge University Press.

GOP condemns Duke. (1989, February 25). *Newsday,* p. 9.

Hardy, C. L., & Van Vugt, M. (2006). Nice guys finish first: The competitive altruism hypothesis. *Personality and Social Psychology Bulletin, 32,* 1402–1413.

Herrnstein, R., & Murray, C. (1996). *The bell curve: Intelligence and class structure in American life.* New York. Free Press.

Huntington, S. P. (2004, March/April). The Hispanic challenge. *Foreign Policy,* pp. 1–2.

Jobling, I. (2003, October–November). *Competitive altruism and white self-destruction.* Retrieved January 7, 2008, from http://www.amren.com/ar/2003/10/index.html

Lee, M. A. (2003, Spring). Insatiable. *Intelligence Report*, pp. 52–60.

Levin, M. (2005). *Why race matters.* Oakton, VA: New Century Books.

Lind, W. (1998, July 10). *The origins of political correctness.* Paper presented at the 13th annual summer conference of Accuracy in Media, Washington, DC. Retrieved January 10, 2008, from http://www.academia.org/lectures/lind1.html

Lynn, R. (2002). Race and psychopathic personality. *American Renaissance, 13*(7). Retrieved December 15, 2007, from http://www.amren.com/ar/2002/07/

Lynn, R. (2006). *Race differences in intelligence: An evolutionary analysis.* August, GA: Washington Summit.

MacDonald, K. (2006–2007). Psychology and white ethnocentrism. *Occidental Quarterly*, pp. 7–40.

McMillan, N. (1971). *The Citizens' Council: Organized resistance to the second reconstruction, 1954–1964.* Urbana: University of Illinois Press.

Mehler, B. (1999, Winter). Race and "reason": Academic ideas a pillar of racist thought. *Intelligence Report*, pp. 27–32.

Mudde, C. (2003). *The ideology of the extreme right.* Manchester, England: Manchester University Press.

Murray, C. (2003). *Human accomplishment: The pursuit of excellence in the arts and sciences, 800 BC to 1950.* New York: HarperCollins.

National Policy Institute. (2005). *Our mission statement.* Retrieved December 15, 2007, from http://www.nationalpolicyinstitute.org/mission.php

New Century Foundation. (2005). *The color of crime: Race, crime and justice in America* (2nd ed.). Oakton, VA: Author.

New Century Foundation. (2006). *Hispanics: A statistical portrait.* Oakton, VA: Author.

Norris, P. (2005). *Radical right, voters and parties in the electoral market.* Cambridge: Cambridge University Press.

Owens, J. (2000). *Ending the race crisis in the 21st century.* Retrieved January 7, 2008, from http://www.cofcc.org/foundation/racecrisis.htm

Pitcavage, M. (1999, February 4). *The Council of Conservative Citizens: Chronology of a scandal.* Retrieved January 7, 2008, from http://www.adl.org/mwd/ccc.asp

Raspail, J. (1995). *The camp of the saints* (5th ed.). Petoskey, MI: Social Contract Press.

Raymond, S. (2007, May 8). *The decline of American Renaissance.* Retrieved January 10, 2008, from http://www.inverted-world.com/index.php/feature/feature/the_decline_of_american_renaissance/

Regnery, W. H. (2005, August 7). *We can kill with kindness—ourselves, that is* [Speech]. Retrieved December 15, 2008, from http://www.nationalpolicyinstitute.org/pdf/regnery_speech.pdf

Rubenstein, E. S. (2005). *The economics of immigration enforcement: Assessing the costs and benefits of mass deportation.* McLean, VA: National Policy Institute.

Sam Francis, columnist, 57, dies. (2005, February 17). *Washington Times*, p. A6.

Simonelli, F. J. (1999). *American fuehrer: George Lincoln Rockwell and the American Nazi Party.* Chicago: University of Illinois Press.

Skinner, R., & Klinker, P. A. (2004). Black, white, brown and Cajun: The racial dynamics of the 2003 Louisiana gubernatorial election. *The Forum, 2*(1). December 10, 2007, from http://www.bepress.com/forum/vol2/iss1/art3

Southern Poverty Law Center. (1999, Winter). Sharks in the mainstream. *Intelligence Report*, pp. 21–26.

Southern Poverty Law Center. (2000, Summer). A league of their own. *Intelligence Report*, pp. 13–17.

Southern Poverty Law Center. (2001a, Spring). Anti-immigration groups. *Intelligence Report*, pp. 16–18.

Southern Poverty Law Center. (2001b, Spring). Blood on the border. *Intelligence Report*, pp. 8–15.

Southern Poverty Law Center. (2001c, Fall). Hands across the water. *Intelligence Report*, pp. 14–23.

Southern Poverty Law Center. (2002a, Winter). Key scientist takes reigns at Pioneer Fund. *Intelligence Report*, p. 4.

Southern Poverty Law Center. (2002b, Summer). Mainstreaming extremism: Citing neo-Nazi and racist sources, Buchanan sounds the alarm. *Intelligence Report*, p. 3.

Southern Poverty Law Center. (2002c, Summer). The puppeteer. *Intelligence Report*, pp. 44–51.

Southern Poverty Law Center. (2006, Summer). The groups: In the world of "academic racism," four groups play leading roles. *Intelligence Report*, pp. 28–29.

Southern Poverty Law Center. (2007a, Winter). Despite "racist" ads, nativist party surges ahead in Bern. *Intelligence Report*, p. 59.

Southern Poverty Law Center. (2007b, Spring). Hate group list. *Intelligence Report*, pp. 52–70.

Stuebner, S. (2002, Fall). In hate's wake. *Intelligence Report*, pp. 44–49.

Swain, C. (2002). *The new white nationalism in America: Its challenge to integration.* Cambridge: Cambridge University Press.

Tanton, J. (1986, October 10). *Memo to WITAN IV attendees.* Retrieved December 14, 2007, from http://www.splcenter.org/intel/intelreport/article.jsp?sid=125

Taylor, J. (1992). *Paved with good intentions.* New York: Carroll & Graf.

Taylor, J. (2004, February 21). *Prospects for our movement* [Speech]. Retrieved November 23, 2007, from http://www.amren.com/news/news04/02/27/jtconf2004talk.html

Taylor, J. (2006, May). *Jews and American Renaissance.* Retrieved December 12, 2007, from http://www.amren.com/mtnews/archives/2006/04/jews_and_americ.php

Taylor, J. (2007, November 14). *Race/IQ explanation gap at Achievement Gap Summit.* Retrieved December 15, 2007, from http://vdare.com/taylor/071113_stumped.htm

Trask, H.A.S. (2002, January). *Who is white?* Retrieved January 7, 2008, from http://www.amren.com/mtnews/archives/2005/06/who_is_white.php

Tucker, W. H. (2002). *The funding of scientific racism: Wickliffe Draper and the Pioneer Fund.* Chicago: University of Illinois Press.

Voice of Citizens Together/American Patrol (Producer). (2000). *Immigration: Threatening the bonds of our union* [Motion picture]. (Available from Voice of Citizens Together/American Patrol, 13601 Ventura Blvd, Sherman Oaks, CA 91423-3701)

Wolf, A. (2004, May–June). Native son: Samuel Huntington defends the homeland. *Foreign Affairs.* Retrieved December 15, 2007, from http://www.foreignaffairs.org/20040501fareviewessay83311/alan-wolfe/native-son-samuel-huntington-defends-the-homeland.html

CHAPTER 8

TOWARD A WORKING DEFINITION OF HATE GROUPS

Randy Blazak

WHAT IS A HATE GROUP?

How many hate groups are there? It is a common question for academics, civil rights activists, and law enforcement. The answer is that it depends. It depends on how you define *hate group*. There are those who might make the case that the definition only suits a small group of racist extremists. There are others who would argue, given histories rooted in racism and homophobia, that large religious groups, including those of radical Islam, Mormonism, and the Roman Catholic Church, could be defined as hate groups.

What are the challenges of defining something that everyone seems already to understand? Concepts like war and peace are generally understood, but is peace just the absence of war? Such concepts are often relative in nature, as one person's trash is another person's treasure, and one people's terrorist is another people's freedom fighter. So is the case with hate. Hate groups rarely view themselves as haters. Those who have been convicted of hate crimes are often viewed by their subcultural reference groups as heroes, even righteous crusaders. A starting point in understanding these groups is formalizing a precise definition. If a hate group is "them" and not "us," we must be clear on the parameters of such a social structure.

Legal scholars have faced a similar challenge in defining *obscenity*. Supreme Court justice Potter Stewart will forever be associated with his comment about obscenity in film. In the 1964 *Jacobellis v. Ohio* case, he wrote that hard-core pornography was difficult to define but that "I know it when I see it" (Dennis, 2007, p. 44). The "I know it when I see it" standard has also been applied to hate groups. There is a general consensus that the Ku Klux Klan (KKK) and neo-Nazi groups, like the National Socialist Movement (NSM), are hate groups, although many of their members would not define them as such. Some skinhead groups, like the Hammerskins, have been identified as hate groups, but what about unaffiliated racist skinheads? There are also anti-racist skinheads (sometimes called SHARPs, for Skinheads against Racial Prejudice) who hate racist skinheads and have committed acts of hateful violence against them.

The difficulty of developing a handy definition of *hate group* mirrors some of the same problems in defining the concept of *hate crime*. Critics typically contend that "every crime is a hate crime," to which defenders list any number of crimes that aren't necessarily motivated by hate. Shoplifting is not a hate crime, leaving the process of defining to listing acts that don't qualify as a hate crime. Similarly, one could contend that "every group is a hate group" since all groups contain humans that are capable of hate. For example, a high school football team may hate its rivals. Does that make it a hate group? During an election year, the bitterness between Republicans and Democrats can be fairly hateful, sometimes becoming criminal (the stealing of yard signs and the Watergate break-in, for example). Are our major political parties also hate groups?

The legal concept of hate crimes has gone through several changes. Evolving out of the federal civil rights laws of the 1960s, hate crime laws emerged on a state-by-state basis in the 1980s and were codified in the federal Hate Crime Statistics Act of 1990, which defined them as follows:

> crimes that manifest evidence of prejudice based on race, religion, disability, sexual orientation, or ethnicity, including where appropriate the crimes of murder, non-negligent manslaughter, forcible rape, aggravated assault, simple assault, intimidation, arson, and destruction, damage or vandalism of property. (Cornell University, 2007, para. 11)

Hate crime laws have faced a couple of definitional issues themselves. First, they needed to include crimes motivated by the perception of the victim. If a Nazi skinhead attacks a man because he or she believes he is Jewish, but he is not Jewish, is it still a hate crime? Second is the issue of protected status. Is someone who hates women and murders females committing a hate crime? Several states have omitted gender and sexual orientation from the list of protected statuses in their hate crime laws. (See Perry, 2001, for a discussion of the debate on including gender in hate crime laws.) The latest federal definition of *hate crime* attempted to clarify these issues. The Local Law Enforcement Enhancement Act (also known as the Matthew Shepard Act), passed by Congress in 2007 (but then withdrawn later that year), defined hate crimes as follows:

> bias-motivated violence by providing the department with jurisdiction over crimes of violence where the perpetrator has selected the victim because

of the person's actual or perceived race, color, religion, national origin, gender, sexual orientation, gender identity or disability. (Human Rights Campaign, 2007, para. 1)

While this definition leaves out property crimes, it gives federal authorities the power to investigate a wide variety of criminal behavior that could be defined as hate motivated.

The challenge of defining hate groups has not had the same legal support. It has largely come from civil rights and watchdog groups, some of which may have a vested interested in overdefining hate groups to emphasize the threat. Since law enforcement agencies cannot legally collect data on groups that are not engaged in criminal activity, it serves no purpose to create a governmental definition of hate groups in the fashion that terrorist groups are defined. What has evolved is a field definition from academics, civil rights groups, the media, and the general public, with a high level of consensus at the core (e.g., high levels of agreement that neo-Nazi organizations qualify as hate groups) and low levels of consensus beyond the core groups (see Figure 8.1). This chapter defines hate groups in a way that assigns inclusion or exclusion to those fringe groups among which consensus is low.

Figure 8.1 The Consensus Model of Hate Groups

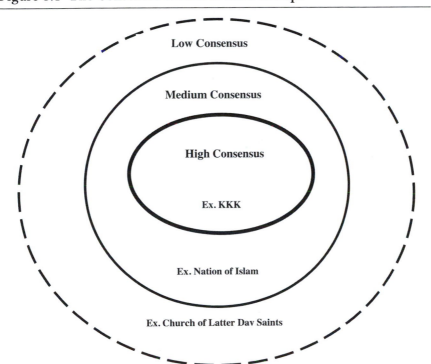

TERRORIST GROUPS

Terrorists groups have been broadly defined as political movements that use violence or the threat of violence as a means to achieve their group goals. One could point out that while this definition can include quasi-political groups, like the Irish Republican Army, it excludes primarily religious groups like al-Qaeda. Section 83 of Canada's Anti-Terrorism Act, passed after the 9/11 attacks, broadly defines a terrorist group as "an entity that has as one of its purposes or activities facilitating or carrying out any terrorist activity." One section of the USA Patriot Act of 2001 includes a "Terrorist Exclusion List" (TEL) that compiles a list of known terrorist organizations that desire to "commit, incite, or aid in the commission of a terrorist act with the intention to cause death or bodily injury against Americans." The designation of a TEL group is the responsibility of the secretary of state and, according to the Department of State Web site, is based on the following criteria:

1. A group that commits or incites to commit, under circumstances indicating an intention to cause death or serious bodily injury, a terrorist activity.
2. A group that prepares or plans a terrorist activity.
3. A group that gathers information on potential targets for terrorist activity.
4. A group that provides material support to further terrorist activity. (U.S. Department of State, 2002)

Groups listed on the TEL are all international entities, including the Islamic Army of Aden (from Yemen), Black Star (from Greece), Turkish Hezbollah (from Turkey), and Ulster Freedom Fighters (from Northern Ireland). As the purpose of this list is to provide a tool to help government agents prevent individuals or groups representing a threat to national security from entering the United States, there are no domestic terrorist groups on the TEL. While domestic groups, such as the Earth Liberation Front and the Army of God, are investigated by the Federal Bureau of Investigation (FBI), they are excluded by the exclusion list. As Mark Hamm (2007) points out in *Terrorism as Crime*, essentially every terrorist attack in the United States, other than the 1993 World Trade Center bombing and the 9/11 attacks in 2001, has been the work of domestic terrorist groups.

Federal authorities do have a significant history of policing domestic terror groups. When the KKK was founded shortly after the end of the American Civil War, it was not described as a hate group. The Confederate veterans dressed as the ghosts of their fallen comrades were viewed by many in the South as the keeper of the Southern ideal, as their night rides harassed newly freed slaves. However, the Klan was seen as a terrorist group by federal authorities. The Force Act of 1870 and the Civil Rights Act of

1871, also referred to as the Anti-Klan Act, were meant to stop their reign of terror in the South, which included acts of violence and the prevention of black voting.

Right-Wing Extremists

Hate groups have typically been associated with the Far Right of the per-haps overly simplistic right-left political spectrum. The tendency is to put American democracy at the center of the continuum, with liberal democrats (represented by the Democratic Party) to the left and conservative democrats (represented by the Republican Party) to the right of the center. Moving left-ward takes you to various forms of socialism and communism, ending in col-lective anarchy. Moving rightward, one travels through corporate oligarchy, authoritarian and fascist states, and individualist anarchy (see Figure 8.2). The continuum assumes that power will be spread more evenly toward the left and concentrated among smaller groups toward the right.

While left-wing terrorist groups exist, the fascist ideology of many hate groups has led them to be described as "right-wing extremists." This right-left

Figure 8.2 The Left-Right Political Spectrum

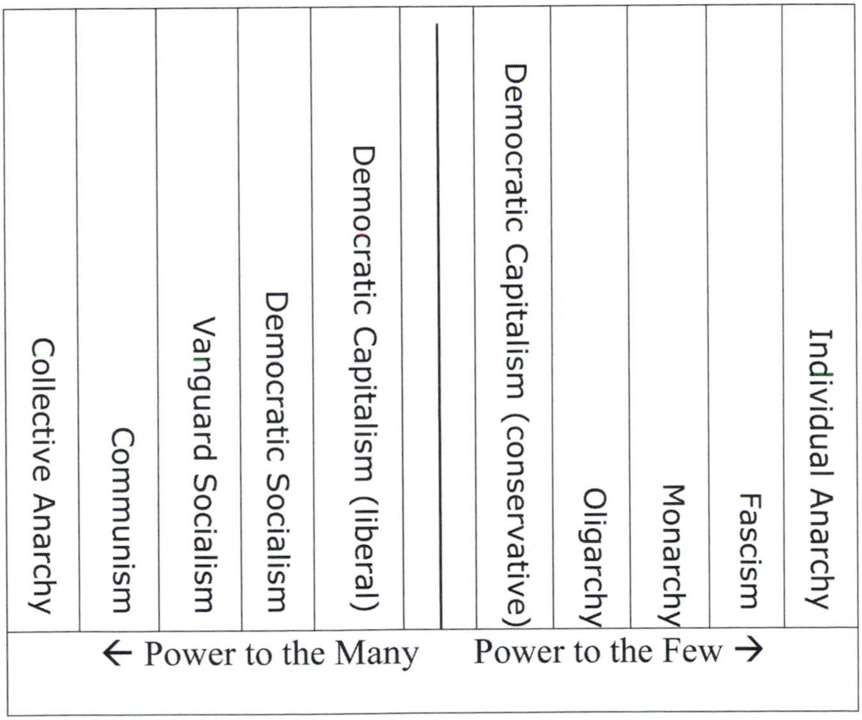

Collective Anarchy	Communism	Vanguard Socialism	Democratic Socialism	Democratic Capitalism (liberal)	Democratic Capitalism (conservative)	Oligarchy	Monarchy	Fascism	Individual Anarchy

← Power to the Many   Power to the Few →

spectrum is surely limiting. Where are Libertarians located? There are communist societies, like China, that have embraced venture capitalism. Similarly, there are groups associated with the Far Right that have many leftist attributes. Most racist groups have expressed opposition to the Iraq War as a war to defend Israel.

In the 1980s, Tom Metzger's White Aryan Resistance (WAR) advocated for a "Third Position." Metzger, a former Klansman and Christian Identity minister, began advocating an alternative to corporate fascism. His brand of racism showed support for the environment and the legalization of drugs. The Third Position allowed for the co-optation of ideas from both the left and the right for the benefit of the racist cause. In an 1998 interview with a skinhead group, Metzger described the Third Position (Anti-Defamation League [ADL], 2007e):

> We reject present international capitalism and international socialism and Marxism as evil threats to our European White race. Beyond that, Third Position adheres totally to the issue of race—all other issues, including economics, come after. There is also room for individual disagreement and dialogue within our associations on all issues except the race issue. (para. 9)

Most often associated with the Far Right is the KKK. The Klan has appeared in different waves throughout its history. Five eras are evident. The first wave was the original Klan that appeared after the Civil War in Pulaski, Tennessee, and was successfully suppressed by federal antiterror statutes. The second wave was the more civically oriented Klan of the 1920s that organized around anti-immigrant sentiments and had a membership as high as 5 million. The third wave of the KKK appeared during the civil rights movement of the 1960s and engaged in terroristic violence. The fourth wave of the KKK emerged in the 1970s and attempted to take a more mainstream approach to racial politics. The fifth era of the Klan emerged in the 1980s, linking the mainstream political approach with an underground paramilitary faction (Ridgeway, 1991).

The Klan has been a consistent presence since its formation in 1866, and the racist violence associated with them has never truly faded. However, each reincarnation has adopted different means to achieve its goal. For example, the 1920s Klan was largely a nativist group that engaged in boycotts of Roman Catholic businesses. In the 1980s, David Duke refashioned his Klan members into the nonviolent National Association of White People (NAAWP). If these versions of the KKK are not using extralegal means to achieve their goals, are they still hate groups?

The post–World War II resentment of Nazis gradually abated enough for the arrival of new (or "neo") Nazi groups in the United States. One thing that kept most social ("Goldwater") conservatives out of the neo-Nazi camp in the

1950s was conservative support for Israel. However, the leftward movement of the youth counterculture in the 1960s allowed Nazi imagery to be adopted by the Far Right, most notably George Lincoln Rockwell's American Nazi Party. The 1970s saw the arrival of William Pierce's National Alliance, and in the 1980s, Nazi skinheads arrived in America, cementing the image of right-wing extremism with racist violence and calls for revolution against the mythical Jewish power pulling the strings of society.

By the 1990s, the Klan had to share the stage with a growing number of hate groups. Monitoring groups, like the Anti-Defamation League (ADL) and the Southern Poverty Law Center (SPLC), provided regular counts of hate groups in publications and online. These counts served to remind the public that Nazis and Klansmen were not artifacts of the past.

What these hate groups have in common is that they occupy the Far Right of the political spectrum, favoring charismatic leadership of a quasi-fascist dictatorship based on ethnic identity or the "war of all against all" individualistic anarchy (favored by many skinheads). They reject most leftist political ideologies that favor distributing power evenly among all people. The alleged Third Position of Tom Metzger only favors sharing powers among a small group of ethnic whites who hold the same narrow ideological view.

Researchers have attempted to create typologies of extremist, terrorist, and white supremacist groups. Chip Berlet and Stanislav Vytosky (2006) create a general typology of white supremacist groups in their overview of the racist movement. While not formerly defining hate groups, Berlet and Vytosky discuss white supremacist groups as relying on three broad metaframes. The first is conspiracism, a belief that larger historical events are shaped by a longstanding conspiracy of secret elites. The second is dualism, a belief that the world is divided into simplistic forces of good and evil, with no middle ground. Finally, such groups share apocalyptic visions of the future. While this conceptualization might include non-white hate groups, Berlet and Vytosky use this framing to create a typology of contemporary right-wing groups. This broad typology breaks such organizations into three sectors: political groups such as the National Socialist Movement, religious groups such as Aryan Nations, and youth cultural groups such as skinheads. This typology can help identify some of the qualities of a hate group, but is not a firm rule on what constitutes a hate group.

DEFINITIONS FROM MONITORING GROUPS

A working concept of hate groups can come from the groups that monitor them. Nongovernmental groups, like the ADL and SPLC, have been leaders in the field of tracking the activities of hate groups and, in some cases, litigating them out of existence. Web sites like Mark Pitcavage's Militia Watchdog in the 1990s keep track of splits and alliances among various subgroups.

Local civil rights groups, like the Oregon Coalition against Hate Crimes, often rely on lists from national groups as well as their own field counts of smaller groups not on the national radar.

Much of the monitoring of hate group activity comes from civil rights groups that represent potential targets of hate crimes and propaganda. The Simon Wiesenthal Center has actively kept track of the prevalence of online hate activity, counting nearly 7,000 "problematic" Web sites and publishing an annual report titled *Digital Terrorism and Hate.* Gay rights groups, like the Human Rights Campaign and the Anti-Violence Project of New York, record hate crimes and incidents against sexual minorities as well as the activities of antigay groups.

The Anti-Defamation League

With regard to tracking hate group activity, one civil rights group has a long history of keeping tabs on the radical right. The Anti-Defamation League of B'nai B'rith was founded in 1913 "to stop the defamation of the Jewish people and to secure justice and fair treatment to all" (ADL, 2007a, para. 1) The ADL has grown into an organization that has crusaded against many forms of bigotry. The ADL lists as one of its mandates scrutinizing and exposing "extremists and hate groups." The organization also has a history of infiltrating groups like the Klan to monitor them internally (Seltzer & Lopes, 1986).

The ADL's Extremism in America project provides a database of symbols associated with anti-Semitism and hate activity, like "88," a common racist shorthand for "Heil Hitler." Their database also includes organizations associated with extremist ideologies. The ADL Web site breaks these entities into four categories. The first is a list of individuals associated with activism, including former Klansman and presidential candidate David Duke and Holocaust denier David Irving. The ADL also lists six "movements" associated with hate (Christian Identity, ecoterrorism, KKK, militia movement, sovereign citizen movement, and the tax protest movement) as well as a small category of hate media (*American Renaissance, The Turner Diaries,* and white power music groups). A fourth category is "hate groups." The ADL currently lists 14 groups:

Aryan Nations
Council of Conservative Citizens
Creativity Movement
Elohim City
Greater Ministries International
Hammerskin Nation
Institute for Historical Review
Little Shell Pembina Band

Militia of Montana
National Alliance
National Socialist Movement
Nazi Low Riders
New Black Panther Party for Self-Defense (NBPP)
White Revolution

Mark Pitcavage, the director of fact-finding for the ADL, is responsible for defining hate groups for the ADL's Web site and publications. Pitcavage is a leading expert on hate group activity and is routinely called on by the media to discuss the problem of organized bigotry. When asked to define hate groups, Pitcavage (personal communication, September 27, 2007) referred to the criteria he created for his law enforcement training:

A hate group is a group whose ideology is centered primarily or substantially on hatred or intolerance of, or prejudice against, people of another ethnic, racial, or religious background, or a different sexual/gender orientation

This could include the New Black Panther Party or Nation of Aztlan as easily as a white supremacist group. The focus is on the ideology. Note too the emphasis on *primarily or substantially*. This means that groups that may in fact be somewhat prejudiced or biased, but whose belief system is not centered substantially on those prejudices, would not be considered a formal hate group.

The ADL list is notable for its inclusion as well as its exclusion. Included are the expected skinhead and neo-Nazi groups as well as the New Black Panther Party and the Little Shell Pembina Band, a Native American group. Absent are domestic Jewish groups, like the Jewish Defense League (JDL), the militant Jewish group listed as a terrorist organization by the FBI. The JDL has been linked to violent attacks against Soviet interests in the United States and the murder of an Arab American named Alex Odeh (Kushner, 2003). In 2001, JDL leaders Irv Rubin and Earl Krugel were arrested and charged with plotting an attack against the office of Arab American congressman Darrell Issa as well as a mosque in California. The ADL has publicly condemned the JDL, stating that the group is a "gross distortion of the position of Jews in America" on its Web site (ADL, 2007b). Yet, unlike the SPLC, the ADL does not list the JDL as a hate group.

The Southern Poverty Law Center

The organization most widely associated with monitoring hate groups is the SPLC. The SPLC was founded in 1971 in Montgomery, Alabama, as an advocate for the legal rights of poor and minorities in the region. The

SPLC first took on the KKK in 1979 after a Klansman attacked a civil rights gathering in Decatur, Alabama. That lawsuit led to the creation of Klanwatch in 1981, which monitored Klan activity. Klanwatch became the Intelligence Project, designed to monitor a wide variety of hate groups, including several black nationalist groups. In addition to its regularly updated Web site, an accounting of hate group activity is published quarterly in the *Intelligence Report*.

In its annual "Year in Hate" issue, the SPLC's (2008) *Intelligence Report* listed 888 hate groups active in 2007, a 5 percent increase from their count in the previous year. The count emphasizes *active* groups, engaging in activities in the previous year, including "marches, rallies, speeches, meetings, leafleting, publishing literature or criminal acts" (p. 52). The count excludes Web sites, which are kept in a second tally because a Web site may actually be one person representing himself or herself as a group. SPLC counted 643 U.S.-based hate Web sites in 2007.

Coming from news reports, law enforcement agencies, citizen reports, field sources, and its own research, the SPLC has developed a categorization system of hate groups in the United States. The seven categories include ones with high levels of consensus as well as more disputed groups:

1. Ku Klux Klan (155): Includes 29 chapters of the Brotherhood of Klans Knights of the Ku Klux Klan
2. Neo-Nazi (207): Includes 13 chapters of the National Alliance
3. White nationalist (125): Includes 44 chapters of the Council of Conservative Citizens
4. Racist skinhead (90): Includes 14 chapters of Volksfront
5. Christian Identity (36): Includes three chapters of Christian Guard
6. Neo-Confederate (104 chapters of the League of the South)
7. Black separatist (81): Includes 64 chapters of the Nation of Islam (NOI)
8. General Hate (90): Includes six subcategories

   a. Anti-gay (9): Includes the Family Research Institute
   b. Anti-immigrant (14): Includes four chapters of Save Our State
   c. Holocaust denial (7): Includes the Institute for Historical Review
   d. Racist music (14): Includes Final Stand Records
   e. Radical traditionalist Roman Catholic (14): Includes the Alliance for Catholic Tradition
   f. Other (32): Includes 4 chapters of Fundamentalist Latter Day Saints and 13 chapters of the JDL

This comprehensive list includes groups with high consensus (the 23 Aryan Nations groups, for example). There are also groups with low consensus (the California Coalition for Immigration Reform, for example). In charge of this process is Mark Potok, editor of the SPLC's *Intelligence Report*. Recognizing that hate is a necessary but not sufficient characteristic for inclusion in the hate group criteria, Potok utilizes broad criteria that provide some parameters for a general definition. First, the group has to be a named entity, not just a collection of people with hateful beliefs toward another group. Second, the group has to have some platform based on the supremacy of their members' reference group. Third, the group has to be involved in some activity emanating from its belief that others are less than them, such as publishing, making speeches, or making T-shirts (M. Potok, personal communication, September 28, 2007).

Potok recognizes that this is an imperfect model and that it is weakest when categorizing antigay groups. Many mainstream religions support the idea that homosexuality is sinful (along with eating pork and working on the Sabbath). Some smaller groups make the "gay sin" issue their primary focus and engage in particularly visceral attacks on members of the sexual minority community. The conservative lobbying group Traditional Values Institute (TVI) is included on the SPLC's list because of its constant use of discredited research that homosexuals are pedophiles and actively recruit children. The TVI's Web site claims that there is a homosexual "agenda" that is both Marxist and based on Hitler's propaganda techniques (Traditional Values Institute, 2005). The Westboro Baptist Church, also on the SPLC list, operates a Web site titled "God Hates Fags" and stages protests at the funerals of Iraq War soldiers (who supposedly have died defending American sodomy).

For groups with low consensus, the SPLC "talks through" the decision whether or not to make a hate group designation. According to Potok, the SPLC went through such a process on how to distinguish British Israelist groups from Christian Identity groups. British Israelism's beliefs are similar to Christian Identity, including the tenet that Britons and other northern Europeans are the Hebrew descendents of the "lost tribes of Israel" (a fact since refuted by the Human Genome Project). Because British Israelism does not hold as a core belief that Jews are the descendents of Satan and are inherently "wicked" (unlike Christian Identity), the SPLC could establish a clear distinction between the two and thus exclude them from the list.

The SPLC has received criticism for the inclusion of groups with low consensus, such as anti-illegal immigration and neo-Confederate organizations, including from CNN host Lou Dobbs. However, the groups that the SPLC argues are hate groups have explicitly racist, homophobic, or bigoted ideologies, and many have substantiated connections to other hate groups. For example, a leading anti-immigrant group, the Federation for American Immigration Reform (FAIR), is led by individuals with connections to white supremacist groups, according to the SPLC. FAIR deputy Wayne Lutton held leadership in four white nationalist groups, including the Council of Conservative Citizens, the *Intelligence Report* alleged in 2007 (Beirich, 2007).

The SPLC's *Intelligence Report* serves as a constant source of hate group activity. The publication keeps track of trends like the "ex-gay" and Nativist movements and lists related groups. For example, 144 groups were classified as "nativist extremist organizations" in the spring 2007 issue. Of these, eight were also included on the "hate groups" list. The report (and its Web site) also lists hate groups by state. California (63 hate groups) and Texas (55 hate groups) have the most, and four states have no identified hate groups (Hawaii, North Dakota, South Dakota, and Rhode Island).

DEFINITIONAL ISSUES

Monitoring groups offer a useful starting point for the definition of hate groups. Hate groups have an ideology "centered primarily, or substantially, on hatred or intolerance" of specific target populations (Pitcavage, personal communication, September 27, 2007) Hate groups are named entities that have ideological platforms and are involved in some activity as an expression of that platform (SPLC, 2008). These criteria raise a handful of interesting definitional issues.

Legal Issues

First, there are legal issues associated with defining an organization as a hate group. Groups defined as criminal or terrorist fall under the domain of government control. For example, the FBI can monitor the activities of groups it believes are involved in racketeering-type crimes under the Racketeer Influenced and Corrupt Organizations (RICO) Act of 1970 statutes. The bulk of activities in which hate groups engage are not criminal and are protected by the First Amendment of the U.S. Constitution. Researchers estimate that only about 5 percent of hate crimes are committed by hate groups (Levin & McDevitt, 1993). Rallies, speeches, CDs, and Web sites are not, in and of themselves, the interest of law enforcement.

However, the FBI has spied on noncriminal domestic groups in the past through COINTELPRO, the FBI's counterintelligence program. COINTELPRO began in 1956 to cause disruption in Communist Party of the USA but was soon extended to disrupt groups ranging from the KKK to Martin Luther King Jr.'s Southern Christian Leadership Conference. The FBI now claims that there are no COINTELPRO investigations of domestic groups, but revelations about the misuse of surveillance techniques under the "war on terrorism" banner have critics accusing the federal government of, again, monitoring noncriminal groups.

The legal issues call into question the ability of government agencies to regulate groups deemed hateful by others. The police cannot prevent Nazis from marching down Main Street if they have a permit. Nor can they stop hate speech or even prevent skinheads from throwing racist flyers in yards.

Groups like the American Civil Liberties Union have gone to court to defend the right of hatemongers to express their First Amendment rights, including the right of Nazis to march in 1977 in Skokie, Illinois, a town that was home to many Holocaust survivors (National Socialist Party of America v. Village of Skokie, 1977). The ruling district court judge in the case said,

> It is better to allow those who preach racial hatred to expend their venom in rhetoric rather than to be panicked into embarking on the dangerous course of permitting the government to decide what its citizens may say and hear. . . . The ability of American society to tolerate the advocacy of even hateful doctrines . . . is perhaps the best protection we have against the establishment of any Nazi-type regime in this country. (Bernard M. Decker, February 23, 1978)

The Constitution prevents any legal classification of hate groups. If the government could define the KKK as a hate group, could it also define a group that hates the president as such? Of course, there are ways around this safeguard. The easiest method is making a case that there is probable cause that a group is engaged in some form of criminal behavior. Once an investigation is opened on a group, it falls under greater legal control.

An example of such a tactic is the parole violation of Kyle Brewster. Brewster was one of the three skinheads convicted of the brutal murder of an Ethiopian graduate student in Portland, Oregon, in 1988. Brewster was sentenced to 15 years in prison and was released on parole in 2002. One of the conditions of his parole was that he not associate with known gang members. Brewster created an online profile in the MySpace community that featured several pictures of himself with members of the Volksfront skinheads. Volksfront had been linked to several crimes in Oregon and Washington. This allowed Brewster's parole officer to define Volksfront as a gang and revoke Brewster's parole. Brewster was returned to prison in 2006 to serve the remainder of his term. On his release in 2007, he was rearrested after one day on an outstanding warrant. While in prison, he had attacked a black prison guard.

Access Issues

There is a certain desire to limit the access that hate groups have to the general public, especially children. The constitutionality of the ability of so-called hate groups to disseminate their materials has been somewhat balanced by the ability of people to regulate what comes into their homes. For example, parents may be able to filter out most hate Web sites from their home computers using screening programs such as Cyber Patrol, SurfWatch, Net Nanny, and Cyber Sitter. These programs allow people to block Web sites deemed objectionable by searching for objectionable words, like *Aryan* or *Nazi*. Of course, these filters are limited in usefulness by defining only Web sites that reflect a high-consensus definition of hate. They will not screen out any of the black nationalist or antigay Web sites associated with organizations defined as hate groups by the SPLC or the ADL. In addition, the programs will also not block the more sophisticated Web sites that do not use typical hate group jargon. For example, Stormfront, a hate site owned by a former Grand Wizard of the KKK, operates martinlutherking.org, a fairly discreet racist Web site dedicated to discrediting Martin Luther King Jr.

Schools have also wrestled with the issue of hate group access to students. Private schools may restrict First Amendment expression on their property (Corry v. Stanford University, 1995), allowing for the prohibition of hate flyers, rallies, and Web sites, as defined by them. Public schools have not had clear legal guidelines in defining hate materials or hate speech, let alone hate groups. Given the high amount of bullying and cyberbullying in schools, much behavior could be defined as hateful. If a group of sophomores hates freshmen and commits criminal attacks against them, would they be defined as a hate group? If a subculture of students, like punk rockers, incorporates swastikas into its subcultural style, would they also be included in the definition? Again, the common tool has been to associate materials with criminal behavior. For example, many schools have banned gang-related clothing from schools, leaving it up to administrators to define what qualifies as "gang related." Some such bans have been extended to whole cities. In 1993, Harvard, Illinois, banned all gang clothing from the city. Individuals could receive six months in jail and a fine of up to $500 for wearing clothing associated with known gangs (Fritsch, Caeti, & Taylor, 1999).

The private sector has wrestled with defining hate speech and access to hate group materials in the workplace. Many Web servers have clear policy against hosting hate materials on their servers. In 2004, the *Web Host Industry Review*, an online industry journal, urged that Web servers place restrictions against hate speech in their acceptable use policies (AUP; King, 2004). For example, Alabanza, a Web host that removed neo-Nazi Web sites from its server in 2003, has an AUP that prohibits

> transmitting or storing any material that is unlawful, obscene, harassing, libelous, abusive, hateful, encourages unlawful acts, or may be interpreted as violating the civil rights of others. (NaviSite, 2008, para. 12)

Businesses have sought to prohibit hate speech in company forums. For example, the Oracle, a California-based tech company, has been the target of racist materials because of its high number of Asian employees. In an effort to limit hate materials, the company Web policy states,

You agree not to . . . post . . . any Content that: (a) is false or misleading; (b) is defamatory; (c) is harassing or invades another's privacy, or promotes bigotry, racism, hatred or harm against any group or individual; . . . or (g) violates any applicable laws or regulations. (Burleson, 2007, para. 5)

For both Web servers and private businesses, it is an administrative judgment call to define what is hateful material.

Access has also been a definitional issue in prisons and jails. Materials from hate groups have traditionally been banned as disruptive and inciteful. Prison officials must routinely make decisions that balance the rights of inmates with the security and safety of correctional facilities. In 2006, Pennsylvania death row inmate Ronald Banks argued that his denial of written material violated his First Amendment rights. The case went before the Supreme Court, where the prison's right to restrict written material was upheld (Beard v. Banks, 2006). The loophole is with regard to religious material (and legal material protected under habeas corpus rights).

What can be prohibited as hate material often is allowed as religious material. Owing to the demand that Muslim inmates be allowed the freedom to practice their religion, the Supreme Court ruled in 1964 that religious materials must be allowed in prisons (Cooper v. Pate, 1964). This opened the door for racists to receive previously banned material from groups if it could be classified as religious. The primary beneficiaries of the *Cooper v. Pate* ruling have been racist Odinists who have co-opted the Viking pagan belief system. Odinist priests hold meetings in state and federal prisons across the country. Some of the most notable proponents of this faith have been David Lane and Richard Kemp, members of the Order, a racist gang of armed robbers that murdered a Jewish radio personality in an attempt to start a race war in the 1980s.

The definitional issue creates problems in limiting access to hate group materials. Without clear criteria for hate groups, it is impossible for parents to limit their children's access to hate group materials. This can only be done on a case-by-case, ad hoc basis that depends on parents understanding the subtle techniques used by groups that espouse bigoted views. Schools and prisons shy away from attempting such definitions for fear of violating First Amendment rights, relying on the prohibition of materials that are disruptive and placing hate group materials in the same nebulous category as pornography.

Counting Issues

The lack of a clear definition makes counting hate groups an impossible task. There may be some merit in counting high-consensus groups. As mentioned, the SPLC counted 155 chapters of the KKK in 2007. Counting the low-consensus groups is another matter. What should a count of antigay groups include? The KKK is antigay, as are most Southern Baptist churches. Should each Klan chapter and every individual Southern Baptist church be included?

The high-consensus group counts have their own issues. Of the 165 Klan chapters in the SPLC count, there are 34 different Klan groups (the Empire Knights of the KKK is different than the National Knights of the KKK), some with dozens of chapters across the country. Does this represent 165 hate groups, 34 hate groups, or one hate group, the KKK? The SPLC Klan count also includes the Klan Store in Ocala, Florida, and the Redneck Store in Laurens, South Carolina. One can assume that the proprietors of these businesses are members of one or more of the other 163 Klan entities in the count.

Another issue with the counting of hate groups is the multiple memberships many individuals may hold. A member of the National Socialist Movement in Seattle may also be a member of the National Vanguard, which also has a Seattle chapter. It has long been common for members of skinhead groups, like Hammerskins, to also hold memberships in the KKK and Aryan Nations, leading some observers to wonder if the same handful of white supremacists are being counted multiple times.

Of course, any count is impossible because of the fluid nature of the extremist underground. Some groups are small and unnamed, adopting the leaderless resistance approach pioneered by militia groups in the 1990s and Muslim extremists in the 2000s. Instead of a structured organization with a hierarchical leadership, leaderless groups share a common ideology and agenda but no identifiable figurehead. This makes the policing and disruption of such groups much more difficult. If a small group of neo-Nazi skinheads is spreading anti-Semitic flyers and graffiti in a town but has no name, are they a hate group?

Other groups might just be off the radar of those who count them. According to the SPLC, there are no hate groups in the Dakotas. Finally, many hate groups have short life-spans and disappear as quickly as they appear. The Tualatin Valley Skinheads in Oregon (included in the SPLC's 2005 count) were essentially three people claiming to be a large operation. One member was arrested for vandalizing a Jewish cemetery; the second member was the leader's girlfriend, who broke up with him; and finally, the one-member skinhead group became a one-member chapter of the NSM and was included in the 2006 SPLC count. Should a "group" like this be counted along with larger groups, like the National Alliance? And once a group like this ceases to exist, as the Oregon NSM chapter did in 2007, how long should it continue to be counted as a hate group?

Patriot Militias

The presence of patriot militia groups gained global attention when it was revealed that the two primary conspirators in the 1995 bombing of a federal building in Oklahoma City had been active in the militia movement. Timothy McVeigh and Terry Nichols had drifted in and out of the shadowy world of antigovernment militias before plotting the attack that killed 168 Americans. The research of Mark Hamm (2002) contends that the Oklahoma City bombers were also supported by a gang of racist bank robbers called the Aryan Republican Army.

At the time of the 1995 bombing, the militia movement was largely responding to the perception that the federal government was increasingly overstepping its constitutional authority and becoming a dictatorship, evidenced by disastrous events in Ruby Ridge, Idaho, in 1992 and Waco, Texas, in 1994. These two well-known events culminated in standoffs between federal authorities and citizens that resulted in the preventable deaths of civilians (as well as law enforcement personnel) and were viewed by the radical Right as the unconstitutional authoritarian rule of the federal government.

Militia groups are a part of the larger "patriot" movement that tends to see a growing federal government encroaching on the rights of the individual. The patriot movement sees the United States as falling under the control of the "New World Order." Militias themselves are not hate groups. Some have diverse memberships and focus on issues of wide appeal, like opposition to the Internal Revenue Service (IRS). Minority-based organizations that have been called hate groups, like the JDL and New Black Panther Party, could also be described as militia groups.

The SPLC has tracked militia groups since 1994. Six months before the Oklahoma City bombing, SPLC chief legal council Morris Dees sent a letter to Attorney General Janet Reno warning her of the threat of radical militias. However, the SPLC counts patriot groups separately, largely because any bigotry expressed by individual groups is secondary to their primary focus on constitutional opposition to the federal government. In 2006, the SPLC counted 147 patriot groups.

The varied world of antigovernment militias has best been described by Kenneth S. Stern in his 1996 book, *A Force upon the Plain: The American Militia Movement and the Politics of Hate*. Stern utilizes a funnel model to describe the issues that attract individuals to militia activism (see Figure 8.3). At the top of the funnel (stage 1), individuals are brought in by a wide variety of issues, including Second Amendment opposition to gun control, tax protests, and the "wise use" opposition to environmental laws. Once in the militia movement, some sink into stage 2, a rabid antigovernment belief system. Some believe in the *organic constitution,* which posits that the original 1897 Constitution is the only true federal mandate and any other constitutional amendments after the Bill of Rights are invalid, including the establishment of the IRS. Stage 2 militia members are likely to see the federal government as authoritarian and not truly democratic. Stage 3 sees the arrival of conspiracy theories about the government. These are often linked to beliefs

Figure 8.3 The Funnel Model of Militia Involvement

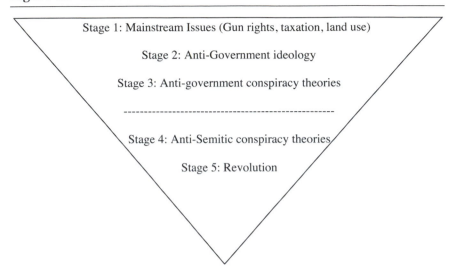

Stage 1: Mainstream Issues (Gun rights, taxation, land use)

Stage 2: Anti-Government ideology

Stage 3: Anti-government conspiracy theories

Stage 4: Anti-Semitic conspiracy theories

Stage 5: Revolution

about the Illuminati, Freemasons, the United Nations, or even aliens. Stage 3 militia members typically view federal authorities as under the control of an international shadow government that controls both the Republican and Democratic parties. Stage 4 sees those conspiracy theories become anti-Semitic. The shadow government is named as the Zionist Occupation Government (ZOG). Belief in ZOG is widely held among neo-Nazis and other organized racists. The belief has a small cabal of Jewish rabbis orchestrating the events in several nations and is reinforced by a long-discredited document known as *The Protocols of the Elders of Zion* (which has found a new audience with Muslim extremists).

The final stage of Stern's (1996) model promotes the idea of an armed racial uprising. If the U.S. government is controlled by ZOG at every level, stage 5 militia members contend, the only response is a "second" American revolution. The racist novel *The Turner Diaries* provides the model of such an insurrection and was a guidebook for McVeigh. In the late 1990s, many stage 5 militia members predicted societal collapse sparked by the Y2K bug in 2000, and there were a handful of terrorist plots foiled by the FBI. Stern contends that while most militia members enter at the nonbigoted stage 1, many are pulled down into deeper levels. Small cells pulled into stage 5, like McVeigh and Nichols, could commit massive acts of hate-motivated terrorism.

The problem, then, is whether or not to classify patriot militias as hate groups. The media hysteria after the 1995 bombing saw all militia and patriot groups linked to the acts of McVeigh and Nichols. Some groups saw the two men as heroes striking a blow against ZOG. Others saw McVeigh and Nichols as victims of an inside job by the government that would give federal authorities more support for clamping down on patriot groups. And many militia groups sought to distance themselves from the bombers and the racist Right altogether.

An individual patriot group, like the Constitution Party of Arkansas, may not publicly espouse anti-Semitic calls for revolution, but may have members who are at stage 4 or 5. It is not uncommon to find hate group materials, like *The Turner Diaries*, at gun shows that are popular with militia members, but does having members who subscribe to a far-right ideology make an organization a hate group?

Minority Hate Groups

The stereotype of the hate group is that it is an organization of white bigots. Can minorities organize around hateful ideology as well? The SPLC has raised some eyebrows by highlighting the rise of antigay rhetoric in traditionally black churches and describing black nationalist organizations, like the NOI, as hate groups. Both the SPLC and ADL list the New Black Panther Party as a hate group. Does it make sense to conceptualize those who have long been the victims of institutional and organized racism as bigots themselves? Or is this the "hate that hate produced"?

The NOI has held antiwhite conspiracies as truths since its founding in 1930. NOI founder Wallace Fard Muhammad and his disciple Elijah Muhammad promoted the idea that the white race was the result of a breeding experiment by an evil scientist named "Yacub," allowing the "white devils" to rule over blacks for 6,000 years. The NOI has also long been accused of anti-Semitism. The leader of the NOI since 1978, Louis Farrakhan has been recorded referring to Judaism as a "dirty religion" and Jews as "blood suckers." He has routinely denied the anti-Semitism theme in the NOI. Mainstream/Middle Eastern Muslims consider the NOI to be a heretical group.

In 1998, one of the more vocal anti-Semites in the NOI, Khalid Muhammad, became the leader of the NBPP, a black nationalist group modeled after the Black Panther Party of the 1960s. Muhammad took the Panthers to Jasper in 1998 to protest the dragging death of James Byrd. According to the ADL report, he told the rally of black protestors, "Black people, we can take these bastards. . . . We can run over the damn police and take their ass. Who's with me?" (ADL, 2007d, para. 22). Muhammad's rhetoric against whites and Jews was continued after his death in 2001 by his disciple Malik Zulu Shabazz, who inherited the leadership of the NBPP.

Another entity not listed as a hate group by monitors, but identified by many community members as such, is the Nation of Aztlán (NOA). The NOA is a Chicano nationalist group that calls for the restoration of the southwestern territory of the United States to Latino control. Aztlán is based on the belief that this region is the mythic homeland of the Aztecs. According to the ADL (2007c), "the group's nationalist message is blurred by frequent appeals to anti-Semitism, anti-Zionism, homophobia and other expressions of hatred" (para. 1). An online zine called *La Voz de Aztlán* (The Voice of Aztlán) has reportedly published articles attacking Jews and Zionism.

The Aztlán movement has been linked to Movimiento Estudiantil Chicano de Aztlán (MEChA) groups. MEChA is a movement that promotes unity among Chicano students. There is nothing in MEChA charters that makes claims of Chicano supremacy or calls for ethnic nationalism or separatism. MEChA groups are typically Hispanic college students who use MEChA to publicize the issues and concerns of the Latino community. However, MEChA has been listed as a hate group by the American Patrol. The American Patrol is a California-based anti-immigration group that SPLC has listed as a hate group and that the ADL has described as a "virulently anti-Hispanic group" (ADL, 2005, para. 15). Can one hate group list another entity as a hate group? If not, why?

Low-Consensus Groups

If it were only racist anti-immigrant groups making the claim that a Chicano organization is a hate group, it would easily be dismissible. However, the *National Review*, a mainstream conservative publication, referred to MEChA as a "bizarre Chicano-separatist group" (Graham, 2003, para. 11). This highlights the tendency of those on the right side of the political spectrum to see groups that might be closer to left-wing ideologies as hate groups.

Environmental and animal rights groups, like the Earth Liberation Front (ELF) and the Animal Liberation Front, have been listed as domestic terrorist groups by the FBI. While these groups are not known for violence against people, their activities have been tied to millions of dollars in damage from arson and vandalism. A 2006 indictment against 11 ELF members in Oregon linked the group to 65 counts of arson. Fires had been set at energy facilities, ski resorts, and ranger stations, among other targets (Oregon Department of Justice, 2006). One of the arson targets was the University of Washington Horticulture Center. The ELF Web site took credit for trying to destroy the research of H. D. Bradshaw, who the group mistakenly believed was researching genetically altered trees. The fire caused more than $2 million in damages and destroyed 20 years of colleagues' research, according to Bradshaw, who referred to ELF as a band of bigots. "They can't possibly understand anything about the environment or science. They are a hate group, and what they hate is science," he told the press in 2001 (Hebel, 2001, p. 1).

That year, Oregon State senator Gary George introduced a law that would classify crimes motivated by a dislike of capitalism as hate crimes. Inspired by the smashing of a Starbucks window by anarchists during an antiglobalization protest, the law would have added five years to prison sentences for those who commit ecosabotage and crimes motivated by a hatred of people who "support capitalism" or advocate a "balance with nature" (Counterpunch, 2001). The bill failed, but George, a Libertarian, had hoped to raise the debate about the nature of hate crime laws. Would anticorporate anarchists now be classified as hate groups? What about people that just hate Starbucks?

It should be noted that both the SPLC and ADL have been described as hate groups by members of the radical Right. Two Web sites in the 1990s regularly accused the groups of promoting hate against whites and Christians: ADL Watch and Dees Watch (named after SPLC founder Morris Dees's Klanwatch). The ADL has been accused of Jewish supremacy and as acting as a foreign agent for Israel. The ADL has also been successfully sued for the defamation of others. In 2000, the Denver ADL described William and Dorothy Quigley as violent anti-Semites in a press conference after the couple had a series of petty altercations with Jewish neighbors. The couple sued the ADL for defamation, and a federal judge awarded them a $10.5 million judgment (Finnigin, 2000). Both the ADL and SPLC have been accused of attempting to limit free speech and of being intolerant of intolerance.

There has been high consensus about the classification of right-wing political groups as being hate motivated. Could left-wing political groups be described similarly? If Marxist groups hate the wealthy, shouldn't they receive the same treatment as groups who hate poor immigrants? There is also the case of SHARPs, the antiracist skinheads. SHARPs hate racist skinheads have violently attacked them. Can you have an antihate hate group?

Defining Hate

The root of the problem is in the definition of hate itself. Dictionary definitions offer some help. Webster's defines *hate* as such: "to dislike strongly, to bear malice to, to detest" (Webster's, 1984, p. 567). The *Online Dictionary* describes hate as such: "dislike intensely; feel antipathy or aversion toward; 'I hate Mexican food'; 'She detests politicians'?" (Freedictionary.com, 2003) Is the hatred of Mexican food the same as the KKK's hatred of Mexican Americans?

Groups with low consensus are not likely to see themselves as hatemongers. Anti-immigrant groups see themselves as defending legality and protecting jobs, wages, crime victims, and national security, not as hating immigrants. Antigay groups see themselves as protecting the innocent from sin, not as hating homosexuals (with the possible exception of the Westboro Baptist Church). One can assume that radical Mormon, Roman Catholic, and Jewish groups, like the JDL, just see themselves as taking necessary steps to defend the existence of their faiths. Included in this definition would be radical Muslim groups that espouse virulent anti-Semitism and theories about ZOG.

Low-consensus groups often express anger when included on a monitoring group's hate group list. When the Cutting Edge Ministry was listed in the Wiesenthal Center's *Digital Hate 2001* report, the response was surprise that a group that defended Israel would be included on a list with neo-Nazis. The author of the Web site, which features many anti-Catholic messages, responded, "Hate has become fashionably defined as disagreeing with anyone in the Politically Correct Movement. . . . This obnoxious listing of 'Hate Groups' is one more indication the noose is growing tighter around all those who love the Lord Jesus Christ" (Cutting Edge, 2002, para. 25).

High-consensus groups also shy away from framing themselves as haters. White supremacists have taken to referring to themselves as more politically correct white separatists. They still clearly believe in the superiority of the white race, but their rhetoric has shifted to masking the bigotry. They are not racists, but "racialists," who just want to be left alone. Increasing numbers of skinhead groups are describing themselves as European heritage groups. The Klan has attempted to refashion itself as a white civil rights organization.

Typical of the white civil rights approach is former grand wizard of the Louisiana KKK David Duke. As a Klansman, Duke publicly promoted legality and nonviolence, describing himself as a "white nationalist" and "racial realist." Duke left the Klan in 1980 and founded the NAAWP, modeled after the National Association of Colored People. Duke argued that if minorities can have special interest groups to defend their rights, whites deserve the same opportunity.

This is a common tactic among "racialists." They are not engaging in racial hatred, but balance. If African Americans can express their racial anger in rap music, whites should be allowed to express theirs in white power rock. If there can be a black student union, there should be a white student union. If Chicano pride is celebrated, so should white pride. This is not hate, they would argue, but equality.

A recent online post defending a 2007 rally of the Hammerskin skinhead group illustrates this sentiment:

What's wrong with the preservation of the white race? We certainly hear enough about racial pride in the black and latino community but for some reason anytime a white person claims any racial pride they are branded as racist bigots and hate group members. While the so-called minority communities seek to encourage this double standard most intelligent white folks know it's just that, a hypocritical double standard. If your [*sic*] "white" be proud of your heritage (German, French, Croatian, Russian, etc). And like it or not in America, Hammerskin Nation enjoys freedom of speech as do the rest of us. Stop crying and deal with it! (Frrost, 2007)

What determines the gradations of a spectrum in which the hatred of Jews is at one end and the hatred of rainy days is at the other? Fortunately, there is a legal guideline. Similar questions arose during the creation of the first hate crime laws. Who should such laws protect? Should hate crime laws protect the poor, political groups, and the left-handed? The response was to restrict the laws to the coverage of specific protected categories. These are categories of people (not things, like Starbucks and rainy days) who have historically been victimized by bias-motivated criminality. There is a history of the victimization of African Americans because they are black. There is not a similar history of the victimization of Democrats because they are Democrats.

Protected categories are based on high levels of consensus. Because of historical victimizations of racial and ethnic minorities, immigrants, and religious minorities, like Roman Catholics and Jews, hate crime laws seek to punish crimes motivated by bias based on race, ethnicity, national origin, and religion. This includes crimes against majority groups as well as minority ones. There is less of a consensus on other categories, such as sexual orientation, disability status, class, and gender, although an increasing number of states are including these categories in their hate crime laws.

DEFINITION OF A HATE GROUP

Each of these issues allows to us be mindful of the importance of a meaningful definition of hate groups that takes into account these concerns. Along with the legal concerns discussed, there are also civil issues of officially defining an organization as a hate group. Such designations can be viewed as libelous to those who believe that their group is doing good for the community and not engaging in "hatemongering." To be listed as a hate group by organizations as recognized as the ADL and SPLC could permanently stigmatize a group and its members. Cities have had similar problems in the past with the creation of "gang member lists" to limit the activity of individuals believed to be members of street gangs. Such gang injunctions have been challenged in courts as both unconstitutional and defamatory (American Civil Liberties Union, 2001). Civil suits in cities like Garden Grove, California, and Portland, Oregon, have found the inclusion of individuals on such gang lists to be a violation of due process rights (American Association for Justice, 1994). After having his group included on the SPLC's 2007 hate group list, Kyle Barstow, leader of the Michigan State University (MSU) chapter of Young Americans for Freedom (YAF), told the *Intelligence Report* he was considering legal action against the SPLC for defamation (Holthouse, 2007).

The Seven-Stage Hate Model

In 2003, the FBI published "The Seven-Stage Hate Model: The Psychopathology of Hate Groups" in a attempt to help the agency develop strategies to counter hate crimes by organized racists. Authored by two FBI agents who had investigated skinhead groups in Southern California over a seven-year period, the report offers a possible structure to the definition of hate groups. The model follows a path from group formation to the realization of the group's ultimate goal.

> *Stage 1: The haters gather.* In this introductory phase, bigots find peers to validate their negative attitudes toward other groups. The formation of a group provides both empowerment and anonymity.
>
> *Stage 2: The hate group defines itself.* The group creates a name for itself (possibly using already existing group names). The group will claim symbols and clothing styles to represent its collective beliefs. Group rituals will be established, including possible initiation rituals to demonstrate commitment to the group.
>
> *Stage 3: The hate group disparages the target.* The members of the group collectively express their hatred for target groups. This could be in publications, song lyrics, or speeches at rallies. Verbal debasement of others serves to enhance the haters' self-image.
>
> *Stage 4: The hate group taunts the target.* Members begin to confront the objects of their hate, perhaps shouting disparaging comments from afar or threatening targeted individuals who are found in territory the group as claimed as theirs. Nazi salutes and graffiti are other methods of taunting.
>
> *Stage 5: The hate group attacks the target without weapons.* Verbal abuse by haters becomes physical abuse. Typically, a group will seek out individual victims for a thrill-seeking attack. The violence bonds the group and further isolates them from society.
>
> *Stage 6: The hate group attacks the target with weapons.* While guns are used during hate crimes, more common are weapons that require the attackers to have close contact with the victim of their hate, such as broken bottles, baseball bats, or belt buckles.
>
> *Stage 7: The hate group destroys the target.* The ultimate goal is to destroy (kill) the victim as a symbolic act of destroying the victim's group (Schafer & Navarro, 2003).

The model has a wide variety of applications. It was developed based on the formation and criminality of racist skinhead gangs. It could also easily fit the formation of nativist groups that form around a common hatred of Latino immigrants. The authors also contend that the model could also explain workplace harassment, in which, in stage 7, the victim must leave the workplace because of intolerable conditions created by a group of co-workers.

Obviously, a group does not to have to progress through all seven stages to be certified as a hate group. Most recognized hate groups do not move past stage 3, keeping their disdain for target populations within their reference group. However, the criteria for the first three stages give us a foundation for a useful definition.

A Working Definition

The FBI piece attempts to make a distinction between rational and irrational hate. The authors state, "Unjust acts inspire rational hate. Hatred of a person based on race, religion, sexual orientation, ethnicity, or national origin constitutes irrational hate" (Schafer & Navarro, 2003, p. 1). Of course, organized bigots see their hatred as very rational; they rationally oppose groups they feel threaten them. But as a starting point, the hate of hate groups must be defined as a generalized hatred toward a large group of people (e.g., hating Asian people, instead of hating a specific Asian individual):

> *Criterion 1: A hate group is a collection of people who hold a common disdain for one or more large categorizations of people.* This malice is based on a belief that the target group is somehow inferior to the members of the hate group. This excludes a family who has a long hatred for a rival family or sports teams and political parties that have longstanding rivalries. Fans of the Atlanta Braves may, on occasion, hate fans of the New York Yankees, but they do not, as a group, believe that Yankees fans are inferior as human beings. Christian Identity groups, as a rule, believe Jews are inferior human beings. Groups that hate corporations would not be included because corporations are things and not groups of people.
>
> *Criterion 2: A hate group is a named entity.* A hate group must name itself or accept a name given to it by others. This prevents cliques, crowds, and other transitory groups of people from being named as hate groups. Hate group names may be the adoption of larger organizations, like the KKK, or they may be self-starter groups, creating new names for themselves. Named groups typically adopt symbols, styles, and rituals to identify who is a member and who is not. It is not necessary for hate group members to display "proof" of membership (such as group patches, tattoos, or membership cards). Claiming membership is sufficient.
>
> *Criterion 3: A hate group desires the oppression of one or more large categorizations of people based on historical circumstances.* Disdain for other groups is not sufficient for classification as a hate group. Some Christian groups may harbor a common animosity toward Jews or Muslims but have no desire to see them punished. This oppression is based on a desire to continue the oppression of a group or to oppress the group who has historically been viewed as the oppressor. This criterion would include groups who want to see the continued oppression of homosexuals or oppress whites because of historical white racism. It would not include groups that want to oppress

Californians because there is no historical oppression of Californians and, as a group, Californians have not historically oppressed any group.

Criterion 4: A hate group must act on its collective disdain of other groups. The final criterion requires the group to engage in some activity that is an expression of its desire to oppress one or more groups. This can include holding regular meetings, publishing a Web site or newsletter, attending rallies as a group, producing music, or engaging in criminal acts, including hate crimes and terrorism. These acts are based on two group goals. The first is to promote their group beliefs and encourage others to accept their group views. The second goal of the activity is to disparage, taunt, attack, and/or destroy the targets of their group animosity. This can include the promotion of conspiracy theories that allege that the target group conspires against the hate group's reference group. These actions must be sanctioned by the group and not be actions of rogue members.

This criterion would exclude groups that may have a historical bias toward a group but do not, as a group, act on it. For example, the Book of Mormon, the sacred text of the Church of Latter Day Saints, contains racist descriptions of "dark skinned" people, and early Mormon leaders Brigham Young and Joseph Fielding Smith made clearly racist comments. However, in 1963, the Church issued a statement opposing racism and supporting the civil rights movement and has since publicly opposed racism (Ostling & Ostling, 2000).

These four criteria are meant to reinforce the inclusion of high-consensus groups as well as scrutinize the inclusion of low-consensus groups. For example, the MSU-YAF might be seen as a low-consensus group. The YAF had traditionally been a relatively mainstream conservative group since its founding by William F. Buckley in 1960. However, the MSU chapter of the YAF clearly fits the proposed hate group criteria. The MSU-YAF is a small group of people bounded by their common disdain for immigrants, Muslims, homosexuals, and other minorities, evidenced by the fact that the majority of the group's activities express negative views toward these large categorizations of people (criterion 1). The MSU-YAF has named itself (criterion 2). The MSU-YAF desires the oppression of large groups based on historical circumstances. This is illustrated based on the group's campus activities, including a "Straight Power" rally in 2006, in which members held antigay signs displaying slogans like "Go Back in the Closet." The group has also held a Koran desecration competition and a "Catch an Illegal Alien Day" contest (criterion 3). Finally, the MSU-YAF has acted on its collective disdain, including hosting a Holocaust denier on campus in 2007 (criterion 4; Holthouse, 2007).

Groups identified as antigay or anti-immigrant may be excluded from hate group lists if they do not explicitly express disdain for certain populations as well as desire to oppress those groups. A religious group that organizes in opposition to homosexuality may "love the sinner, but hate the sin." A border patrol group may not desire to oppress immigrant populations, just protect native populations. Of course, these assessments are made on subjective judgments. An anti–illegal immigration group may publicly decry racism in the nativist movement but only target nonwhite undocumented immigrants in its literature.

SUMMARY

A hate group is a named entity that holds a common disdain for one or more large categorizations of people, desires to oppress those people based on historical circumstances, and acts on that desire. This definition has multiple uses. This definition can be used by academics and monitoring groups so both can share a common conceptualization when discussing the issue. For example, if certain black nationalist groups fit the criteria and are counted by monitoring groups, they should be included in academic research on hate groups. Second, as suggested by the FBI's Seven-Stage Hate Model, a proper definition of a group allows law enforcement to differentiate at which point hate groups engage in criminal activities. For example, an identified group at stage 3 ("disparaging target") may engage in racial intimidation. A stage 4 group ("taunting target") may engage in bias-motivated vandalism.

The formal definition can also help with some of the issues discussed in this chapter. This definition clearly states that hate groups act on their desire to oppress large groups of people. This sets the bar fairly high, allowing constitutionally protected activities to continue, but giving law enforcement clear guidance with regard to group conspiracies to deprive others of their constitutional rights (which are regulated by federal civil rights laws). The proposed Matthew Shepard Act would extend these civil rights to all Americans, regardless of sexual orientation. The standard would also make it more difficult for individuals to sue on behalf of their listed groups, as the group would have to clearly act on an expressed disdain for other populations.

The definition could also help parents, schools, and businesses with access issues. While Web filter programs may not be able to screen out all Web sites based on the four criteria, the definition can give those who are responsible for access a guideline for what materials are the product of named hate groups. For example, a brief observation of martinlutherking.org would quickly reveal that it is linked to the Stormfront Web site and fully with the criteria of inclusion on a list of hate group materials.

Counting hate groups can also be a more uniform process with a clear definition. One problem remains here, and this is the counting of chapters as separate groups. By this definition, if a chapter has a (slightly) different name, it should be counted as its own group. If the White Revolution chapter in Brooks, Georgia, is the Brooks White Revolution, for example, it is a separate group. If it is composed just of members of White Revolution who live in Brooks, it is part of one national group and should be counted as such. Without this distinction, hate groups can be counted wherever two or more hate group members live (the South Elm Street Brooks White Revolution, the North Elm Street Brooks White Revolution, and so on).

The definition is most helpful in distinguishing hate group designations among some of the more contested groups. Clearly many patriot militias are not hate groups, keeping their focus on issues like gun rights. Others have slipped into stages 4 and 5 of the militia funnel and rightly deserve inclusion. Minority groups that express disdain for other populations and desire to oppress them also deserve inclusion. Such groups, however, desire extra scrutiny before being labeled as hate groups. For example, the NOI clearly expresses disdain for the "white devil" and acts on this disdain, making speeches and publishing articles in *Mohammed Speaks*. But does the NOI, as a group, desire to oppress whites? If not, they should not be defined as a hate group. Despite the criticism of MEChA, no one has yet linked them to a platform promoting the oppression of non-Hispanics. Such a standard can be useful in distinguishing low-consensus groups, like the ELF, from white separatists whose sanitized rhetoric still reflects a desire to oppress racial and ethnic minorities.

It is hoped that this exploration will spark an ongoing discussion on the value of an operational definition of *hate group*. Once formalized, comparative research can be conducted, for example, comparing the recruiting techniques of black and white nationalist hate groups. At the moment, the discussion tends to compare apples to oranges because of floating and unclear definitions. "I know it when I see it" is not a sufficient criterion for classifying a social construct as persistent as this.

REFERENCES

American Civil Liberties Union. (2001, May 10). *ACLU wins higher legal standards for gang injunctions*. Retrieved September 12, 2007, from http://www.aclu.org/crim justice/juv/10290prs20010510.html

Anti-Defamation League. (2007a). *About ADL*. Retrieved September 12, 2007 from http://www.adl.org/main_about_adl.asp

Anti-Defamation League. (2007b). *Backgrounder: The Jewish Defense League*. Retrieved September 12, 2007 from http://www.adl.org/extremism/jdl_chron.asp

Anti-Defamation League. (2007c). *Backgrounder: The Nation of Aztlan*. Retrieved September 12, 2007 from http://www.adl.org/learn/Aztlan/default.asp

Anti-Defamation League. (2007d). *Extremism in America: New Black Panther Party for self-defense*. Retrieved September 12, 2007, from http://www.adl.org/learn/ext_us/Black_Panther.asp?LEARN_Cat=Extremism&LEARN_SubCat=Extremism_in_America&xpicked=3&item=Black_Panther

Anti-Defamation League. (2007e). *Extremism in America: Tom Metzger/White Aryan Resistance*. September 12, 2007, from http://www.adl.org/learn/ext_us/Metzger.

asp?LEARN_Cat=Extremism&LEARN_SubCat=Extremism_in_
America&xpicked=2&item=7

Beard v. Banks, 548 U.S. 521 (2006).

Beirich, H. (2007, Winter). The Teflon nativists. *Intelligence Report*, pp. 40–45.

Berlet C. & Vytosky S. (2006). Overview of U.S. white supremacist groups. *Journal of Political and Military Sociology*, 34,11–58.

Burleson, D. (2007, June 18). *Hate speech enters Oracle forums.* Retrieved October 1, 2007, from http://www.dba-oracle.com/oracle_news/news_hate_speech.htm

Cooper v. Pate, 378 U.S. 546 (1964).

Cornell University. (2007). *U.S. Code Collection, Title 28, Part II, Chapter 33, § 534.* Retrieved October 1, 2007, from http://www.law.cornell.edu/uscode/uscode28/usc_sec_28

Corry v. Stanford University, Case No. 74309 (Sup. Ct. Santa Clara County, 1995).

Counterpunch. (2001, May 14). *Hate-crime follies.* Retrieved May 31, 2001, from http://www.counterpunch.org/hatefollies.html

Cutting Edge. (2002). *Cutting Edge Ministries is listed as a hate group!* Retrieved October 1, 2007, from http://cuttingedge.org/news/n1427.cfm

Dennis, D. (2007). Obscenity law and its consequences in mid-nineteenth-century America. *Columbia Journal of Gender and Law, 16*, 43–53.

Finnigin, D. (2000, May 2). $10.5 mil award in Quigley case. *Hollywood Reporter*, p. 3.

Fritsch, E. J., Caeti, T. J., & Taylor, R. W. (1999). Gang suppression through saturation patrol, aggressive curfew, and truancy enforcement: A quasi-experimental test of the Dallas anti-gang initiative. *Crime & Delinquency, 45*, 122–139.

Frrost, T. (2007, October 3). Post in response to "Skin cancer: A white supremacist group comes to Portland to celebrate its 20th anniversary." Retrieved December 12, 2007, from http://wweek.com/editorial/3347/9634/

Graham, T. (2003, October 8). Schwarzeneggernaut: The national media gave him a licking, but he kept on ticking. *National Review Online.* Retrieved October 1, 2007, from http://www.nationalreview.com/comment/tgraham200310080847.asp

Hamm, M. S. (2002). *In bad company: America's terrorist underground.* Boston: Northeastern University Press.

Hamm, M. S. (2007). *Terrorism as crime: From Oklahoma City to Al-Qaeda and beyond.* New York: Routledge.

Hebel, S. (2001, June 4). Earth Liberation Front takes credit for fire at U. of Washington Horticulture Center. *Chronicle of Higher Education*, p. 1.

Highlights of Anti-Terrorism Act, RSC 2001 (2001). www.justice.gc.ca/eng/news-nour/nv-cp/2001/doc_27787.html

Holthouse, D. (2007, Winter). Black hats on campus. *Intelligence Report*, pp. 26–31.

Human Rights Campaign. (2007). *The Local Law Enforcement Hate Crimes Prevention Act/Matthew Shepard Act, H.R. 1592/S. 1105.* Retrieved October 1, 2007, from http://www.hrc.org/laws_and_elections/5660.htm

Jacobellis v. Ohio, 378 U.S. 184 (1964).

King, R. O. (2004, May 21). Solutions and policy combat spreading hate. *WHIR News.* Retrieved October 1, 2007, from http://www.thewhir.com/features/hate-sites.cfm

Kushner, H. W. (2003). *Encyclopedia of terrorism.* Thousand Oaks, CA: Sage.

Levin, J., & McDevitt, J. (1993). *Hate crimes: The rising tide of bigotry and bloodshed.* New York: Plenum.

National Socialist Party of America v. Village of Skokie, 432 U.S. 43 (1977).

Navisite. (2008). *Acceptable use policy (AUP)*. Retrieved September 3, 2008, from http://www.navisite.com/about-navisite/legal/aup.php

Oregon Department of Justice. (2006, January 20). *Animal Liberation Front (ALF) and Earth Liberation Front (ELF) members indicted by federal grand jury on conspiracy and arson charges* [Press release]. Salem, OR: Author.

Ostling, R., & Ostling, J. K. (2000). *Mormon America: The power and the promise*. New York: HarperCollins.

Perry, B. (2001). *In the name of hate: Understanding hate crimes*. New York: Routledge.

Ridgeway, J. (1991). *Blood in the face: The Ku Klux Klan, Aryan Nations, Nazi skinheads, and the rise of a new white culture*. New York: Thunder Mountain Press.

Schafer, J. R., & Navarro, J. (2003). The seven-stage hate model: The psychopathology of hate groups. *FBI Law Enforcement Bulletin, 72*(3), 1–7.

Seltzer, R., & Lopes, G. M. (1986). The Ku Klux Klan: Reasons for support or opposition among white respondents. *Journal of Black Studies, 17*, 91–109.

Shoop, J. G. (1994). Image of fear: Minority teens allege bias in "gang profiling." *Trial, 30*, 12–15.

Southern Poverty Law Center. (2008, Spring). The year in hate. *Intelligence Report*, pp. 48–69.

Stern, K. S. (1996). *A force upon the plain: The American militia movement and the politics of hate*. New York: Simon & Schuster.

Traditional Values Institute. (2005). *Homosexual urban legends*. Retrieved October 1, 2007, from http://www.traditionalvalues.org/urban/

U.S. Department of State. (2002). *Terrorist exclusion list*. Retrieved May 1, 2007, from http://www.state.gov/s/ct/rls/fs/2002/15222.htm

Webster's II: New Riverside Dictionary. (1984). Boston: Riverside, p. 567.

CHAPTER 9

DEFINING AND MEASURING HATE CRIME:
A POTPOURRI OF ISSUES

Susie Bennett, James J. Nolan, and Norman Conti

In June 1998, three espoused racist white males in a pickup truck gave a lift to an unsuspecting James Byrd, a 49-year-old black man who had been walking along the road. As he jumped in the back of their pickup truck, one of the occupants of the truck became angry that the driver had "picked up a nigger." The three decided to assault the black male, so they drove him to a deserted and winding rural road. One of the white men was reported to have said, "We are going to start *The Turner Diaries* early," referring to the fiction novel by a noted white supremacist about a race war with the ultimate goal of an all-white nation. The men wrapped a chain around Byrd's ankles and dragged him down the bumpy road. As they started down the road, one of the white males was alleged to have said (while laughing), "That fucker's bouncing all over the place." During the incident, Byrd's head and right arm were ripped off. According to news reports, his remains were found in 75 places along a 1.2-mile stretch of road (Nolan & Akiyama, 2002).

Hate crime was the term used to capture the motivation behind what happened to James Byrd. Hate crime—as a new category of crime—came onto the political landscape in the late twentieth century with a good deal of support as well as controversy. Sociologists explain the conceptual emergence of hate crime as a consequence of the civil rights movement, the crime victims' movement, the women's movement, and the gay and lesbian movement (Grattet & Jenness, 2001). The term itself is attributed to early efforts by the Anti-Defamation League (ADL), an interest group founded in 1913 to fight bigotry, anti-Semitism, and racism. Justifications for adding hate crime as a new and distinct crime category are well documented and include their more serious nature (Levin, 1999; McDevitt, Balboni, Garcia, & Gu, 2001), more harmful aftermath (Herek, Gillis, Cogan, & Glunt, 1997), more threatening element to civil disorder, and their creation of fissures in the social fabric. Hate crime is considered more harmful as the original act permeates from the victim to the victim's family, group, and society at large (Sullaway, 2004). Notorious cases, such as the vicious murder of James Byrd in Texas, exemplify the brutality and collateral community damage associated with hate crime. However, the Byrd case differs from the majority of potential hate crimes in that the bias motivation was very clear.

The development of hate crime laws was hailed as a breakthrough for combating bias-related violence and intimidation by some, but criticized as nothing more than a symbolic gesture by others. To say the least, hate crime—as a special category of crime—has been controversial. This is interesting since other crime categories, such as domestic and intimate violence, carjacking, and stalking, had been implemented during the same general time period without much fanfare. Some of the arguments challenging hate crime laws have been based on misconceptions and fear, while others have been well grounded in political, legal, and moral arguments (Dunbar & Molina, 2004; Jacobs & Henry, 1996).

An overarching theme in many of the arguments against hate crime laws is that they are ambiguous and therefore difficult to define, identify, investigate, and measure, particularly for law enforcement officials, who are charged with putting the "law in action" (Jenness & Grattet, 2005). The myriad definitions and indicators make detection and identification challenging, and are compounded by the ambiguous and often conflicting nature of the events themselves. This chapter addresses the issue of ambiguity inherent in the definition of hate crime and seeks to provide some clarity to the term. We focus first on the ambiguity caused by the variety of hate crime laws and definitions, specifically those related to criminal acts and penalties, data collection, and law enforcement training. We then outline some of the incentives, disincentives, and other factors that affect law enforcement participation in identifying and reporting hate crime. Next, we identify some of the problems law enforcement officers face while trying to identify hate crime. In the final section, we include a conceptual framework that may prove useful in resolving these problems and suggest how this may help law enforcement identify hate crime. This will be particularly beneficial as the National Incident-Based Reporting System (NIBRS) becomes more fully implemented.

HATE CRIME LAWS AND DEFINITIONS

The diversity of hate crime laws can create confusion at times for those charged with identifying, investigating, and reporting them. For law enforcement purposes, there are three main types of hate crime law: criminal conduct, data collection, and law enforcement training.

Criminal Statutes

Laws that define criminal conduct and related penalties provide police officials with the legal standing to arrest and prosecute individuals and groups for committing hate crimes. State penal codes regarding hate crime are defined in many ways, but most seem to have two primary components: (1) some underlying criminal act (such as an assault or act of intimidation) and (2) the choice of victims *because of* their group affiliation (or the act itself was a manifestation of extreme prejudice on the part of the offender). In some states, hate crime laws provide for penalty enhancements or increase an underlying misdemeanor offense to a felony. In other states, hate crime is a separate offense for which offenders can be convicted in addition to the underlying crime. Some state laws identify only certain underlying criminal acts, such as "intimidation," as being eligible for hate crime status, whereas other states regard *any* crime as a hate crime if there is a bias motivation or if the victim was selected based on group membership. Examples of hate crime laws that apply to criminal behavior include the following:

West Virginia's Hate Crime Statute, in Pertinent Part

If any person does by force or threat of force, willfully injure, intimidate or interfere with, or attempt to injure, intimidate or interfere with, or oppress or threaten any other person in the free exercise or enjoyment of any right or privilege secured to him or her by the Constitution or laws of the state of West Virginia or by the Constitution or laws of the United States, because of such other person's race, color, religion, ancestry, national origin, political affiliation or sex, he or she shall be guilty of a felony, and, upon conviction, shall be fined not more than five thousand dollars or imprisoned not more than ten years, or both. The fact that a person committed a felony or misdemeanor, or attempted to commit a felony, because of the victim's race, color, religion, ancestry, national origin, political affiliation or sex, shall be considered a circumstance in aggravation of any crime in imposing sentence. (West Virginia State Criminal Code § 61–6-21)

New York's Hate Crime Statute, in Pertinent Part

A person commits a hate crime when he or she commits a specified offense and either: (a) intentionally selects the person against whom the offense is committed or intended to be committed in whole or in substantial part because of a belief or perception regarding the race, color, national origin, ancestry, gender, religion, religious practice, age, disability or sexual orientation of a person, regardless of whether the belief or perception is correct, or (b) intentionally commits the act or acts constituting the offense in whole or in substantial part because of a belief or perception regarding the race, color, national origin, ancestry, gender, religion, religious practice, age, disability or sexual orientation of a person, regardless of whether the belief or perception is correct. (New York State Criminal Code § 485.05)

California's Hate Crime Statute, in Pertinent Part

A criminal act committed, in whole or in part, because of one or more of the following actual or perceived characteristics of the victim: 1) disability, 2) gender, 3) nationality, 4) race or ethnicity, 5) religion, 6) sexual orientation, 7) association with a person or group with one or more of these actual or perceived characteristics. (California Penal Code § 422.55)

Hate Crime Data Collection

The most significant and comprehensive hate crime data collection law to date is the Hate Crime Statistics Act of 1990 (HCSA). The HCSA was a mandate by Congress that charged the U.S. attorney general with collecting data regarding hate crime. The attorney general assigned the task to the director of the Federal Bureau of Investigation (FBI), who transferred responsibility to the Uniform Crime Reporting Program (UCR). In response to the congressional mandate, the UCR program developed and implemented the National Hate Crime Data Collection Program.

The HCSA (as amended, 28 U.S.C. § 534) reads as follows:

§ [Sec. 1.] a.   This Act may be cited as the "Hate Crime Statistics Act."

b.   1.   Under the authority of section 534 of title 28, United States Code, the Attorney General shall acquire data, for each calendar year, about crimes that manifest evidence of prejudice based on race, religion, disability, sexual orientation, or ethnicity, including where appropriate the crimes of murder, non-negligent manslaughter; forcible rape; aggravated assault, simple assault, intimidation; arson; and destruction, damage or vandalism of property.

2.   The Attorney General shall establish guidelines for the collection of such data including the necessary evidence and criteria that must be present for a finding of manifest prejudice and procedures for carrying out the purposes of this section.

3.   Nothing in this section creates a cause of action or a right to bring an action, including an action based on discrimination due to sexual orientation. As used in this section, the term "sexual orientation" means consensual homosexuality or heterosexuality. This subsection does not limit any existing cause of action or right to bring an action, including any action under the administrative Procedure Act or the All Writs Act [5 USCS §§ 551 et seq. or 28 USCS § 1651].

4.   Data acquired under this section shall be used only for research or statistical purposes and may not contain any

information that may reveal the identity of an individual victim of a crime.

5. The Attorney General shall publish an annual summary of the data acquired under this section.

c. There are authorized to be appropriated such sums as may be necessary to carry out the provisions of this section through fiscal year 2002.

Sec. 2. a. Congress finds that—

1. the American family life is the foundation of American Society,
2. Federal policy should encourage the well-being, financial security, and health of the American family,
3. schools should not de-emphasize the critical value of American family life.

b. Nothing in this Act shall be construed, nor shall any funds appropriated to carry out the purpose of the Act be used, to promote or encourage homosexuality. (Federal Bureau of Investigation [FBI], 2004)

The HCSA was amended in 1994 to include bias against persons with disabilities, for which data collection commenced in 1997. The intent behind the HCSA was to capture information about the nature and frequency of bias crime as it relates only to those crimes already being collected by the UCR program in the United States, without adding additional procedures to law enforcement.

Figure 9.1 shows that although the number of police agencies who participate in the FBI's hate crime reporting program grew dramatically after the inception of the HCSA, spiking from around 2,000 agencies in 1991 to around 11,000 agencies by 1997, participation has leveled off and remained fairly stable, with between 11,000 and just under 14,000 agencies participating over the past 10 years. Although these agencies "participate" in the program, the vast majority, around 85 percent, report that zero hate crimes have occurred in their jurisdictions. The problem of "zero reporting" is often attributed to the ambiguous nature of hate crime laws (Nolan & Akiyama, 2002; McDevitt, Balboni, & Bennett, 2000).

LAW ENFORCEMENT TRAINING FOR HATE CRIMES

Along with laws that define hate crime for criminal justice and data collection purposes, many states have laws that require hate crime training for law enforcement officers. Some states, like New Mexico, require officers to be trained to "detect, investigate, and report crimes motivated by hate" (N.M. Stat. Ann. § 31–18B-5). Other states, for example, New Jersey, have laws that require cultural diversity training for law enforcement personnel (N.J. Stat. Ann. § 52:9DD-9). State training laws can be a source of confusion

Figure 9.1 Police Agencies Reporting Zero Hate Crimes Compared to Those Reporting One or More

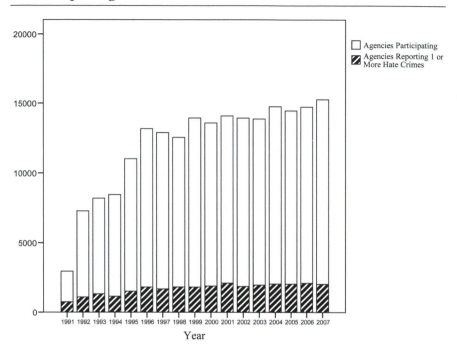

Source: FBI-UCR Hate Crime Statistics, 1991–2006. Retrieved March 23, 2008, from http://www.fbi.gov/ucr/ucr.htm

when they define different acts as hate crimes or pertain to different groups, depending on whether they are for training, criminal investigation, or data collection. For example, in Oregon, the criminal hate crime statute relates to the crime of "intimidation because of the perpetrator's perception of that person's race, color, religion, national origin or sexual orientation" (Ore. Rev. Stat. § 166.155, § 166.165), whereas the hate crime training law is more expansive and covers "investigation, identification and reporting of crimes motivated by prejudice based on the perceived race, color, religion, national origin, sexual orientation, marital status, political affiliation or beliefs, membership or activity in or on behalf of a labor organization or against a labor organization, physical or mental handicap, age, economic or social status or citizenship of the victim" (Ore. Rev. Stat. § 181.642).

In summary, the diversity of hate crime laws for varied purposes can create confusion inside and outside law enforcement. In some states, hate crime laws relate only to specific crimes and certain forms of bias. In other states, any crime can be a hate crime if it is motivated by bias or if the victims were selected because of their group membership. In almost every state, the definition of hate crime for data collection purposes under the FBI's UCR program is different from the state's criminal statute. And even within states, the laws that identify hate crimes for criminal prosecution, data collection, and law enforcement training may define hate crimes differently.

HATE CRIME MEASUREMENT BY OTHER ORGANIZATIONS

What we know about hate crime is contingent on how it is defined but ultimately rests on how it is measured. In addition to the national hate crime reporting program and NIBRS (to be discussed), a number of nonprofit community organizations and special interest groups around the country compile and analyze their own statistics on hate crime (Haider-Markel, 2006). As both hate groups and prejudiced loners appear to flourish in the cyber world (Levin, 2002), so, too, are the groups dedicated to exposing and combating them. Many of these monitoring groups operate primarily via the Internet and provide detailed information, assistance, and encouragement for individuals to detect and report hate activity that they see or experience. The Southern Poverty Law Center (SPLC), an organization developed by attorneys in 1971 to pursue civil rights issues, publishes an annual report known as the *Intelligence Report* that tracks hate groups, militias, and other extremist groups across the country. The *Intelligence Report* began documenting hate activity in 1981 and continues to show increases in hate group activity. In 2007, they reported 888 hate groups in the United States, a 48 percent increase since 2000 (Southern Poverty Law Center, 2007). This figure represents both Web-based hate groups and other extremists. This information is distributed to law enforcement, policy makers, educators, and the general public to raise awareness of hate group activities.

The ADL (2008) plays a vital role in tracking and logging hate-related incidents in the media as well as community and legal responses. They have been instrumental in conducting or collaborating in survey and opinion polls that show that Americans continue to foster negative attitudes toward minority and immigrant groups. They also provide a "blueprint" for action in combating bias crime that includes information for the public as well as training for law enforcement.

Many community and neighborhood organizations play an important role in collecting hate crime data and educating community and law enforcement. For example, the Los Angeles County Commission on Human Relations has been collecting and analyzing data about hate crimes and prosecution in Los Angeles County since 1980. They report that the number of hate crimes reported in Los Angeles County in 2006 was at its second lowest level since the HCSA was implemented in 1991 (Los Angeles County Commission on Human Relations, 2006). Of the 514 hate crime incidents reported, law enforcement referred 152 cases to the Los Angeles County district attorney's office. Eighty-five percent of these cases resulted in criminal charges being filed. Neighboring Orange County's Human Relations Commission collects information on both hate crimes and hate incidents and reports that in 2007, hate crimes declined 20 percent from 101 to 81, while noncriminal hate incidents increased by about 30 percent, from 34 to 45 (Orange County Human Relations Commission, 2008).

There are a host of additional nonprofit groups that measure hate crime and incidents to further inform our understanding of the scope of hate crime throughout the country. For example, the United Methodist Church hosts a Hate Crime Data Collection Project that provides resource sheets on their Web site to encourage individuals to aid in their efforts to track local media and newspaper segments that refer to bias (United Methodist Church, 2008).

Incentives, Disincentives, and Other Factors That Influence Hate Crime Reporting

As we mentioned at the outset of this chapter, law enforcement officials are charged with identifying, investigating, and reporting hate crime. However, there are incentives, disincentives, and other forces within the field of law enforcement that affect police participation (Nolan & Akiyama, 2002; Shively, Cronin, & McDevitt, 2001). In the two situations presented subsequently, filing a hate crime was viewed as a disincentive by law enforcement officials. Both of these situations clearly fit the FBI definition of hate crime ("motivated in whole or in part by the offenders' bias"), but in neither case were hate crime charges initially brought against the defendants.

On a bright afternoon in March 2008, Lavareay Elzy, a six-year-old black male, was shot in the head while riding with his family through Harbor Gateway, California. Activists and local residents implored prosecutors to file hate crime charges against the two Latino suspects because they were known members of a gang reputed for its hatred of African Americans and that had been establishing a pattern of race-based attacks in the area. Since the Elzy family was unknown to the assailants, they were assumed to have been targeted solely based on race. Prosecutors opted for gang enhancements instead of hate crime charges because they believed that the act of flashing gang signs before opening fire on the vehicle pointed more clearly to gang-related motivation than hate crime (Maddaus & Woodhouse, 2008).

In September 2007, Megan Williams, a 20-year-old African American woman, was kidnapped and tortured for six days in a Big Creek, West Virginia, home by seven white defendants. Williams was repeatedly stabbed, mutilated, sexually abused, and forced to drink toilet water and eat animal feces, while her tormentors verbally abused her with racial slurs. As of this writing, local authorities in the case have only filed hate crime charges against one of the defendants after much prodding by local and national advocacy groups (Associated Press, 2008). For the remaining six defendants, prosecutors have preferred to focus on the crimes that carry the stiffest penalties: kidnapping, which is punishable by life imprisonment, and sexual assault, which is punishable by up to 35 years in prison. Prosecutors in the case have been reluctant to pursue hate crime charges because the victim had had a previous "social relationship" with one of the offenders and was therefore not a random target.

In the California case, the victims were clearly selected because of their race. However, the gangland nature of the case was arguably clearer, so filing a hate crime charge may have seemed like a distraction for the police and prosecutors. In the West Virginia case, the victim was also selected because of her race; however, the fact that she had had a social relationship with one of the defendants may have made the hate crime charge somewhat murky compared to the other charges, such as kidnapping and rape. In both cases, there were *disincentives* to identifying the crimes as hate crimes, even though there was public outcry from citizens and advocacy groups to do so.

On the other hand, there are also *incentives* to adding a hate crime charge in some cases. Consider the following situation from New York: in Queens, in February 2008, Alexandra Gilmore, a 36-year-old white female, was charged with a hate crime for taking advantage of Artee McKoy, a 93-year-old white male Alzheimer's patient, by claiming to be his daughter to swindle him out of $800,000. Gilmore and her accomplice, 30-year-old Rebecca Tharpe, were charged with second-degree larceny, motivated by hate, and face up to 25 years if convicted (Livingston, 2008).

This case showed clear evidence of material and economic motivation, but prosecutors found the crimes so despicable that they tacked on hate crime charges as well since New York's definition requires simply that a crime be motivated *in part* because the victim is perceived to be from a different group. Whether the prosecutors felt that the crimes against Mr. McKoy were based on age or disability is somewhat unclear; however, there was obviously an incentive to filing hate crime charges against the defendants, regardless of whether the crimes are truly recognized by citizens and advocacy groups as such.

In addition to these incentives and disincentives, there are other forces that affect police participation in hate crime reporting. Using focus groups and survey research, Nolan and Akiyama (2002) identified a list of "social forces" that either encourage police participation or discourage it. Table 9.1 provides a summary of these findings.

In addition to these forces for and against participation in hate crime reporting, other research has sought out various ways police officials overcome obstacles to reporting hate crime such as implementing a bias crime investigations unit or having a second-level review of suspected bias crime reports (Bell, 2002; Cronin, McDevitt, Farrell, & Nolan, 2007).

Table 9.1   Forces that Affect Whether Law Enforcement Agencies Report Hate Crimes

"Encouraging" forces, agency level	"Discouraging" forces, agency level
• Ability to assess intergroup tensions in community	• Not deemed important by department
• Desire to give support to communities	• Perception on part of police that no problem exists
• Belief that hate crime reporting will improve police-community relations	• Insufficient support staff to process, record, and submit hate crime data.
• Belief that police help set level of acceptable behavior in the community	• Perceived as not being "real" police work
	• A belief that reporting hate crimes will make things worse for victims
• Understanding that community wants police to report hate violence	• A belief that reporting hate crimes will make things worse for communities
• Need to know extent of problem as first step to developing solutions	• Perception that some minority groups complain unnecessarily
• Lets community know that department takes hate crimes seriously	• Not a priority of local government
	• Identifying a crime as a hate crime will have no effect on the outcome
• A belief that victims will get help	• A belief that it's wrong to make these types of crimes "special"
• Will help diffuse racial tensions within the police department	• A belief that hate crime reporting will result in negative publicity for the community
• The right thing to do "politically"	
• The right thing to do "morally"	• A belief that hate crime reporting supports the political agendas of gay and minority groups (which is seen as a negative thing)
• Will help maintain department's good relationship with diverse groups	
• Consistent with values of department	• It creates too much additional work
• A belief that identifying problem will keep others safe	• Hate crimes are not as serious as other crimes (i.e., a lower priority)
• Citizens appreciate the hate crime reporting efforts of the police	• Agency does not have the adequate technological resources

Source: From J. J. Nolan and Y. Akiyama, "Assessing the climate for hate-crime reporting in law enforcement organizations: A force-field analysis," *Justice Professional* 15, no. 2 (2002): 87–103.

A CONCEPTUAL FRAMEWORK FOR HATE CRIME IDENTIFICATION AND REPORTING

According to the American philosopher John Dewey (1910/1997), terms like *hate crime* take on shared meaning through the dual processes of *intension* and *extension. Intension* means defining the term; *extension* means identifying things that do and do not fit this definition. Consider, for example, the term *house*. We've come to know a house when we see one, regardless of size, color, or geographic location. Given cultural relativity, we are also able to distinguish a house from a garage, barn, storage facility, and apartment complex (Craig & Waldo, 1996). Defining the term *house* is what we mean by *intension*, while distinguishing the house from other similar structures is what we mean by *extension*. Where *intension* is the meaning in principle, extension is the group of things being separated and distinguished (see Nolan, McDevitt, Cronin, & Farrell, 2004).

Defining Hate Crime Through Intension

As previously stated, a hate crime is defined by the FBI (2004) as a "criminal offense committed against a person or property which is motivated, in whole or in part, by the offender's bias against race, religion, disability, ethic/national origin group, or sexual orientation group." This definition provides a description of what is intended to be categorized under the term *hate crime*. The difficulty arises when law enforcement officials attempt to apply this seemingly clear definition to murky, real-life situations.

Identifying Hate Crimes Through Extension: A Rational Exercise

In this section, we will use standard mathematical set notation to depict the process of extension. In preparation for the extension of the term *hate crime* to real-life events, it is important to identify the universal set (denoted as U) of all possible hate crime–like events. Since hate crimes are manifestations of intergroup conflict, we identify three forms of such conflict as our starting point: noncriminal acts, criminal acts not reported to the police, and criminal acts that are reported to the police. Therefore the universal set of *possible* hate crimes U is the set of all acts on the part of individuals and groups that are motivated by some form of intergroup conflict. This set includes acts of discrimination and crimes that are motivated in whole or in part by bias. But, because we are examining hate crimes within the field of all acts that result from interpersonal and intergroup conflicts, this set also includes behaviors that are caused by ongoing disputes between neighbors; disagreements that result from failed interpersonal or business relationships; and day-to-day conflicts that erupt in public places like restaurants, city buses, subways, and on the street, among many other forms. The universal set comprises three subsets: (I) the set of all noncriminal acts, (II) the set of all criminal acts that were not reported to police, and (III) the set of all criminal acts that were reported to and recorded by the police. We therefore denote the universal set as U = IIIIII (see Figure 9.2).

Figure 9.2 Universal Set and Subsets of Crime. Inside the Universal Set are Three Subsets: {A} Set of all Events (Crimes and Non-Crimes Having Some Bias Indicators), {B} Set of Crimes Fitting Federal Hate Crime Statistics Act of 2004, and {C} Set of Crimes Fitting Local and State Criminal Definitions

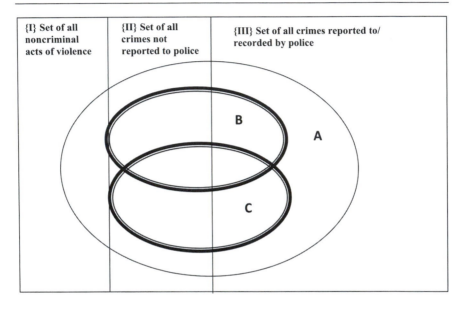

Inside the universal set are three subsets that relate to hate crime (see Figure 9.2). The first is set A. This is the set of events that show some indication that bias on the part of the offender may be a motivating factor. For example, racial or ethnic epithets may have been used by the offender when a crime was committed, or the victim and offender were from different racial or ethnic groups. Without more information, a determination that the event was a hate crime or hate incident cannot be confirmed. Set A also contains events that have the impact of a hate crime, even though the offenders' motivations were known or were confirmed to be something other than bias. For example, suppose a church is burned to the ground in an African American community. Some might think that the motivation was bias or hate, when in fact, the true motivation may have been insurance fraud. Since this is the type of crime that may be perceived by the community as a message of hate, we include it in set A.

Set B is a subset of A, denoted as BA. Set B contains all crimes that fit the FBI's definition used for statistics gathering in response to the HCSA. Set C, on the other hand, contains all crimes that fit the federal, state, and local criminal hate crime laws. C is a subset of A (CA), but it is not a subset of B (CB). In other words, all crimes that fit the statistical definition of bias crime do not necessarily fit the criminal definition. In some cases, the state and local criminal statute will include different bias or crime types. In a study of hate crime reporting in the United States, Cronin and colleagues (2007) found a jurisdiction that had a local criminal statute called "ethnic intimidation," which included acts of harassment and intimidation aimed at individuals and groups because of their ethnicity only (i.e., not race, religion, etc.). To the police officers in that large city department, a violation of the ethnic intimidation statute meant "hate crime." So when asked to consider a situation in which someone was murdered because of his or her race, the officers argued that this crime would not be called a hate crime in their jurisdiction. In addition, there are states like West Virginia, where the state criminal statute does not included certain categories, that is, sexual orientation, as a bias type. However, for reporting hate crimes to the FBI for statistical purposes, sexual orientation is included.

By viewing hate crime reporting in this way, one can begin to see why certain events are clearly hate crimes, while others are not. In most cases, the clearest hate crimes are those that fit the compound event denoted by B ∩ C, that is, one that fits both the federal statistical and the criminal definitions.

Cronin and colleagues (2007) found that many hate crimes involve bias as a secondary motivation. For example, an offender may want to commit a robbery (i.e., motivated by the need for money) but selects a minority-owned business because of bias. Or consider the offender whose crime is triggered by some other event, such as an argument over a parking spot. The initial argument may escalate into an assault because of the offender's bias. In our conceptual model, set D is the set of crimes that involve bias as a secondary motivation (see Figures 9.3 and 9.4).

Developing a Typology of Hate Crimes by Way of Extension

Once again, where intension is the meaning of the term in principle, extension is the group of things that are being distinguished. The conceptual model presented here is helpful in that it subdivides the universal set of possible bias crime events into 20 different categories of events to consider (see Figure 9.5). Each region created by the overlapping sets is given a number that corresponds to descriptions and examples provided in Table 9.2.[1]

In this conceptual model, we make the distinction between crimes that get reported to the police and those that do not. Therefore crimes that end up being identified in the FBI's hate crime report are those that come from regions 3, 4, 6, and 7. The clearest hate crimes for statistical purposes are

Figure 9.3 Intersections of Subsets of Crime. Set {D} Is a Subset of {A} and Intersects with Sets {B} and {C}. Set {D} Is the Set of Crimes for Which Bias and Hate Are Secondary Motivations.

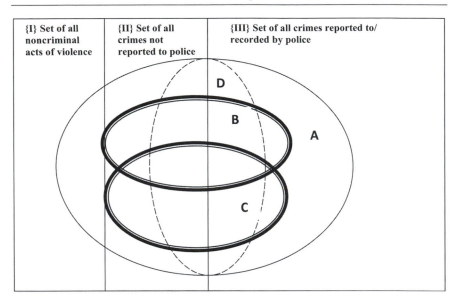

Figure 9.4 Distinguishing Hate Crimes from Other Interpersonal and Intergroup Violence

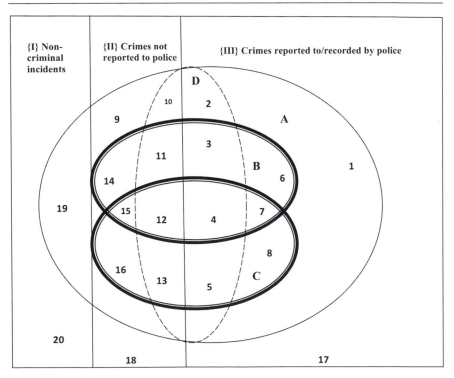

Table 9.2 Types of Hate Crimes

Regions reported	Regions not reported	Description of crime	Examples
1	9	Crimes with bias indicators but cannot confirm whether they fit definitions for statistics or criminal prosecution. Important to know for prevention activities.	An assault in which victim and offender are from different groups, e.g., Asian vs. white, but nothing else is known regarding motivation.
2	10	Crimes with bias as a secondary motivation but do not fit criminal or statistics definitions.	In response to an argument over politics, a man assaults a person whom he identifies as Republican.
3[a]	11[b]	Crimes with bias as a secondary motivation and which fit the definition for statistics, but not for criminal prosecution.	In response to an argument over politics, a man commits an assault. He claims he "hates gay Democrats" (criminal statute doesn't include sexual orientation as a bias category).
4[c]	12[b]	Crimes with bias as a secondary motivation and which fit the definitions for both statistics and criminal prosecution.	In response to an argument over politics, a man commits an assault. He claims he "hates Asian Democrats" (race is included in both criminal and statistics definitions).
5[d]	13[b]	Crimes with bias as a secondary motivation and which fit the definition for criminal prosecution but not statistics.	In response to an argument over politics, a man commits an assault. He claims he "hates female Democrats" (gender is included in the criminal definition but not in the statistics definition).
6[a]	14[b]	Crimes with bias as a primary motivation and which fit the definition for statistics but not criminal prosecution.	Several males assault men exiting a known gay bar. They claim to hate gays. Sexual orientation is a category in the statistics definition but not in the criminal definition.
7[c]	15[b]	Crimes with bias as a primary motivation and which fit the definitions for statistics and criminal prosecution	Several white males burn a cross in the front yard of the home of a black family. They claim to hate black people. Race is a category in both statistics and criminal definitions.

(continued)

Table 9.2   Types of Hate Crimes (*continued*)

Regions reported	Regions not reported	Description of crime	Examples
8[d]	16[b]	Crimes with bias as a primary motivation and which fit the definitions for criminal prosecution but not statistics.	A male shoots only females at a local high school during a shooting spree. Gender is included in the criminal hate crime statute, but not in the statistics definition.
17	18	Crimes with no bias indicators.	Two white males assault each other during a bar fight.

Note: See Figure 9.4 for regions.
[a]Hate crimes for national statistics only.
[b]Unreported hate crimes.
[c]Hate crimes for both national statistics and criminal prosecution.
[d]Hate crimes for criminal prosecution only.

those in which bias was the sole motivation for the crime (regions 6 and 7). More difficult to decide are the criminal behaviors that are motivated only partly by bias (regions 3 and 4). The same is true for criminal prosecution: it is easier to identify hate crimes for prosecution when bias is the sole motivation for the crime (regions 7 and 8) and not when bias is a secondary or partial motivation (regions 4 and 5).

In addition to hate crime that gets reported to the police (regions 3, 4, 5, 6, 7, and 8), there are many other events that get reported to advocacy groups, including crimes that are not reported to police (regions 11, 12, 13, 14, 15, and 16) and noncriminal acts of discrimination such as a Ku Klux Klan rally or the distribution of hate literature in a minority neighborhood (region 19). Advocacy and local neighborhood groups may also become aware of crimes with bias indicators that are reported to the police but have not or cannot be confirmed as hate crimes (regions 1 and 2).

By approaching the topic in this way, one can see that different definitions of hate crime may apply for different purposes. For example, if police officials decide to improve hate crime reporting for criminal prosecutions and for the purpose of gathering statistics, they might start by focusing on crimes that fit into regions 1 and 2. Perhaps by asking specific questions at the scene of the investigation, officers might be better able to confirm whether these crimes really fit into regions 3, 4, 5, 6, 7, or 8. They might also work with neighborhood groups to encourage victims to come forward to report bias crimes that were originally unreported (regions 11, 12, 13, 14, 15, and 16). In addition, they might want to keep track of noncriminal bias-motivated incidents so that they will be able to do more to prevent hate crime from occurring in the first place (region 19).

THE NATIONAL INCIDENT-BASED REPORTING SYSTEM

When looking for the most comprehensive data on hate crime in the United States, most people go to the FBI for the UCR statistics on hate crime. As mentioned previously, the FBI was tasked with implementing the mandates of the HCSA. The program the agency developed involves the collection of bias crime data from state and local law enforcement agencies. Most law enforcement agencies in the country participate in this national program. Hate crimes are reported to the FBI in two formats: (1) a quarterly incident-based form (submitted as an adjunct to the Summary UCR System) and (2) NIBRS. Most police agencies that participate in the hate crime reporting program submit bias crime data using the quarterly report, which has little or no information about the victim and offender. However, NIBRS captures, within each criminal incident, information on offenses, victims, offenders, property, and persons arrested. The ability to link and analyze this detailed information is a significant improvement to the existing UCR program. NIBRS is rich with information about bias crimes reported to the police. Clearly NIBRS is the preferred method of data collection, and its utilization by state and local law enforcement is growing. Between 1995 and 2006, participation in NIBRS grew at a steady rate. In 1995, only 4 percent of the U.S. population was covered by NIBRS reporting agencies; by 2006, that proportion reached 24 percent (see Table 9.3). In terms of hate crime reporting, most police agencies in the United States participate in the UCR Hate Crime Data Collection Program. Between 1995 and 2006, roughly 85 percent of the U.S. population was covered by law enforcement agencies that participate in the program. The proportion of these agencies using NIBRS to report their hate crime data is growing. In 1995, only 5 percent of the hate crime contributors submitted in NIBRS format. That proportion steadily increased to nearly 40 percent in 2006. While NIBRS data cannot be considered a national sample, they do represent a large number of bias crimes from a large and diverse segment of the country. And the data appear to follow the patterns of the full national UCR hate crime program. As more police agencies update their record management systems, the FBI anticipates that a greater proportion of these hate crimes will be reported through NIBRS. Since NIBRS is only as good as the reports submitted by law enforcement, it is very important to clear up some of the ambiguities in reporting hate crimes.

SUMMARY AND CONCLUSIONS

Hate crime is a new term, not a new phenomenon. Unlike other new crime categories introduced in recent years, it is quite controversial. In this chapter, we explain that some of the difficulty in accepting hate crime as a new category of crime arises from the inherent ambiguity in the term.

Table 9.3   U.S. Population Covered by the National Incident-Based Reporting System (NIBRS) and Hate Crime Participants by Year

Year	U.S. population	U.S. population covered by NIBRS agencies		U.S. population covered by hate crime contributors		Percentage of hate crime contributors reporting via NIBRS
1995	262,755,000	10,630,200	4%	197,066,250	75%	5.40%
1996	265,284,000	15,917,040	6%	233,346,702	84%	7.10%
1997	267,637,000	21,410,960	8%	222,856,059	83%	9.60%
1998	270,296,000	27,029,600	10%	216,235,376	80%	12.50%
1999	272,691,000	35,449,830	13%	232,829,887	85%	15.20%
2000	281,421,906	39,399,067	14%	236,929,512	84%	16.60%
2001	284,796,887	42,719,533	15%	241,799,615	85%	17.70%
2002	288,368,698	49,022,679	17%	247,246,683	86%	19.80%
2003	290,809,777	58,161,955	20%	240,906,049	83%	ND[a]
2004	293,656,842	64,604,505	22%	254,193,439	87%	ND[a]
2005	296,507,061	71,161,695	24%	245,006,413	83%	37.80%
2006	299,398,484	71,855,636	24%	255,086,543	85%	39.50%

[a]Data not available.
Source: Federal Bureau of Investigation, Crime in the United States, and Hate Crime Statistics Act of 2004. Retrieved March 23, 2008, from http://www.icpsr.umich.edu/NACJD/NIBRS/

The term *hate crime* is used for a variety of purposes in many diverse environments. Not only do separate purposes and definitions cause problems, but there are also incentives and disincentives for identifying and reporting hate crime, even for law enforcement officials. There are also forces within police agencies that affect how well officers participate. By reducing the discouraging forces and increasing the encouraging forces, law enforcement officials may do a better job of reporting. We introduced a conceptual framework designed to assist those inside and outside law enforcement to better understand the term *hate crime*. This model may help law enforcement officials identify hate crimes for multiple purposes such as criminal prosecution, data collection, crime prevention, and intelligence gathering.

Finally, although police reports will always undercount the true volume of hate crimes, NIBRS can provide an abundance of information about relationships between and among variables. By encouraging law enforcement to recognize hate crimes, they will be better equipped to identify, respond to, investigate, and report hate crimes. This will ultimately result in better national statistics.

NOTE

1. It is important to note that the sizes of the subsets within the universal set are not portrayed in their actual proportions. For example, we expect that noncriminal acts of discrimination {l} is a much larger set of behaviors than the set of reported crimes {lll}.

REFERENCES

Anti-Defamation League. (2008). *Combating hate.* Retrieved March 19, 2008, from http://www.adl.org/combating_hate/

Associated Press. (2008, February 7). West Virginia: Hate crime indictment in torture case. *New York Times*, p. 20.

Bell, J. (2002). *Policing hatred: Law enforcement, civil rights, and hate crimes.* New York: New York University Press.

Craig, K. M., & Waldo, C. R. (1996). 'So, what's a hate crime anyway?' Young adults' perceptions of hate crimes, victims, and perpetrators. *Law and Human Behavior*, *20*, 113–129.

Cronin, S., McDevitt, J., Farrell, A., & Nolan, J. (2007). Bias crime reporting: Organizational responses to ambiguity, uncertainty, and infrequency in eight police departments. *American Behavioral Scientist, 51*, 213–231.

Dewey, J. (1997). *How we think.* Mineola, NY: Dover. (Original work published 1910)

Dunbar, E., & Molina, A. (2004). Opposition to the legitimacy of hate crime laws: The role of argument, acceptance, knowledge, individual differences, and peer influence. *Analyses of Social Issues and Public Policy, 4* (1), 91–113.

Federal Bureau of Investigation. (2004). *Hate Crime Statistics Act (as amended, 28 USC § 534).* Retrieved March 20, 2008, from http://www.fbi.gov/ucr/hc2004/appen dix_a.htm

Grattet, R., & Jenness, V. (2001). Examining the boundaries of hate crime law: Disabilities and the "dilemma of difference." *Journal of Criminal Law and Criminology, 91*, 653–698.

Haider-Markel, D. P. (2006). Acting as fire alarms with law enforcement? Interest group and bureaucratic activity on hate crime. *American Politics Research, 34* (1), 30–62.

Herek, G. M., Gillis, J. R., Cogan, J. C., & Glunt, E. K. (1997). Hate crime victimization among lesbian, gay, and bisexual adults: Prevalence, psychological correlates, and methodological issues. *Journal of Interpersonal Violence, 12*, 195–215.

Jacobs, J. B., & Henry, J. S. (1996). The social construction of a hate crime epidemic. *Journal of Criminal Law and Criminology, 86*, 366–391.

Jenness, V., & Grattet, R. (2005). The law-in-between: The effects of organizational perviousness on policing hate crime. *Social Problems, 52*, 337–359.

Levin, B. (1999). Hate crimes: Worse by definition. *Journal of Contemporary Criminal Justice, 15*(1), 6–21.

Levin, B. (2002). Cyberhate: A legal and historical analysis of extremists' use of computer networks. *American Behavioral Scientist, 45,* 958–986.

Livingston, I. (2008, February 28). 800G rip-off of 93 year old is hate crime. *New York Post,* p. 2.

Los Angeles County Commission on Human Relations. (2006). *2006 hate crime report.* Retrieved March 20, 2008, from http://humanrelations.co.la.ca.us/publications/docs/2006HCR_Corrected06072007.pdf

Maddaus, G., & Woodhouse, A. (2008, March 6). Hate crime charge urged in shooting. *Press Telegram (Long Beach, CA).* Retrieved March 20, 2008, from http://www.highbeam.com/Press-Telegram+Long+Beach,+CA~R~/publications.aspx

McDevitt, J., Balboni, J. M., & Bennett, S. (2000). *Improving the quality and accuracy of hate crime reporting* [Final report]. Washington, DC: Bureau of Justice Statistics.

McDevitt, J., Balboni, J., Garcia, L., & Gu, J. (2001). Consequences for victims: A comparison of bias- and non-bias motivated assaults. *American Behavioral Scientist, 45,* 697–713.

Nolan, J. J., & Akiyama, Y. (2002). Assessing the climate for hate-crime reporting in law enforcement organizations: A force-field analysis. *Justice Professional, 15*(2), 87–103.

Nolan, J. J., McDevitt, J., Cronin, S., & Farrell, A. (2004). Learning to see hate crime: A framework for understanding and clarifying ambiguities in bias crime classification. *Criminal Justice Studies, 17*(1), 91–105.

Orange County Human Relations Commission. (2008). *2007 hate crimes and incidents in Orange County.* Retrieved April 20, 2008, from http://www.ochumanrelations.org/pdf/2007_Hate_Crime_Report.pdf

Shively, M., Cronin, S., & McDevitt, J. (2001). *Understanding the characteristics of bias crime in Massachusetts high schools.* Boston: Center for Criminal Justice Policy Research.

Southern Poverty Law Center. (2007). *Intelligence project.* Retrieved March 24, 2008, from http://www.splcenter.org/intel/

Sullaway, M. (2004). Psychological perspectives on hate crime laws. *Psychology, Public Policy, and Law, 10,* 250–292.

United Methodist Church. (2008). *Hate crime data collection project.* Retrieved March 23, 2008, from http://gbgm-umc.org/programs/antihate/trackingproject.stm

CHAPTER 10

HATE CRIME LAWS: A CRITICAL ASSESSMENT

Jessica S. Henry

Over two decades ago, the first hate crime laws were enacted. In response to calls by advocacy groups and civil rights leaders, politicians in the mid-1980s declared that crimes motivated by certain designated prejudices deserved a separate label and more severe punishment. With the passage of federal and state legislation across the country, criminal conduct that once fell within the parameters of "ordinary" crime was transformed into "hate crime." And with that designation came an ongoing debate among politicians, the media, advocacy groups, and scholars over the necessity and efficacy of a distinct category of crime for offenses motivated by bigotry.

Although the concept of hate crime itself may seem intuitive, hate crimes do not lend themselves to simple definitions. Notwithstanding the title of "hate crime," for instance, a hate crime does not require the presence of actual hate. A man who hates his adulterous wife and her lover will not be charged with a hate crime if he subsequently murders them both in a jealous rage. Conversely, a bored teenager who defaces a Jewish cemetery as a foolish prank may not have any real hatred for Jews, yet hate crime charges would certainly be sustainable.

If hate crime, sometimes referred to as bias crime, does not require the element of hate, then what differentiates a hate crime from other criminal acts? Generally speaking, a hate crime is a crime that is motivated, in whole or in part, by bias or prejudice based on a victim's actual or perceived group affiliation. Under the majority of hate crime statutes, the causation requirement for hate crime is satisfied when it can be established that a victim was selected *because of* his or her membership in a designated group. Under this construct, hate crime laws apply equally to offenses perpetrated against groups historically targeted for bigotry, such as African Americans, and to offenses committed against groups with no history of discrimination, such as whites (Grattet & Jenness, 2001).

Nearly every state and the federal government have adopted some form of hate crime law. Here the various forms of hate crime laws that have been promulgated are analyzed, and questions as to their effectiveness and enforceability are raised. Also, the chapter examines the jurisprudential basis for hate crimes laws and the constitutional implications for freedom of speech and expression. It concludes by considering the continued functionality, viability, and societal implications of hate crime laws.

STATE AND FEDERAL LEGISLATIVE APPROACHES TO HATE CRIME

There are numerous forms of hate crime legislation. First, penalty enhancement statutes increase the penalties for existing criminal offenses that were motivated by bias or prejudice. Second, hate crime statutes create a separate substantive criminal offense for crimes motivated by designated biases or bigotry or for acts of vandalism targeted against designated properties. Third, civil rights laws provide penalties for offenses that interfere with the civil or constitutional rights of members within specifically designated groups. Finally, data collection statutes authorize the collection and reporting of hate crime to state and federal enforcement agencies.

Because of current limits on federal criminal jurisdiction, the prosecution of hate crimes rests primarily with the state. The following section examines various state legislative responses to hate crime, the bias motivations that are included in state statutes, and the variations between states in their approaches to hate. The section also examines the federal government's primary approaches to hate crime, including civil rights legislation, which can be used to target bias offenses; hate crime penalty enhancement statutes; and data collection efforts.

STATE HATE CRIME LAWS

Penalty Enhancement Statutes

Many states have adopted penalty enhancement laws to increase penal sanctions for crimes motivated by statutorily enumerated prejudices. Penalty enhancement statutes do not create a separate criminal offense; rather, a defendant who commits a criminal offense, such as assault, may receive an increased sentence if the crime was motivated by bias. Vermont's hate crime law is one example of a sentencing enhancement statute. Under Vermont's "hate-motivated crime" statute,

A person who commits, causes to be committed or attempts to commit any crime and whose conduct is maliciously motivated by the victim's actual or perceived race, color, religion, national origin, sex, ancestry, age, service in the armed forces of the United States, handicap . . . , sexual orientation or gender identity shall be subject to the following penalties:

1. If the maximum penalty for the underlying crime is one year or less, the penalty for a violation of this section shall be imprisonment for not more than two years or a fine of not more than $2,000.00, or both.

2. If the maximum penalty for the underlying crime is more than one year but less than five years, the penalty for a violation of this section shall be imprisonment for not more than five years or a fine of not more than $10,000.00, or both.

3. If the maximum penalty for the underlying crime is five years or more, the penalty for the underlying crime shall apply; however, the court shall consider the motivation of the defendant as a factor in sentencing. (Vt. Stat. Ann. tit. 13, § 1455).

Under Vermont's sentencing scheme, a defendant who has committed an offense punishable by a maximum of one year imprisonment could receive double that sentence (from one year to two years) if the crime was motivated by hate. In contrast, a defendant who has committed an offense punishable by five years or more (presumably, the most serious criminal offenses) may receive no hate-based enhancement at all. In those cases, the court must consider motive in setting the appropriate sentence but is not required to enhance the punishment.

The recent U.S. Supreme Court decision in *Apprendi v. New Jersey* (2000) has made implementation of penalty enhancement statutes more difficult. In *Apprendi*, the defendant fired shots into the home of an African American family that had recently moved into his neighborhood. He fully confessed that he shot at them because they were black and because he did not want them to live in the neighborhood. Pursuant to a plea agreement, the defendant pled guilty to weapons possession charges, for which he faced a 5- to 10-year sentence. The prosecution retained its right under the plea agreement to seek an enhanced penalty for the offense. The trial court conducted a hearing and determined by a preponderance of the evidence that the defendant's conduct was motivated by racial bias. The defendant was sentenced to 12 years in prison—2 years more than the statutory maximum otherwise available under the plea agreement.

In reversing Apprendi's sentence, the U.S. Supreme Court ruled that judges cannot enhance criminal sentences beyond the statutory maximum based on facts that were not decided by a jury beyond a reasonable doubt (Apprendi v. New Jersey, 2000). Under *Apprendi*, unless a defendant admits bias motivation, the prosecution must prove motive beyond a reasonable doubt to the trier of fact before a biased motive can be used to enhance a sentence.

Other state hate crime laws do not simply authorize a penalty enhancement; rather, these states create a separate category of offense for hate crimes. Many of these substantive bias offenses are based on influential model legislation by the Anti-Defamation League (ADL). The ADL model legislation provides for two main substantive offenses: bias-motivated crimes and institutional vandalism.

Bias-Motivated Crime

Under the ADL model legislation, a person commits a bias-motivated crime

if, by reason of the actual or perceived race, color, religion, national origin, sexual orientation or gender of another individual or group of individuals, he violates Section _____ of the Penal code (insert code provisions for criminal trespass, criminal mischief, harassment, menacing, intimidation, assault, battery and or other appropriate statutorily proscribed criminal conduct). (Anti-Defamation League [ADL], 2001)

Thus, if a person commits an "ordinary" crime, but does so because of an enumerated prejudice, then an additional substantive crime has been committed. In that instance, the ADL recommends that criminal liability for the bias-motivated crime be "at least one degree more serious than that imposed for commission of the underlying offense."

In 2000, the state of New York enacted a comprehensive hate crime statute. It looked to the ADL model statute as its starting point but went even further in defining a distinct substantive crime as a hate crime (Donnino, 2007). Under the New York hate crime law,

A person commits a hate crime when he or she commits a specified offense and either:

    a.   intentionally selects the person against whom the offense is committed or intended to be committed in whole or in substantial part because of a belief or perception regarding the race, color, national origin, ancestry, gender, religion, religious practice, age, disability or sexual orientation of a person, regardless of whether the belief or perception is correct, or

    b.   intentionally commits the act or acts constituting the offense in whole or in substantial part because of a belief or perception regarding the race, color, national origin, ancestry, gender, religion, religious practice, age, disability or sexual orientation of a person, regardless of whether the belief or perception is correct. (N.Y. Penal Law § 485.05)

The specified offenses include varying degrees of assault, menacing, reckless endangerment, manslaughter, murder, stalking, sex offenses, larceny, trespass, and harassment. The net result of New York's hate crime statute is that a defendant who commits virtually *any* substantive criminal offense when motivated by bigotry also may be prosecuted for the separate offense of hate crime.

In addition, New York created mandatory minimum sentences for hate crime offenses. A non-hate-based class B violent felony offense, such as assault in the first degree, is punishable by a determinate sentence of at least five years (N.Y. Penal Law § 70.02). In contrast, a defendant convicted of a hate crime stemming from an assault in the first degree is punishable by a mandatory minimum sentence of eight years' imprisonment (N.Y. Penal Law § 485.10). This is *three* years more than the minimum sentence that would otherwise be available. The hate crime statute carries with it a maximum sentence of 25 years imprisonment.

Institutional Vandalism

Another substantive offense proposed by the ADL is institutional vandalism. Institutional vandalism occurs when a person

knowingly vandaliz[es], defac[es] or otherwise damage[es]:

i.   Any church, synagogue or other building, structure or place used for religious worship or other religious purpose;
ii.   Any cemetery, mortuary or other facility used for the purpose of burial or memorializing the dead;
iii. Any school, educational facility or community center;
iv.   The grounds adjacent to, and owned or rented by, any institution, facility, building, structure or place described in subsections (i), (ii) or (iii) above; or
v.   Any personal property contained in any institution, facility, building, structure, or place described in subsections (i), (ii) or (iii) above. (ADL, 2001)

No bias intent is required; rather, the simple act of defacing a church falls within the statute irrespective of whether the offender was motivated by prejudice. The model statute authorizes penalties based on the cost of the damage caused, including the cost to repair that damage. Institutional vandalism statutes have been adopted by 42 states and the District of Columbia (ADL, 2007).

Whether and when institutional vandalism is charged can significantly impact the size and scope of hate crime. For instance, when a disgruntled student defaces a school with the words "school stinks," it may constitute institutional vandalism under subsection (iii) of the model legislation. But should it count as a hate crime for data collection purposes? If yes, then hate crime data statistics would be vastly inflated. If not, how will states parse out incidents of institutional vandalism motivated by bias from those that are not?

Nearly every state has adopted some form of hate crime law such as those discussed previously. But which groups are included under each hate crime law varies considerably between states and has been the source of divisiveness and debate.

A PATCHWORK APPROACH TO GROUP PROTECTION: WHO SHOULD BE PROTECTED?

Hate crime laws punish offenders who are motivated by statutorily enumerated prejudices. The scope of prejudicial motivations is wide ranging in some states and extremely narrow in others. Indeed, there is no consistency between states, and between states and the federal government, as to which prejudices transform garden-variety offenses into those of hate crime. The result is a patchwork of legislation that does not accurately capture the scope of hate crime incidents.

Wyoming, for instance, has no hate crime laws. In 1998, Matthew Shepard, a gay student at the University of Wyoming, was brutally beaten, tied to a fence, and left to die. Shepard had been targeted for this offense because of his sexual orientation. The two men who committed this crime were charged with capital murder and, ultimately, were sentenced to life imprisonment. The outcry over Shepard's murder came from all corners of the globe, and calls for the passage of a hate crime law resonated throughout the state. Yet the Wyoming legislature defeated a hate crime bill that was proposed in 1999, and no law has ever been passed. This does not mean, however, that victims in Wyoming have never been targeted because of an offender's bigotry. It simply means that such crimes are not recognized as a separate offense under the law.

While no state besides Wyoming abstains entirely from hate crime laws, many severely limit their applicability and scope. Although 45 states and the District of Columbia criminalize bias-motivated violence and intimidation, Arkansas, Georgia, Indiana, South Carolina, and, as stated previously, Wyoming, do not. The hate crime statutes in Arkansas, Georgia, and South Carolina are limited only to the crime of institutional vandalism and do not provide sentence enhancement for crimes motivated by hate against members of specifically enumerated groups (ADL, 2007). Thus a racially motivated attack in Arkansas would not legally constitute a hate crime, although it might be prosecuted as a generic assault.

As noted previously, the vast majority of states with hate crime laws include victims who were targeted because of their race, ethnicity, or religion (ADL, 2007). Other states include gender, disability, and sexual orientation. The latter category, however, has proven to be a lightning rod for criticism and debate.

Sexual Orientation

Only 32 states designate sexual orientation as a prohibited motivation in their hate crime statutes (ADL, 2007). North Carolina, for instance, provides enhanced penalties for crimes based on race, religion, ethnicity, and gender, but not sexual orientation. In West Virginia, the same is true, even though their statute protects crimes motivated by political affiliation—a status recognized in only five other state hate crime statutes. Montana also limits the scope of its protection to crimes based on "race, religion or ethnicity" (ADL, 2007). Thus in Montana, North Carolina, West Virginia, and the other states that do not include sexual orientation in their hate crime statutes, a defendant convicted of a crime motivated by racial animus would be treated more harshly than a defendant convicted of the same underlying crime but who was motivated by bias against gays and lesbians. Indeed, the well-publicized antigay murder of Billy Jack Gaither in 1999 was not counted by Alabama as a hate crime because its state hate crime statute does not include sexual orientation.

Georgia is currently deadlocked over whether to implement a hate crime statute. Georgia passed a hate crime law in 2000. Four years later, in 2004, the Georgia Supreme Court struck down the hate crime statute as unconstitutionally void for vagueness. Current efforts to revive the law are mired over whether to include sexual orientation in the statute. Even though 25 percent of all reported hate crimes in 2006 in Georgia were based on sexual orientation, the inclusion of sexual orientation provoked protest from powerful advocacy groups and will likely prevent the bill from passage (Galloway, 2007).

The Homeless

While the debate over the inclusion of sexual orientation continues in some states, other states have extended the scope of their hate crime protections to include the homeless. For instance, the Maryland Senate recently passed a bill that extends hate crime protection to the homeless (Associated Press, 2008b). Maryland would not be the first state to add homeless status to its hate crime laws. In 2006, Maine included the status of homeless in its hate crime laws. Since then, five additional states, including California, Florida, Massachusetts, Nevada, and Texas, have considered legislation that would include homeless status as a protected category within their state hate crime statutes (National Coalition for the Homeless, 2007).

Critics of the new proposal argue that attacks against the homeless are already covered by existing criminal law and that it is therefore unnecessary to add additional criminal penalties. They further suggest that motivation for crimes against the homeless is not based on animus against homeless people *per se*, but rather reflects the reality that offenders have increased access to the homeless because they live outdoors and, as a result, are more vulnerable targets. Finally, some critics have questioned whether expanding hate crime statutes to include groups such as the homeless dilutes the intended anti-bigotry message of original hate crime laws.

State Data Collection Statutes

Only 27 states and the District of Columbia authorize hate crime data collection. Of the states that have data collection statutes, 16 collect data about crimes motivated by sexual orientation and 9 collect data about crimes motivated by gender (ADL, 2007). These data collection statutes provide the basis of hate crime reporting to the federal government.

In 2006, there were 7,722 reported hate crimes. Of these, according to the Federal Bureau of Investigation (FBI, 2007), "51.8% were motivated by a racial bias, 18.9% were motivated by a religious bias, 15.5% were triggered by a sexual-orientation bias, and 12.7% of the incidents were motivated by an ethnicity/national origin bias. One percent involved bias against a disability" (FBI, 2007). These data represent an 8 percent increase in reported hate crime from 2005.

Hate crime statistics are inherently flawed because the reporting of hate crime data to the FBI by states is entirely voluntary. As a result, numerous police jurisdictions opt not to participate. Indeed, in 2006, almost 5,000 police departments around the country did not participate in the federal reporting program. And of the 12,620 law enforcement agencies in the United States that did participate, only 16.7 percent of participating agencies reported even a single hate crime (ADL, 2007).

In 2006, only four law enforcement agencies in Georgia participated in data collection, recording a total of 16 offenses for the entire year. Alabama reported only one hate crime. Mississippi reported none. California, in con-trast, reported 1,297 (FBI, 2007). Should we infer from these numbers that California is the nation's hate crime capital, while Alabama and Mississippi are among the nation's most tolerant states? Or do the data simply reflect ambivalence or complete disregard by some states for hate crime data collec-tion and reporting?

Furthermore, even when data are collected, they are marred by errors in police reporting. In 2001, the Southern Poverty Law Center (SPLC) is-sued an *Intelligence Report* that documented the frequency of "false zeroes" in hate crime data collection. According to the SPLC, police agencies reported "zero" hate incidents, when, in fact, they had elected not to file reports at all. The result is that agencies that should have been placed in the nonreporting column for hate crime data collection purposes were (and continue to be) in-accurately counted as having no hate crimes in their jurisdictions (Southern Poverty Law Center, 2001).

A further issue undermining federal hate crime data collection efforts is the lack of state training of local law enforcement officials. Only 12 states provide for officer training in the area of hate crimes. Thus many officers do not understand how and whether to classify crimes as bias incidents. Even where training is provided, some officers are reluctant to classify an incident as one of hate because they do not wish to engage in cumbersome paperwork. In addition, officers often elect to look the other way for minor incidents, such as graffiti, rather than pursue more serious hate crime charges, which carry with them greater sanctions.

There also appears to be a great deal of underreporting of hate crime to the police by victims. Individuals may not report a crime to the police for a variety of reasons. Many victims of hate crimes come from populations or communities that traditionally have negative relationships with the police. This may create a fear or reluctance to report hate crime to the police. Victims may experience linguistic or cultural impediments to reporting, fear reprisal or secondary victimization by the police, or simply lack adequate information about hate crime laws.

There are complex reasons for the deficiencies in hate crime data, including narrowly drawn or nonexistent hate crime statutes, poor enforcement, and limited data collection. The result is official FBI reports that lag behind the actual scope of crimes motivated by bigotry.

FEDERAL HATE CRIME LAWS

The federal government has passed its own laws to combat hate-based crimes. These include civil rights laws, penalty enhancement statutes, and data collection statutes.

Federal Civil Rights Legislation

After the Civil War, violence against blacks by whites continued with little enforcement by Southern authorities. Indeed, Southern law enforcement officials and politicians were often involved—either directly or complicitly—in acts of race-based violence. Congress stepped into this enforcement void and passed the first Civil Rights Acts (CRA) in 1871. These CRA enabled the federal government to prosecute individuals who, either working in concert with others (18 U.S.C. § 241) or as an employee of the government (18 U.S.C. § 242), had deprived others of their civil rights. Congress also enabled individuals to sue a state or local government employee in federal court when that employee interfered with a civil or constitutional right.

In 1968, Congress enacted 18 U.S.C. § 245, which authorized the federal prosecution of a person who "by force or threat of force willfully injures, intimidates or interferes with . . . any person because of his race, color, religion or national origin and because he is or has been" engaged in specific federally protected activities such as attending school, voting, or serving on a jury. Criminal sanctions under this law can be quite severe, including capital punishment, depending on the circumstances of the underlying offense.

Yet the CRA are limited as a hate crime enforcement tool because of limits on federal jurisdiction. Much of Congress's ability to regulate criminal conduct derives from acts that impact interstate commerce. In 2000, however, the U.S. Supreme Court significantly scaled back Congress's ability to rely on the interstate commerce clause in making and enforcing criminal and civil rights laws. In *United States v. Morrison* (2000), the Supreme Court struck down a section of the Violence against Women Act, which would have permitted rape victims to sue for civil damages in federal court. The Supreme Court in *Morrison* reasoned that Congress has exceeded its authority under the commerce clause in passing that law. Whether Congress continues to have broad authority to regulate hate crime remains an unanswered question (Hasenstab, 2001).

Moreover, the scope of federal protection under the CRA is limited. Indeed, the CRA provide protection only for victims who were selected based on "race, color, religion or national origin" (18 U.S.C. § 245). Notably absent from the CRA are protections for crimes motivated by sexual orientation. Since 1999, Congress has attempted to pass legislation to address this deficiency. There has been staunch opposition by religious fundamentalists and conservative politicians to the inclusion of sexual orientation in a federal hate crime bill.

Nowhere was this more apparent than in Congress's latest attempt in 2007 to extend federal protections to hate crimes motivated by gender, sexual orientation, gender identity, or disability through the passage of the Local Law Enforcement Hate Crimes Prevention Act of 2007, popularly known as the Matthew Shepard Act. In addition to expanding the categories of qualified motivations for federal hate crimes, the Matthew Shepard Act would have eliminated the requirement that the victim be engaged in a federally protected activity at the time of the offense such as voting or attending school. It also would have expanded the authority of the federal government to investigate hate crimes.

James Dobson, founder and chairman of the politically powerful religious-based organization Focus on the Family, called on legislators to vote against the Matthew Shepard Act because its intent "is to muzzle people of faith who dare to express their moral and biblical concerns about homosexuality" (Stout, 2007, p. A19). And indeed, President Bush threatened from the outset to veto the proposed hate crime legislation (Costello, 2007).

Notwithstanding these threats, passage of the Matthew Shepard Act appeared closer than ever before. The bill handily passed in the House of Representatives. In an effort to avoid a presidential veto, the U.S. Senate added the Matthew Shepard Act as an amendment to the Department of Defense

Authorization for 2008 (the DOD bill). Legislators assumed, given the ongoing Iraq War and the need to fund U.S. troops, that the DOD bill would pass and, along with it, the Matthew Shepard Act. President George W. Bush, however, threatened to veto the entire DOD bill, with its accompanying hate crime amendment. Ultimately, Congress did not have adequate votes for its passage, and the Matthew Shepard Act was removed from the DOD bill, signaling its legislative demise for at least another year ("Caving In," 2007).

Federal Sentencing Enhancement Statutes

As part of the 1994 crime bill, Congress enacted the Hate Crime Sentencing Enhancement Act of 1994, which required the U.S. Sentencing Commission to increase the penalties for crimes in which the victim was selected "because of the actual or perceived race, color, religion, national origin, ethnicity, gender, disability, or sexual orientation of any person." In 1995, as mandated by Congress, the U.S. Sentencing Commission implemented a three-level sentencing guideline increase for hate crimes (U.S. Sentencing Guidelines § 3A1.1[a]). These enhancements are limited only to crimes that fall within the federal government's jurisdiction. Interestingly, and notwithstanding the absence of federal protection for sexual orientation in its civil rights laws, Congress included sexual orientation within the ambit of its mandatory sentencing guidelines.

Application of the sentencing guideline is dependent on a number of factors, including a defendant's criminal history and the underlying offense. Assume an individual commits an aggravated assault on another person in a national park, resulting in serious bodily injury. Because the aggravated assault took place on federal property, the federal government would have jurisdiction over the incident, and federal law would apply. Assume further that the individual who engaged in the aggravated assault had no criminal history. That individual would typically face, under the sentencing guidelines, a 30- to 37-month federal prison term. Application of the hate crime sentence enhancement would increase the penalty to 41 to 51 months.

The U.S. Supreme Court has declared that all federal sentencing guidelines are advisory and no longer mandatory (United States v. Booker, 2005). It remains to be seen whether federal courts, no longer bound by stringent sentencing guidelines, will elect to apply the hate crime sentencing enhancement at all.

Federal Data Collection Statutes

A final federal law devoted to hate crime is the Hate Crimes Statistics Act of 1990 (HCSA). In its current form, HCSA calls for data collection of crimes "that manifest evidence of prejudice based on race, religion, disability, sexual orientation, or ethnicity, including where appropriate the crimes of murder, non-negligent manslaughter; forcible rape; aggravated assault, simple assault, intimidation; arson; and destruction, damage or vandalism of property" (HCSA, 1990). The FBI annually publishes the data provided to it under the HCSA. But because the HCSA is voluntary and has never enjoyed adequate fiscal or full state support and cooperation, the resulting data are inherently unreliable. Indeed, given the limitations of the data provided to the FBI, it is virtually impossible to extrapolate *any* conclusions about the state of hate crime in the United States.

INCREASED SENTENCES: ENTRENCHING BIGOTRY?

Regardless of their form, many state and federal hate crime laws discussed in this chapter result in increased prison sentences for hate offenders. The purpose of this, as explained by the New York state legislature, is to "provide clear recognition of the gravity of hate crimes and the compelling importance of preventing their recurrence" (N.Y. Penal Law § 485). In other words, one intended function of hate crime is to deter offenders from committing bigoted crime in the future.

Ironically, increased prison terms for hate crime offenders may have unintended consequences. Prisons are breeding grounds for recruitment by and membership in extremist hate groups (ADL, 2002). Consider the horrific murder of James Byrd Jr. On June 7, 1998, James Byrd, an African American, was walking home from a party in the small town of Jasper, Texas, when he was offered a ride from John King, Russell Brewer, and a third man who also lived in town. The three white men beat Byrd, sprayed his face with black paint, chained him to the back of their pickup truck, and dragged him down a dirt road to his death. Byrd was decapitated; his mangled body parts were found strewn along the road. King and Brewer had met in prison, where they joined a white supremacist prison gang and developed the racist ideologies that would ultimately contribute to Byrd's death (Temple-Raston, 2002).

Exposure to extremist ideology is certainly one potential outcome from increased prison sentences. This is particularly troubling since the vast majority of hate offenders are "thrill seekers," who participate in hate offenses because they are "looking for some fun" and not because they are particularly biased (Levin & McDevitt, 1993; McDevitt, Levin, & Bennett, 2002). Given exposure and recruitment opportunities, hate offenders could likely leave prison far more committed to bigotry than when they first arrived. In addition, in some cases, the mere label of "hate offender" could provide increased status to new prison inmates among entrenched members of extremist groups (Henry, 2007). This would certainly undercut any rehabilitative function of punishment in the bias crime context.

As detailed previously, state and federal hate crime laws vary in their scope, application, and enforcement. These laws also raise significant challenges in both the legal and policy arenas. These challenges will be considered in the next section.

THE CONSTITUTIONAL AND POLICY QUAGMIRE OF HATE CRIMES

Most crimes consist of two main elements: the overt criminal act (*actus reas*) and the criminal intent (*mens rea*). Motive is generally not an element of a criminal offense. Yet intent and motive are often and erroneously confused. While intent refers to a person's conscious objective to engage in a particular action or cause a particular outcome, motive refers to the reason why a person commits an offense.

Most non-hate-based crimes do not include motive as an element of the offense. Consider, for instance, a husband who murders his wife. It is legally irrelevant whether he murdered her because he despised her and wanted to leave her for another woman or because she was terminally ill and begged him to end her suffering. If the prosecution can prove beyond a reasonable doubt that he intended to kill her (the *mens rea*) and did so (the *actus reas*), the crime of murder has been committed, regardless of the motivation for the offense.

Hate crimes are unusual in that motive is a central element of the offense. Indeed, the distinguishing factor between a hate crime and any other crime is whether the offender was motivated by bias or prejudice. Yet motive can prove to be a highly murky concept. Consider a fight that begins over a sought-after parking spot. The two drivers, one white and one black, leap from their cars. The white man punches the black man in the nose, screaming, "That was my parking spot," followed by a racial epithet. If the white man uses a racial epithet during the fight, is what might otherwise be an ordinary assault transformed into a hate crime? If the white man uses a curse word, but not one that is racially charged, would it still be a hate crime? If the white man said nothing at all but had racist thoughts during the fight, would that be a hate crime? Was the fight actually motivated by racial bias, or tension over a lost parking spot? Was the use of racial slurs indicative of overt prejudice in the context of that assault, or was it simply indicative that the white man carried prejudices with him that were revealed only in the heat of battle?

Consider further the case of Megan Williams. In early September 2007, Megan Williams, a 20-year-old African American woman from Big Creek, West Virginia, was kidnapped. For over a week, Ms. Williams was sexually assaulted, beaten, and tortured by six white men at a remote hillside location. Throughout her captivity, Ms. Williams was choked with a cable cord, sexually assaulted, forced to drink from a toilet bowl, and scalded with hot water. An assailant called Ms. Williams by a racial epithet as he stabbed her in the ankle. The perpetrator even told Ms. Williams that she had been victimized because she was black. Ms. Williams's ordeal and the arrest of her captors captured national and international news.

Although one of the perpetrators explicitly told Ms. Williams that she was victimized because of her race and used racial slurs throughout her ordeal, state prosecutors initially refused to bring hate crime charges in the case (Mohajer, 2007). The federal government also declined to press civil rights charges (Harki, 2007). Prosecutors apparently did not pursue hate crime charges because there were mixed motives in the attack, and hate crime charges may have been too difficult to prove. Ms. Williams had a prior social relationship with one of the perpetrators, Bobby Brewster (Mohajer, 2007). Indeed, Ms. Williams had been to Brewster's house before the incident and, several months earlier, had filed charges against him for domestic battery and assault. After months of international, national, and local pressure, hate crime charges were finally filed in February 2008 against the one perpetrator who used a racial epithet against Ms. Williams as he stabbed her in the ankle. No additional hate crime charges were filed against any other participant in the crime (Associated Press, 2008b).

The Williams case demonstrates the complexities of motive. If Ms. Williams was targeted, at least in part, because of her prior relationship with Brewster, should prosecutors nonetheless have brought hate crime charges against all the defendants given the explicitly racist comments made throughout the offense? Or where there are multiple motives, should hate crime charges be avoided due to evidentiary issues?

Constitutional Objections to Hate Crime Laws

There are also complex constitutional questions that arise in establishing motive. In the context of hate crimes, the prosecution must often resort to the words of the offender to establish motive. In the Williams case, for instance, the word *nigger* could be deemed evidence of racial motivation in the commission of the offense. The First Amendment, however, guarantees the freedoms of speech and expression, even speech that society may find abhorrent or offensive. As Justice Holmes eloquently opined many years ago, the Constitution guarantees the "principle of free thought—not free thought for those who agree with us but freedom for the thought we hate" (United States v. Schwimmer, 1929). It is equally true, however, that the First Amendment does not protect all speech such as words that incite violence or words that are obscene.

Critics argue that hate crime unconstitutionally punish hate thoughts and speech (Jacobs & Potter, 1998). For example, if one man punches a gay man because the latter was a New York Mets fan instead of a New York Yankees fan, no hate crime would have been committed. If that same man punches a gay man because of his sexual orientation, a hate crime would have been committed. The sole difference between the two assaults was not the conduct, given that both involved a single punch by one man to another. The difference stems from the thought that was in the perpetrator's head as he threw the punch. And if it is the thought that results in additional hate crime sanctions, then doesn't that amount to "thought" punishment, in violation of First Amendment protection?

To further highlight this result, imagine that the man in the first example screamed "down with the Mets" as he engaged in the assault, while the man in the second example screamed "down with gays." The first assault would surely not result in hate crime charges, while the second assault surely would. The distinguishing factor between the two is the content of the speech. But does that not infringe on the First Amendment?

Supporters of hate crime laws argue that hate crime laws are not impermissible content-based restrictions of thought or speech, but rather, are regulations of unlawful conduct. The U.S. Supreme Court appears to have accepted that argument, at least in the context of hate crime penalty enhancement statutes. In 1993, in *Wisconsin v. Mitchell*, the Supreme Court unanimously upheld the constitutionality of penalty enhancement hate crime laws. In *Mitchell*, a group of African American teenagers were discussing a scene in the film *Mississippi Burning*, in which a white adult male assaulted a black child. Nineteen-year-old Todd Mitchell exhorted his friends, "Do you all feel hyped up to move on some white people?" When a 14-year-old white boy walked by the group shortly after, Mitchell shouted, "You want to fuck somebody up? There goes a white boy; go get him." Mitchell and his friends beat the white boy into a coma, from which he emerged four days later (Wisconsin v. Mitchell, 1993).

Mitchell was subsequently convicted of aggravated battery, which carried a maximum two-year prison term. The jury, however, found that Mitchell's crime was motivated by racial animus under Wisconsin's penalty enhancement statute. Wisconsin's enhancement statute provided for an increased sentence when a person

> intentionally selects the person against whom the crime . . . is committed or selects the property which is damaged or otherwise affected . . . because of race, religion, color, disability, sexual orientation, national origin or ancestry of that person or the owner and occupant of that property. (Wisconsin v. Mitchell, 1993)

Under this statute, Mitchell was sentenced to four years in prison, twice the minimum permitted by law.

On appeal, the Wisconsin State Supreme Court struck down the statute. That court expressed skepticism at the distinction between conduct and speech:

> The hate crime statute enhances the punishment of bigoted criminals because they are bigoted. The statute is directed solely at the subjective motivation of the actor—his or her prejudice. Punishment of one's thought, however repugnant the thought, is unconstitutional. (State v. Mitchell, 1992)

Finding that the underlying assaultive conduct was already criminal under Wisconsin law, the Wisconsin court concluded that the statute impermissibly targeted "offensive motive or thought" in violation of the Constitution (State v. Mitchell, 1992).

The U.S. Supreme Court disagreed. In a unanimous decision written by then chief justice Rehnquist, the U.S. Supreme Court reversed the Wisconsin State Supreme Court and declared the Wisconsin statute to be constitutional. According to the *Mitchell* court, the statute punished criminal *conduct* and not constitutionally protected viewpoints. Thus the statute did not run afoul of First Amendment protections (Wisconsin v. Mitchell, 1993).

The U.S. Supreme Court has also upheld legislation targeting offensive conduct in the context of cross burnings. In 2003, a defendant in Virginia was convicted of cross burning under a statute that allowed the jury to infer intent to intimidate from the act itself of burning a cross. The defendant appealed, arguing that the statute abridged his First Amendment rights. The Supreme Court confirmed that cross burning is a symbolically protected form of speech under the First Amendment. It went on to hold, however, that cross burning with the intent to threaten or intimidate is not. Although the Court held the Virginia statute as written to be unconstitutional, the Court made clear that anti-cross-burning statutes could be constitutional if properly drafted to prohibit intimidation (Virginia v. Black, 2003).

The decision in *Black* marked a significant retreat from a nearly identical cross burning case the Court had decided in 1992. In *R.A.V. v. St. Paul*, a white juvenile and several other defendants set fire to a cross on the lawn of a black family. The U.S. Supreme Court was unanimous in invalidating a Minnesota city's ordinance making it a crime to burn a cross with the knowledge that the act would "arouse anger, alarm or resentment in others on the basis of race, color, creed, religion or gender." Although unanimous in outcome, the justices relied on different reasons for striking down the statute. The majority opinion in *R.A.V.*, written by Justice Anton Scalia, held that the St. Paul ordinance criminalized offensive viewpoints:

> [The statute in St. Paul] proscribed fighting words of whatever manner that communicate messages of racial, gender or religious intolerance.

Selectivity of this sort created the possibility that the city is seeking to handicap the expression of particular ideas. (R.A.V. v. St. Paul, 1992)

The *R.A.V.* majority emphasized that while the government can regulate fighting words, it cannot regulate only those fighting words that express a disfavored or unpopular viewpoint. The Minnesota ordinance was fatally flawed because it represented content-based discrimination.

The Supreme Court appears to have reached a compromise on the issue of cross burning and the First Amendment. Under *Black*, cross burning is protected only when it is intended to be expressive speech. A cross burning at a Ku Klux Klan rally may fall within the First Amendment given its historical and symbolic significance. Conversely, the burning that occurred in *R.A.V.*—a cross burned on the private property of a black family—is arguably not protected expression where the prosecution can establish that the burning was intended to intimidate or harass the recipient.

CONCLUSION

It has been over two decades since the first hate crime laws were passed. The results have been somewhat haphazard. States vary greatly in the scope of protections provided and in their commitment to enforce their own laws. Some states, like California and New Jersey, should be recognized for their attention to hate crime enforcement. States like Wyoming continue to dismiss hate crime laws out of hand, while still other states define hate crime narrowly or take a lackadaisical approach to their enforcement. Hate crime data collection efforts range from effective and comprehensive, on one hand, to inaccurate, incomplete, or nonexistent, on the other. And even where data collection is attempted, reporting varies greatly by law enforcement agencies within state jurisdictions. So, too, the federal government continues to drag its heels on comprehensive hate crime legislation that would include sexual orientation and otherwise give teeth to the enforcement of hate crimes by meaningfully expanding federal jurisdiction.

Given the disarray among state and federal hate crime laws, it makes sense to revisit the functionality of hate crime laws. Hate crime laws are largely perceived as expressing

> strong social condemnation of bias crimes. . . . Condemnation of hate crimes implies a general affirmation of the societal value of the groups targeted by hate crimes and a recognition of their rightful place in society. Hate crimes legislation is seen as reinforcing the community's commitment to equality among all citizens. (Beale, 2000, p. 1255)

Indeed, scholars have consistently emphasized the symbolic function of hate crime legislation in sending a message that crimes motivated by bias will not be tolerated (Grattet & Jenness, 2001; Jacobs & Henry, 1996; Jacobs & Potter, 1998; Lawrence, 1999).

Symbolic politics fueled the passage of hate crime laws. The Senate Judiciary Committee's report on the HCSA declared,

> The very effort by the legislative branch to require the Justice Department to collect this information would send an additional important signal to victimized groups everywhere that the U.S. Government is concerned about this kind of crime. (S. Rep. No. 21 1989)

In signing New Jersey's ethnic intimidation law, then governor Jim Florio declared, "This legislation does more than punish. . . . It says something about who we are and about the ideals to which this state is committed" (Levinson, 1990). New York's former governor Mario Cuomo implored his state legislature to support that state's Bias Related and Violence Intimidation Act and "make it clear to the people of this state that behavior based on bias will not be ignored or tolerated" (Cuomo, 1991).

Hate crime laws may well send a message of intolerance for bigotry and prejudice, on one hand, and also a message of tolerance and acceptance toward those groups specifically designated for protection, on the other. But what message is sent to groups, or even individual crime victims, not designated for hate crime protection?

Many states and the federal government do not include crimes motivated by bias based on sexual orientation in their hate crime statutes. The omission is not because hate crimes do not occur against gays and lesbians; rather, conservative politicians fear that inclusion of sexual orientation may send a message that they are endorsing homosexuality. Indeed, the HCSA, which included sexual orientation in its data collection statute, was passed only with the inclusion of compromise language, insisted on by conservative senators, including Senator Jesse Helms, which stated that "nothing in this Act shall be construed . . . to promote or encourage homosexuality" (Toner, 1990, p. A17). Helms and his cohort successfully used the passage of HCSA to send a clear message of intolerance for gays and lesbians—surely a perversion of the law's intended spirit.

Or consider the initial decision by West Virginia and federal prosecutors not to pursue hate crime charges in the Megan Williams case. Their decision provoked outrage throughout the nation and, indeed, the world. Online petitions were circulated urging the government to bring hate crime charges (*Megan Williams Case*, 2007). State legislators from outside West Virginia urged prosecutors to employ hate crime laws ("Congresswoman," 2007). National civil rights activists, including the Reverend Al Sharpton, attended a rally calling for hate crime charges in the case (Mohajer, 2007). Ms. Williams and her family continue to experience disappointment over the absence of hate crime charges, even though the perpetrators face potential life sentences. Ultimately, five months after the attack and under immense pressure, prosecutors filed a single hate crime charge against only one defendant.

The absence of hate crime charges became a rallying cry in the Williams case. As such, the Williams case serves as an excellent illustration of the symbolic importance of hate crime laws and the harm that can be caused when the government declines to apply them. If hate crimes have a largely a symbolic function, then more attention must be paid to their enforcement and to the messages of disinclusion sent by national politicians disavowing sexual orientation or local prosecutors refusing to bring hate crime charges. Otherwise, state and federal hate crime laws and their inconsistent enforcement may send a potent, and surely unintended, message of ambivalence, intolerance, and divisiveness.

REFERENCES

Anti-Defamation League. (2001). *ADL approach to model legislation.* Retrieved January 7, 2008, from http://adl.org/99hatecrime/text_legis.asp

Anti-Defamation League. (2002). *Dangerous convictions: An introduction to extremist activities in prison.* New York: Gorowitz Institute. Retrieved January 4, 2008, from http://www.adl.org/LEARN/Ext_Terr/dangerous_convictions.pdf

Anti-Defamation League. (2007). *State hate crime statutory provisions.* Retrieved January 7, 2008, from http://www.adl.org/99hatecrime/state_hate_crime_laws.pdf

Apprendi v. New Jersey, 530 U.S. 466 (2000).

Associated Press. (2008a, February 21). *Senate passes homeless hate crime bill.* Retrieved February 28, 2008, from http://www.nbc4.com/politics/15364903/detail.html

Associated Press. (2008b, February 7). West Virginia: Hate crime indictment in torture case. *New York Times,* p. A17.

Beale, S. S. (2000). Federalizing hate crimes: Symbolic politics, expressive law, or tool for criminal enforcement? *Boston University Law Review, 80,* 1227–1281.

Caving in on hate crimes. (2007, December 10). *New York Times.* Retrieved December 13, 2007, from http://www.nytimes.com/2007/12/10/opinion/10mon3.html

Congresswoman, legal advisor discussed Williams torture case. (2007, December 13). *National Public Radio.* Retrieved December 20, 2007, from http://www.npr.org/templates/story/story.php?storyId=17201595

Costello, C. (2007, May 3). *White House threatens to veto hate-crimes bill.* Retrieved December 8, 2007, from http://www.cnn.com/2007/POLITICS/05/03/hate.crimes.bill/index.html

Cuomo, M. (1991, August 16). Letter from the governor of the state of New York to the New York legislature. Available at Lexis.Nexus (subscription required).

Donnino, W. (2007). Practice commentaries, McKinney Cons. Laws of NY, Book 39, Penal Law § 485.00.

Federal Bureau of Investigation. (2007, November). *Hate crime statistics, 2006.* Retrieved January 7, 2008, from http://www.fbi.gov/ucr/hc2006/index.html

Galloway, J. (2007, December 27). Hate crimes: Debate on gays, lesbians Mires bill. *Atlanta Journal-Constitution,* p. D21.

Grattet, R., & Jenness, V. (2001). Examining the boundaries of hate crime law: Disabilities and the "dilemma of difference." *Journal of Criminal Law and Criminology*, *91*, 653–697.

Harki, G. (2007, September 13). No hate charges in torture case: Victim went to rural mobile home "of her own free will," prosecutor says. *Charleston Gazette & Daily Mail*, p. 1A.

Hasenstab, D. (2001). Is hate a form of commerce? The questionable constitutionality of federal "hate crime" legislation. *St. Louis University Law Journal*, *45*, 973–1017.

Hate Crime Sentencing Enhancement Act, 28 U.S.C. § 994 (1994).

Hate Crime Statistics Act, Pub. L. No. 101-275, 104 Stat. 140 (1990).

Henry, J. S. (2007). Treating bigots like pedophiles: Posting personal data of convicted bias offenders on the Web. *American Criminal Justice Association: LAE Journal*, 16–19.

Jacobs, J. B., & Henry, J. S. (1996). The social construction of a hate crime epidemic. *Journal of Criminal Law and Criminology*, *82*, 336–391.

Jacobs, J. B., & Potter, K. (1998). *Hate crimes: Criminal law and identity politics*. New York: Oxford University Press.

Lawrence, F. M. (1999). *Punishing hate: Bias crimes under American law*. Cambridge, MA: Harvard University Press.

Levin, J., & McDevitt, J. (1993). *Hate crimes. The rising tide of bigotry and bloodshed.* New York: Plenum Press.

Levinson, L. (1990, 8 August). Florio Signs Bias Bill, UPI. Available in Lexis.Nexis (subscription required).

Matthew Shepard Local Law Enforcement Hate Crimes Prevention Act, S. 1105 (2007).

McDevitt, J., Levin, J., & Bennett, S. (2002). Hate crime offenders: An expanded typology. *Journal of Social Issues*, *58*(2).

Megan Williams case petition. (2007, September 13). Retrieved December 20, 2007, from http://www.gopetition.com/petitions/the-megan-williams-case.html

Mohajer, S. T. (2007, December 19). Sharpton speaks at Williams rally. *Charleston Gazette & Daily Mail*, p. 5C.

National Coalition for the Homeless. (2007, February). *Violent crimes against the homeless on the rise*. Retrieved February 15, 2008, from http://www.nationalhomeless. org/getinvolved/projects/hatecrimes/pressrelease.html

R.A.V. v. St. Paul, 505 U.S. 77 (1992).

Southern Poverty Law Center. (2001, Winter). Discounting hate: Ten years after federal officials began compiling national hate crime statistics, the numbers don't add up. *Intelligence Report*, retrieved February 18, 2008, from http://www.splcenter. org/intel/intelreport/article.jsp?aid=157

State v. Mitchell, 485 N.W.2d 807 (1992).

Stout, D. (2007, May 4). House votes to expand hate-crime protection. *New York Times*, p. A19.

Temple-Raston, D. (2002). *A death in Texas: A story of race, murder and a small town's struggle for redemption*. New York: Henry Holt.

Toner, R. (1990, February 9). Senate, 92 to 4, wants U.S. data on crimes that spring from hate. *New York Times*. Retrieved February 20, 2008, from http://query.nytimes. com/gst/fullpage.html?res=9C0CE1D7133EF93AA35751C0A966958260

United States v. Booker, 542 U.S. 200 (2005).

United States v. Morrison, 529 U.S. 598 (2000).
United States v. Schwimmer, 279 U.S. 644 (1929).
U.S. Congress, Senate. (1989). 101st Cong., 2d sess., S. Rep. 21.
Virginia v. Black, 538 U.S. 343 (2003).
Wisconsin v. Mitchell, 508 U.S. 476 (1993).

CHAPTER 11

WEIGHING GENOCIDE

Timothy Pytell

In 1994, the renowned Marxist historian Eric Hobsbawn conceptualized the twentieth century as the age of extremes. Hobsbawn's concern was the ideological conflicts between capitalism, communism, fascism, and nationalism. However, a more accurate conceptualization of the twentieth century should focus on the pervasive mass death and genocide. For example, according to R. J. Rummel (2008), a conservative estimate of the number of people killed by wars, massacres, and other atrocities in the twentieth century is 262 million. The omnipresent devastation leads us to the uncomfortable conclusion that we live in an age of mass death and genocide, and if there is any hope of stopping, or at least slowing down, the onslaught, we need to confront this reality.

Although the twentieth century represents a new level of genocidal killing, the truth is that mass killing of humans by other humans has been occurring from time immemorial. Indeed, the desire to completely annihilate another human group different from one's own is articulated in the classic foundational text of Western civilization, *The Iliad*, by Homer, when he has Agamemnon state, "My dear Menelaus, why are you so chary of taking men's lives? Did the Trojans treat you as handsomely as that when they stayed in your house? No; we are not going to leave a single one of them alive, down

Acknowledgments: I would like to thank Professor Brian Levin for inviting me to contribute to this important volume. I addition, I would like to thank the Teaching Resource Center at California State University, San Bernardino, for providing me the opportunity to team teach a course on comparative genocide with Professor James Fenelon. I am indebted to and appreciative of both Professor Fenelon and the students at CSUSB.

to the babies in their mothers' wombs—not even they must live. The whole people must be wiped out of existence, and none be left to think of them and shed a tear" (as quoted in Chalk & Jonassohn, 1990, p. 58).

If the ultimate goal of genocide is the nullification of another or human group, the Other, it appears that this aptitude is deeply ingrained in our nature. Indeed, according to the social psychologist James Waller (2007), our "evolutionary heritage" and "natural selection" has "primed us for the capacity for evil—including the perpetration of genocide and mass killing" (p. 287). Waller's work, along with the pioneering effort of the historian Christopher Browning (1993) and his highly acclaimed book *Ordinary Men: Reserve Police Battalion 101 and the Final Solution in Poland,* forces us to confront the rather unsettling fact that all of us have the capacity for extraordinary evil. History also shows that this capacity is all too easily activated by a peculiar mix of cultural, psychological, and social realities. Fully conscious of the human tendency and capacity for beastliness, Waller (2007) concludes with the rather disheartening claim that "it is hard to argue that we can do something beyond merely make the world a little less horrible" (p. 298). Waller's distress is common to many Holocaust and genocide scholars. The great hope of Holocaust scholarship in the last decades of the twentieth century was to promote enough awareness of the unimaginable destruction wrought by Hitler and his regime that another atrocity like the destruction of European Jewry would never occur again. But sadly, since the end of World War II, the world has witnessed genocidal acts in Cambodia, Guatemala, Iraq, Rwanda, Bosnia, and Darfur. These atrocious events have had a humbling effect on scholars but have also made the necessity of understanding the mechanisms of genocide to prevent it all the more urgent.

One of the more sensitive souls to the heightened violence in the last century was the lawyer of Polish-Jewish descent Raphael Lemkin. Lemkin was born in 1900 and was educated in linguistics and law. Lemkin not only coined the term *genocide* in 1944, but also dedicated his entire life to raising awareness within the international community that a legal response was needed to what he described to the League of Nations in 1933 as "acts of barbarism." In 1933 the particular acts of barbarism and vandalism that motivated Lemkin to action have become known to historians as the Armenian genocide. This genocide was perpetrated by Turkey against ethnic Armenians inside the crumbling Ottoman Empire during the First World War. Setting the stage for the atrocious twentieth century, nationalists in Turkey murdered 1.5 million Armenian civilians and forcibly removed thousands during the First World War. Tragically, Lemkin's initial plea fell on deaf ears, and the response was ominous since Hitler assumed power in Germany the same year. In 1939, in response to the Nazi attack on Poland, Lemkin joined the Polish army and was wounded when he fought against the Nazi takeover of Warsaw. He evaded capture, though, and made his way to the United States, but 49 members of his family were killed in the Holocaust. In America, he joined the War Department in 1942 and began work on his landmark study of legal practices in Nazi-occupied Europe, published in 1944 as *Axis Rule in Occupied Europe*. In the book, Lemkin (1944) coined the term *genocide* and defined it in these terms:

> By "genocide" we mean the destruction of a nation or of an ethnic group. This new word, coined by the author to denote an old practice in its modern development, is made from the ancient Greek word genos (race, tribe) and the Latin cide (killing). . . . Generally speaking, genocide does not necessarily mean the immediate destruction of a nation, except when accomplished by mass killings of all members of a nation. It is intended rather to signify a coordinated plan of different actions aiming at the destruction of essential foundations of the life of national groups, with the aim of annihilating the groups themselves. Genocide is directed against the national group as an entity, and the actions involved are directed against individuals, not in their individual capacity, but as members of the national group. (p. 80)

Lemkin's focus on how genocide intends to destroy national groups was a prescient insight into how the advent of the nation-state was leading to novel levels of violent conflict and destruction. Significantly, his definition of genocide and his assertion that genocide be viewed as a violation of international law became one of the legal bases for the Nuremberg trials in 1946. Lemkin also served with the team of Americans at Nuremberg, where the term *genocide* was first used in the indictment against the Nazis. However, to make genocide a "crime" in legal terms, Lemkin needed the sanction of international law.

Samantha Power's (2002) best-selling book *"A Problem from Hell": America and the Age of Genocide* movingly describes Lemkin's tireless efforts to lobby nations and influential leaders to make the United Nations approve the Convention on the Prevention and Punishment of Genocide. Lemkin's effort paid off when, on December 9, 1948, the United Nations approved the convention. Lemkin spent the rest of his life lobbying nations to pass legislation in support of the convention. Lemkin died in 1959, exhausted and impoverished by his efforts.

The United Nations' definition of genocide expounds on Lemkin's and has been the subject of unending controversy. According to the second article of the convention,

> genocide means any of the following acts committed with intent to destroy, in whole or in part, a national, ethnical, racial or religious group, as such:
>
> a. Killing members of the group;
> b. Causing serious bodily or mental harm to members of the group;

    c.   Deliberately inflicting on the group conditions of life calculated to bring about its physical destruction in whole or in part;

    d.   Imposing measures intended to prevent births within the group;

    e.   Forcibly transferring children of the group to another group.

Scholars have found a great deal to quibble about in this definition, and subsequently, the issue of genocide is fraught with controversy. The current definition is a typical political "compromise" worked out by the United Nations and has led to little consensus. One minor issue is the phrase "as such," which, depending on how you interpret the meaning, seems to both limit the definition and make it too inclusive. It seems unclear whether the term is referring to "the group" or individual members of the group. If it were the former, then destroying individual members without the intent to destroy the group as a whole would not be genocide. If it means the latter, then destroying individuals or even *an* individual because of their membership in a group becomes genocide if "intent" is proven.

The most important issue that has led to a lack of consensus is due primarily to the focus on "national, ethnical, racial or religious" groups, which glaringly omits groups that have been annihilated because of their political position or social class. For sure, these latter categories are more permeable than the former because divesting your status as a bourgeoisie, or a member of the Communist Party, is more plausible than divesting your status as a Jew or Muslim, or as an Albanian or Tutsi. Also, renouncing your social or political position is not a "condition for survival" of your group. However, it is certainly insensitive and deeply problematic not to recognize the Soviet Union's purge in the 1930s of their wealthy peasants (*kulaks*) to manufacture a proletariat that led to at least 6 million deaths—as genocide (see Weitz, 2003). In this case, the targeted "group" had only a limited connection to social or political reality because it was primarily based on the ideological fantasy of the perpetrator.

Given these circumstances, it is not surprising that the omission of politics and class in the United Nations definition was done in deference to the wishes of the Soviet Union and their concern that Stalin's mass murders would be conceived as genocidal. In response to this omission, a groundswell is emerging among genocide scholars like Daniel Feierstein (2008), director of the Center of Genocide Studies in Buenos Aires, Argentina, that it is time to revise this article of the convention because "the annihilation processes (at least in our modern times) are always 'politically' charged" (para. 1) and the omission serves to protect some people, while failing to protect others.

Another issue raised by the genocide convention is the problem of intent. In criminal law, there are different levels of intentionality, and most crimes require purposefulness. However, the fact that a crime occurred, regardless of intentionality, can lead to prosecution. Subsequently, in genocide scholarship, the issue of intent has been brought into contention. According to the perspective of Robert Gellately and Ben Kiernan (2006), "intent is irrelevant" in the sense that all that is necessary is to prove that the criminal act "was intentional not accidental" (p. 15). Therefore a "conquest or a revolution that causes total or partial destruction of a group, legally qualifies as intentional and therefore as genocide whatever the goal or motive, so long as the acts of destruction were pursued intentionally" (p. 15). From this legal perspective, "genocidal intent also applies to acts of destruction that are not a specific goal but are predictable outcomes or by-products of a policy, which could have been avoided by a change in that policy" (p. 15). This perspective raises the issue of colonialism and genocide and the controversial issue of whether the widespread and enduring atrocities against the indigenous people of the territory of the United States were genocide.

It seems profoundly insensitive not to recognize the destruction of the indigenous people of North America as genocide. However, it apparently has been easy to do so. The reasons we are in cultural denial about the genocide of the indigenous peoples are multilayered. For one, it is a genocidal process that began in 1492 with disease and conflict, escalated after the Jamestown Massacre in 1622, and continued as Manifest Destiny pushed the pioneers westward across the frontier. Indeed, according to Russell Thornton (1987) in *American Indian Holocaust and Survival: A Population History since 1492*, there were, at the minimum, 5 million Native peoples in the land currently known as the United States in 1492. In a steady decline afterward, the population bottomed out in the 1880s at 250,000. It is hard to conceptualize a genocide almost 500 years in the making. Without a doubt, during this period, an unknown but surely monstrous amount of mass murder and death by disease and starvation occurred. In addition, there are also the better-known genocidal massacres, such as the Trail of Tears, the Sand Creek Massacre in Colorado, and Wounded Knee in the Dakotas, that occurred as the "frontier" moved westward. According to the historian Brendan Lindsay (2007), the process of westward expansion culminated in an "openly arrived at and executed genocide of Native peoples in order to secure property" (p. 4) in California in the years 1846–1916. According to Lindsay's unsettling argument, the initiative behind the genocide was not a state-sanctioned policy originating from Washington, D.C., but rather, from local populations "through the democratic processes and institutions" that called for and garnered the resources from either the state or local community and created the militias that perpetrated genocidal massacres. In addition to these local initiatives, state governments outfitted militias and even offered rewards for the scalps of Native peoples.

David Stannard (1993), in his book *American Holocaust: The Conquest of the New World*, captured the genocidal subconscious of the majority of Americans when he quoted Theodore Roosevelt's statement, "I don't go so far as to think that the only good Indians are dead Indians, but I believe nine out of ten are, and I shouldn't like to inquire too closely into the case of the tenth" (p. 245). This statement reads like a precursor to Heinrich Himmler's complaint in the midst of the Nazi Holocaust that every German has his "good Jew," and it is well known that Hitler admired America's "extermination" of Native peoples. Finally, Clifford Trafzer and Joel Hyer (1999) described how many Californians during the gold rush expressed their genocidal consciousness with their calls for the "extermination" of Native peoples because, just like the Nazi attitude toward the Jews, they no longer recognized the humanity of Native peoples. It seems that slowly, but surely, a consensus is emerging among scholars that genocide occurred in the Americas.

However, it will take a generation of new historians to uncover more fully our genocidal past, comprehend the nuances and differences between more "modern" genocides, and incorporate "our" genocide into the American historical canon. This process will be difficult because including genocide into the story of America will require a radical shift in consciousness. This is because, despite the strong evidence and nuanced arguments that assert a pervasive genocidal intent among colonial Americans, most Americans claim it is an exaggeration to suggest we committed genocide. This line of reasoning claims that rather than genocide, America perpetrated what has become known in the lexicon as *ethnic cleansing*. *Ethnic cleansing* is a poor euphemism for forms of culturcide, ethnocide, ghettoization, displacement of people to reservations, and forced removal of populations. As we shall see, this is often an initial step in the process of genocide and fits the United Nations convention's definition of "deliberately inflicting on the group conditions of life calculated to bring about its physical destruction in whole or in part."

The key argument in the American denial of genocide is the point that America never became a genocidal regime, and subsequently, the vast amount of Native people died "inadvertently," not intentionally by disease. To be sure, we have only limited evidence that the prime killer of smallpox was spread *intentionally* among Native peoples, and it doesn't appear to have been common (Stannard, 1993). Nevertheless, those who believed their Manifest Destiny was to engage in a "civilizing mission" inadvertently spread the disease, and as often as not, they saw the destruction waged by the disease as a reflection of their own superiority and/or God's will. The uncomfortable truth is that even if we frame the civilizing mission of Europeans in the Americas as a "positive," which is questionable, given that it was premised on culturcide, the *consequences* of the mission were a key component of genocide. Arguably, until we view the Native peoples as *equals*, and not as "redskins" or "warriors" or "Indians," we will not be conscious enough of these people's humanity to include them in our "national" community. In contrast, we have had much more success incorporating the reality of slavery into our national consciousness. This is not only because the genocide of Native peoples is very uncomfortable to confront, but also, the genocidal destruction more or less led to a "vanishing" of these peoples. Indeed, for most Americans, there was no genocide, and Native peoples have vanished into the myth of Pocahontas and Geronimo.

One reason scholars are coming around to viewing the Native American experience in terms of genocide is because they are less concerned with legal issues and the criminal prosecution of genocide and therefore tend to rely on definitions that include social and political groups as well as consequences and not just intentions. For example, the senior genocide scholar Helen Fein (2007) defines genocide as the "sustained purposeful action by a perpetrator to physically destroy a collectivity directly or indirectly, through interdiction of the biological and social reproduction of group members, sustained regardless of the surrender or lack of threat offered by the victim" (p. 132). Fein's reliance on the phrase "directly or indirectly" allows for the factoring in of consequences, while the "interdiction of biological and social reproduction" suggests that outright killing is not always necessary. Finally, "sustained" offers a time element, and the phrases "surrender" and "lack of threat" suggest that innocents are being destroyed. On the basis of this definition, it is easy to conclude that America conducted a sustained genocide against Native peoples.

Despite the strength of this argument, other scholars (Weitz, 2003) claim that genocide is a phenomenon of Western modernity in general, and the twentieth century specifically. This position is based on a number of factors. For one, as we have seen, Lemkin coins the term in 1944 to describe novel acts of barbarism that occurred during his lifetime. Second, the number of human beings killed by states in the twentieth century, a phenomenon the political scientist R. J. Rummel (2008) defines as *democide*, is 262 million. This number surpasses the imagination, but to give some perspective, R. J. Rummel (2008) claims that "if all these bodies were laid head to toe, with the average height being 5 feet, then they would circle the earth ten times. Also, this democide murdered 6 times more people than died in combat in all the foreign and internal wars of the century. Finally, given popular estimates of the dead in a major nuclear war, this total democide is as though such a war did occur, but with its dead spread over a century" (Rummel, 2008). What makes the mass death of the twentieth century unique in human history is certainly the sheer numbers (see Table 11.1). We know that the cause of this destruction was dependent on two interrelated phenomena: the rise of the nation-state and industrialization. The dangers of these phenomena became very apparent in the First World War (1914–1918). Motivated by nationalism and the call to arms, nearly 10 million European males went to their deaths in the Great War, while almost another 20 million were wounded. The ubiquitous death and casualties were a consequence of new forms of warfare that relied on heavy artillery, machine guns, a multitude of incendiary devices, mustard

Table 11.1   Number of Victims and Percentage of Victim's Group

Dates	Perpetrator	Victims	No.	Percentage of victims
1915	Ottoman Empire	Armenians	1,200,000	66
1933	Soviet Union	Ukrainians	>3,100,000	>10
1941–1945	Germany and others	Jews	5,500,000– 6,000,000	67
1941–1945	Germany and others	Russian prisoners of war	3,300,000	58
1941–1945	Germany and others	Roma	500,000– 1,500,000	–
1975–1979	Kampuchea	Khmer and ethnic minorities	>1,671,000	>21
1987–1988	Iraq	Kurds	100,000	8
1992–1995	Bosnia-Herzegovina	Non-Serbs	>10,000	–
1994	Rwanda	Tutsis	507,000	70

Source: From H. Fein, *Human Rights and Wrongs: Slavery, Terror, Genocide* (Boulder, CO: Paradigm, 2007).

gas, and, by the end of the war, armored cars and tanks. Indeed, the shadow of destruction of the First World War enveloped the entire century. It comes as no surprise, then, that the first modern genocide also occurred during the war.

The Armenian genocide shares many of the characteristics that mark genocides in modernity. In 1914 the Ottoman Empire entered the First World War on the side of the Axis powers, Germany and the Austro-Hungarian Empire, with the hope of offsetting some of the territorial losses and decline of prestige that the Ottomans had been experiencing throughout the nineteenth and early twentieth centuries. In addition, many of the government leaders of the Ottoman Empire were members of the Young Turks, who had conducted a coup in 1908 to restore a constitutional monarchy. These leaders were committed to pan-Turkism and pan-Islamic ideology to make Turkey into a modern nation-state. The impetus to murder innocent Armenians was taken by the Young Turks and, in particular, the minister of war, Enver Pansher. In 1915 the war against the Russians was going badly for the Ottomans. In addition, the allies had landed at Gallipoli, forcing the Ottomans into a two-front war. Under these extreme circumstances of total war, Pansher and the Young Turks began to blame the ethnically distinct and Christian Armenians for treason and supporting the Russians. In what Donald Bloxham (2005) has described as "cumulative radicalization," the genocide was triggered by a constellation of events—the advance of the Russian army in the Caucasus; the Anglo-French attack at the Dardanelles; the growing fears concerning the loyalty of the Ottoman Empire's most important remaining Christian minority, the Armenians of Anatolia. Under these circumstances, Pansher first demobilized all Armenians fighting in the Ottoman army, and the vast majority were subsequently murdered. In May of 1915 another Young Turk, Mehed Talaat Pasha, requested that the government issue a temporary deportation order. Under this order, the Armenian genocide ensued. The numbers are uncertain, but well over a million Armenians, out of a population of 2.1 million, were murdered during their forced deportation from their traditional homeland to the Syrian Desert. Women and children were separated from men, and most of the men were immediately shot. The government provided no water, food, or other resources during these forced marches. During these treks, hundreds of thousands were murdered, raped, and robbed by either government soldiers or the marauding bands that preyed on the refugees. Armenian intellectuals, priests, and educators were also murdered.

In contrast to the genocide against the Native peoples in North America, the Armenian genocide marks the beginning of the "modernity" of genocides. As we shall see, these genocides share characteristics with the previous colonial genocides but are also marked by a newly developed ideological intensification that has different attributes and are always directed with virulence against a group that is conceived of as being outside of the community of obligation. In addition, twentieth-century genocides are usually state sponsored and thus mobilize all the resources of the state, including bureaucracies, armies, and an energized citizenry, who carry out extreme acts of violence with a vengeance. From this perspective, the genocide that was conducted against Native peoples was an embryonic form of the full-fledged violence of the twentieth century.

The emblematic genocide of the twentieth century is, without a doubt, the Nazi Holocaust against the European Jews. The iconic status of the Holocaust is due to a number of factors. The enormity of scale and the clarity of Nazi ideology and its subsequent intent are central. The Nazis murdered nearly 6 million Jews. By mobilizing the vast resources of the Nazi European empire, Hitler and his henchmen carried out the sinister and diabolical destruction of Jewish life in Europe. Historians have longed been baffled by the fact that a large proportion of the Nazi war effort was diverted to focus on the genocide against the Jews. This included the construction of ghettos, concentration camps, and death camps. Also, ministries and departments were established to organize the destruction of the Jews. The perpetrators included bureaucrats, policemen, ordinary soldiers, SS death squads, and camp administrators. In Auschwitz, the horror became surreal when special commandos of political prisoners and fellow Jews were forced to prepare and gas Jews.

For a number of years after the Holocaust, historians struggled to come to terms with the enormity of the event. The famous theoretician and cultural critique Theodore Adorno set the tone by claiming after Auschwitz "poetry cannot be written." However, in 1961, Raul Hillberg's epoch tome *The Destruction of the European Jews* reconstructed how the Nazis went about achieving their aims. Slowly, the field of Holocaust studies emerged, and today, the Nazi genocide is perhaps the most documented and discussed historical event.

As the historiography of the Holocaust progressed, in the 1980s, an anxious and fruitful debate emerged between two schools of scholars: the intentionalists and the functionalists. Succinctly put, the intentionalists claimed that Hitler and his peculiar brand of anti-Semitism was the source of Auschwitz, despite the fact that historians never discovered a written order by Hitler, while the functionalists claimed that Auschwitz was the culmination of not only anti-Semitism, but a wide variety of factors such as the science of eugenics, dehumanizing technology, instrumental rationality, bureaucracy, total war, and so on. This debate climaxed in the late 1990s when Daniel Goldhagen's (1997) *Hitler's Willing Executioners* and Christopher Browning's (1993) *Ordinary Men* came to contrary conclusions on what motivated Police Battalion 101 to round up and murder Polish Jews. According to Browning's more functionalist view, these were "ordinary men" who succumbed to social-psychological pressures of military culture, conformity to authority, and group solidarity. In contrast, Goldhagen's (1997) more intentionalist view conceived of these men as "Hitler's willing executioners," who, like Hitler, were motivated by an ideology of "eliminationist anti-Semitism," which was deeply ingrained in German society. Indeed, Goldhagen traced the origins of this ideology back to the Germanic Middle Ages. Since Goldhagen was trained as a political scientist, historians expressed outrage over his less than refined explanation for the Nazi Holocaust. In addition, the vast popularity of Goldhagen's book among lay readers in both America and Europe baffled historians, especially since they had spent decades developing a nuanced version of how Hitlerian intent interplayed with the Nazi state and party, ideological indoctrination, military culture, circumstances of total war, and social and psychological pressures to create the Holocaust.

The Goldhagen (1997) controversy, along with the debate between intentionalists and functionalists, has subsided, and the historiography of the Holocaust has moved on to new territory. From the perspective of 2008, it is clear that the Goldhagen controversy represented the initial reformulation of the genocide against the Jews in light of new historical understanding of Eastern Europe. This fresh perspective was based on the newly opened archives that occurred with the fall of Communism in 1989. This slow process is aptly described as the "East Europeanization of the Holocaust" and has blended the intentionalist/functionalist positions into a "twisted road to Auschwitz."

Despite the fact that we have no written order by Hitler, a general consensus has nevertheless emerged among historians that the decision to annihilate European Jews was made in the summer or fall of 1941 (see Browning, 2004). Browning's refined analysis and conclusion are primarily based on the fact that from the outbreak of the war in 1939 until the decision was made, mass murder of Jews occurred, perhaps a million people, but the solution to the so-called Jewish question centered on emigration, deportation to Madagascar, or a reservation in the east. Indeed, it wasn't until October 23, 1941, that Jewish emigration from Europe was banned. This change in Nazi policy on the Jewish question is attributable to Operation Barbarossa and Hitler's decision to invade the Soviet Union in June of 1941. As Hitler's armies successfully marched across eastern Poland and the Ukraine, large populations of Jews came under Nazi control. The rapid success of the German army in Eastern Europe, in combination with the difficulty of conscience the SS and the Einsatzgruppen had when marching innocent Jewish men, women, and children into the forest, where large pits had been dug, where their bodies could fall after shooting them in the back of the head, led to the final solution. According to this interpretation, to deal with all the new Jews under their control, and to alleviate this "burden" of shooting innocents, a "twisted road to Auschwitz" occurred, where death became mechanized and "massafied."

Some historians even argue that the "final solution" can be attributed to the euphoria of the initial victories in the east. Indeed, the Wannsee Conference, which was the organizational meeting by Reinhard Heydrich to plan and mobilize the necessary resources for the final solution in January of 1942, was originally intended for December 9, 1941, and was obviously scheduled while the German armies were winning in the east. But the conference had to be postponed due to the Japanese attack on Pearl Harbor, which led to Hitler's declaration of war on America. In addition, by December 1941, it was becoming clear that Germany's war fortunes were changing as their army became bogged down at Stalingrad during a fierce Russian winter (see Roseman, 2002).

In the circumstances of total war, what had been mass murder of Jews, again, perhaps a million dead at this point, mutated into full-fledged genocide. Indeed, although the killing continued until the end of the war, the majority of Jews were murdered from March 1942 to February 1943. Without a doubt, the Wannsee Conference organized and sustained the momentum for the implementation of the final solution. Perhaps the most striking fact about the conference that we learn from the meeting's minutes is the scale of Nazi intent, where "approximately eleven million Jews [were to be killed] in the final solution of the European Jewish question" (see Yale Law School, n.d., para. 13). The number of 11 million reveals Nazi genocidal grandiosity, and the number is based on Jews in both Nazi-occupied territory and *unoccupied* territory, including Jews in the Union of Soviet Socialist Republics, Ireland, and the "European portion of Turkey."

The Nazis' diabolical focus on Jews no doubt drew impetus from Hitler's rabid anti-Semitism and perverted racial worldview. However, the implementation of the Holocaust required much more. Not only was there mass participation of German soldiers, policemen, and citizens, but also Poles, Ukrainians, Romanians, Croats, and countless others. Accordingly, the Holocaust was a multinational operation on a scale that surpasses all other genocides, and in this regard, the Holocaust was "unique."

Recently, however, historians have begun to question the claim of the uniqueness of the Holocaust because they have come to realize that the assertion has a number of pitfalls. For one, the claim makes the Holocaust a metaphysical, almost religious event that stands outside of historical time. In addition, it seems insensitive to make one people's suffering "unique" or somehow worse than all others. The reality is that all genocides are unique. For example, in a brief period of 100 days, around 1 million Rwandans were murdered, and astoundingly, primarily by machetes. According to Waller (2007), that is "five and a half lives terminated every minute," which "represents a rate of death nearly three times the rate of Jewish dead during the Holocaust" (p. 225).

In addition to no longer framing the Holocaust as *unique*, historians are beginning to focus on the more *universal* aspects of the Holocaust. For example, although the Holocaust will remain a primary event in Jewish history, there is also an emerging recognition that the Nazis had a vision of "serial" genocide (see Gellately & Kiernan, 2006). Estimates vary, but according to Richard Lukas (1997), perhaps as many as 3 million non-Jewish Polish nationals died at the hands of the Nazis. Without a doubt, if the Nazis had been successful in their efforts, we would no longer speak of the people of Poland. There were also a number of other "human groups" singled out for persecution and eventual destruction by the Nazis, such as the Roma and Sinti (gypsies), homosexuals, and all those considered handicapped. From this perspective, Hitler's "biocracy" had little room for anyone other than Aryans. According to the historian Henry Friedlander (1995), the "opening act" of the Nazi genocide began with euthanasia and the T-4 program, which was implemented in 1939 under Hitler's order and led to the gassing of around 30,000 mentally and physically handicapped German citizens. Therefore, as the historiography moves forward, it appears in the twenty-first century that the Holocaust is not only slowly becoming a key event in Jewish history, but is also being "universalized" into a defining genocidal event in Western history.

Another example of this shift is the development of the field of comparative genocide in the 1990s. Many of these scholars were originally trained in Holocaust studies and began to branch out to other issues and concerns. No doubt, the continual occurrence of genocides in the second half of the twentieth century led many to question the premise of Holocaust scholars that by raising awareness about the Nazi genocide, it would never again happen.

One of the key insights that the comparative genocide perspective has generated is that genocides have a number of similar constituting features, and by recognizing these features, we may be able to diagnose and predict when genocides are about to occur (see Table 11.2). In any genocide, the central component is the ideological or culturally constructed worldview. Prime examples are the creation of an idealized "national" community, as in the case of America's Manifest Destiny, Turkey's pan-Turkism and pan-Islamism, Nazi Germany's biocracy, and Rwandan's Hutu supremacy. In the idealization of the nation, there are characteristics of purity, or homogeneity. For example, in the case of the Soviet Union, status was based on adhering properly to Communist ideology. In all cases, the idealized community depends on establishing the second component of genocides—the Other. The socially constructed Other removes groups from the community of obligation, for instance, Native peoples, Christian Armenians, Jews, Slavs, Tutsi, homosexuals, handicapped, or those deemed deviant in some manner.

The *process* of genocide begins with the social marginalization of these Others such as through legal restrictions, ghettotization, and so on. In this stage, the progression often escalates into *ethnic cleansing* and sporadic violence. When the correct mix of circumstances is present, most often, war or social conflict, rituals of violence occur. In this stage, mass murder, genocidal massacres, and eventually, the development of full-blown genocide occur. Again, what arguably distinguishes the American genocide from the genocides of the twentieth century is the role of the state. Unlike in the Armenian genocide, the Holocaust, Pol Pot's regime, or the Rwandan regime, there was no state-sanctioned attempt by the U.S. government in concerted action to

Table 11.2 Stages of Genocide

Stage no. and title	Description
1. Classification	Categorize groups into "us" vs. "them."
2. Symbolization	Give names to the categories: Jews, Gypsies, Bourgeois, etc.
3. Dehumanization	Deny the humanity of the group through vilifying propaganda.
4. Organization	State militias are formed to carry out tasks to allow the state to deny responsibility
5. Polarization	Moderates and dissenters are targeted and eliminated.
6. Preparation	Groups are physically divided and death lists are formed.
7. Extermination	Mass killing of groups determined to be subhuman.
8. Denial	Evidence is covered and witnesses are intimidated.

Source: From G. Stanton, "The 8 Stages of Genocide," http://genocidewatch.org/aboutgenocides/8stagesofgenocide.htm.

kill all of the Native peoples; that is, the United States remained in a continual state of genocidal actions as opposed to becoming a genocidal regime.
Perhaps this is because we never experienced the crisis of total war, as did
Turkey and Nazi Germany, although many of the genocidal massacres in the
United States were carried out by Civil War veterans. In the United States,
genocide was localized. For example, Waller (2007) describes how, in the
buildup to the Sand Creek Massacre in Colorado in 1864, the publisher of
the *Rocky Mountain News*, William N. Byers, wrote, "Eastern humanitarians
who believe in the superiority of the Indian race will raise a terrible howl
over this policy [of extermination], but it is not time to split hairs nor stand
upon delicate compunctions of conscience" (p. 26). Around 150 men, women,
and children were murdered at Sand Creek. In contrast, the genocide against
the Armenians clearly had state sanction in the deportation order, and yet,
the genocide unfolded on the ground in a somewhat haphazard fashion. As
mentioned, as the Armenians were rounded up and forced to march into the
desert, renegade soldiers and bands of marauders raped and pillaged them.
Many starved to death or collapsed and were left to die. Some even committed suicide by drowning themselves.

It is clear that Hitler learned the lessons of the American and Armenian
example. It is also highly unlikely that Hitler "planned" Auschwitz, but rather,
Auschwitz emerged as a phenomenon of Nazi Germany in total. Again, this is
why Nazi Germany represents the apex of genocidal regimes. In Auschwitz,
genocide became industrialized and mechanized. Vast amounts of resources
were directed toward genocide, and it appears that had the Nazis been successful, the European Jews would be just the first of a number of human
groups to be destroyed.

Since 1945 genocidal acts have been carried out on every continent, with a
majority occurring in Africa. On the basis of the level of atrocities, Cambodia
under the Khmer Rouge, the Rwandan destruction of Tutsis, the Guatemalan
military's destruction of Native peoples, and finally, Bosnia Serb's attack on
Muslims stand out. Today, genocide is occurring in Darfur. These realities
seem to confirm Waller's (2007) dour claim that all we can hope for is to
make the world a little less horrible.

The question arises, Why are the United Nations and the United States
failing so miserably to live up to Lemkin's clarion call and enforce the convention? Samantha Power's book *"A Problem from Hell": America and the Age
of Genocide* attempts to provide some answers. Power's survey of America's
response to genocide in the twentieth century argues that our failure cannot be attributed to a lack of knowledge or capacity, but rather reflects a
lack of will. According to Power (2002), America's response to the Armenian
genocide set a pattern where "time and again," the United States would be
reluctant to "denounce" another state, and when knowledge was gained that
huge numbers of civilians were being murdered, "the uncertainty about the

facts and their rationalization that a firmer U.S. stand would make little difference" (p. 13) was the response.

Slowly, too slowly, the international community is taking stock of the genocidal violence that epitomized the last century. But to quote Bob Dylan, "Times are a-changing." Power, genocide scholars, and countless concerned global citizens are beginning to take responsibility to protest and demand action when crimes against humanity are about to occur. We have the understanding to determine when and where the elements that lead to genocide exist—acting on this knowledge is the way to *prevent* genocides. Finally, only by honestly confronting and comprehending the horrors of recent history can we become motivated to promote a new universalism in human consciousness, to see our own face in the face of the Other, to see our humanity in the humanity of the Other. Only then will genocide become a thing of the past.

REFERENCES

Bloxham, D. (2005). *The great game of genocide: Imperialism, nationalism and the destruction of the Ottoman Armenians*. Oxford: Oxford University Press.

Browning, C. (1993). *Ordinary men: Reserve Police Battalion 101 and the final solution in Poland*. New York: HarperCollins.

Browning, C. (2004). *The origins of the final solution: The evolution of Nazi Jewish policy, September 1939–March 1942*. Lincoln: NE: University of Nebraska Press.

Chalk, F., & Jonassohn, K. (1990). *The history and sociology of genocide: Analyses and case studies*. New Haven, CT: Yale University Press.

Feierstein, D. (2008, January 28). Re. Kenya and genocide definitions. Message posted to http://www.h-net.org/~genocide/

Fein, H. (2007). *Human rights and wrongs: Slavery, terror, genocide*. Boulder, CO: Paradigm.

Friedlander, H. (1995). *The origins of Nazi genocide: From euthanasia to the final solution*. Chapel Hill: University of North Carolina Press.

Gellately, G., & Kiernan, B. (Eds.). (2006). *The specter of genocide: Mass murder in a historical perspective*. New York: Cambridge University Press.

Golhagen, D. (1997). *Hitler's willing executioners: Ordinary Germans and the holocaust*. New York: Vintage.

Hillberg, R. (1961). *The destruction of the European Jews*. Chicago: Quadrangle Books.

Hobsbawn, E. (1994). *Age of extremes: A history of the world, 1914–1991*. New York: Random House.

Lemkin, R. (1944). *Axis rule in Europe*. Retrieved October 17, 2007, from http://www.preventgenocide.org/lemkin/AxisRule1944-1.htm

Lindsay, B. (2007). *Naturalizing atrocity: California's Indian genocide, 1846–1916*. Unpublished doctoral dissertation, University of California, Riverside.

Lukas, R. (1997). *Forgotten Holocaust: The Poles under German occupation, 1939–1944*. New York: Hippocrene Books.

Power, S. (2002). *"A problem from hell": America and the age of genocide*. New York: HarperCollins.

Roseman, M. (2002). *The Wannsee Conference and the final solution: A reconsideration.* New York: Henry Holt.

Rummel, R. J. (2008). *Freedom, democracy, peace; power, democide and war.* Retrieved October 20, 2007, from http://www.hawaii.edu/powerkills/

Stannard, D. (1993). *American Holocaust: The conquest of the New World.* Oxford: Oxford University Press.

Thornton, R. (1987). *American Indian holocaust and survival: A population history since 1492.* Norman: Oklahoma University Press.

Trafzer, C., & Hyer, J. (Eds.). (1999). *Exterminate them! Written accounts of the murder, rape, and enslavement of Native Americans during the California gold rush.* East Lansing: Michigan State University Press.

United Nations General Assembly. (1948, December 9). *Convention on the prevention and punishment of the crime of genocide.* Retrieved October 19, 2007, from http://www.hrweb.org/legal/genocide.html

Waller, J. (2007). *Becoming evil: How ordinary people commit genocide and mass killing.* New York: Oxford University Press.

Weitz, E. (2003). *A century of genocide: Utopias of race and nation.* Princeton, NJ: Princeton University Press.

Yale Law School. (n.d.). *Wannsee Protocol, January 20, 1942.* Retrieved February 8, 2008, from http://www.yale.edu/lawweb/avalon/imt/wannsee.htm

CHAPTER 12

FROM *BIRTH OF A NATION* TO STORMFRONT: A CENTURY OF COMMUNICATING HATE

Sara-Ellen Amster

What began with Holocaust denial on the Internet for 22-year-old Eric Hunt erupted into a full-time obsession and then an attack on Nobel Peace Prize winner Elie Wiesel in a San Francisco hotel elevator.

For law enforcement, the incident was greater proof that hateful words posted on a Web site—a perfectly legal act—could inspire real violence. Hunt was charged with attempted kidnapping, false imprisonment, elder abuse, stalking, and the commission of a hate crime (Martin, 2007).

"I had planned to bring Wiesel to my hotel room where he would truthfully answer my questions regarding the fact that his nonfiction Holocaust memoir, 'Night,' is almost entirely fictitious," Hunt wrote last year using his real name in a February 6 post on an anti-Semitic Web site (Reuters, 2007b, p. 1).

American extremists continue to excel at embracing new technology to spread their messages and boost their ranks, expanding the influence of "leaderless resistance" to reach potential lone adherents in their own living rooms without the need for leaflets, rallies, or meetings. By 2000, domestic hate groups using the Internet were making genuine inroads by employing new media. The expanded use of the Internet gave individuals like Matt Hale and his World Church of the Creator and William Pierce's hate rock movement unprecedented, direct access to impressionable young people. Now the influence of the Internet has exploded, and so have social networking sites and video-sharing locations. There is also a plethora of assistance for newcomers to put up professional-looking Web sites, although some sites appear dormant, except for their recognizable names, such as kukluxklan.org and naawp.net.

Researcher Denise M. Bostdorff (2004) at the University of Wooster in Wooster, Ohio, contends that the Klan is engaged in "community building of a most egregious sort" on the Internet. "In this context, community is built through opposition to other groups and through angry, persistent messages of hate that discourage dissenting points of view. Klan website messages create a virtual tribal identity of white masculinity to attract white men, while some Klan groups exploit the Internet's audience segmentation to make specialized community-building appeals to women and to youth and children" (p. 340).

Brian Marcus, who monitored domestic hate groups for the Anti-Defamation League (ADL), agreed. "The technology has made it so simple. It has become easier and easier for people to put up a Web site and make it look good. The National Socialist movement will host you on their Web site and provide you help putting one up" (B. Marcus, personal communication, March 5, 2008).

While society has embraced the Internet for positive purposes, it also has remained the perfect tool for communication among far-flung racist young people, mostly out of the oversight of parents, teachers, or anyone who might disapprove. The concern continues to focus on such organizations as Stormfront, run by Don Black, a convicted federal felon; groups affiliated with regional or national Ku Klux Klan (KKK) chapters; neo-Nazi groups advocating white power and anti-Semitism; and even homeschooling sites with tips for raising proud, white, racialist children. Locations that are less overt about racism bring more moderate white women into the white racialist movement. The KKK is no longer a major force in American culture, but there are still between 6,000 and 8,000 Klan members nationally (Garland, 2008). "The pervasive nature of the Internet not only opened the Klan up to new audiences, but also changed the Klan's identity—the invisible empire was suddenly able to become visible and tout its separatist message without raising public indignation," writes the *New Zealand Herald*'s Christopher Garland (2008, para. 16). Pastor Thom Robb, leader of one of the largest KKK organizations in the United States, told Garland that the media used to carry the Klan's message willingly. "But we don't really need the media anymore—that's the absolute truth. The only thing we need is the Internet" (Garland, 2008, para. 17).

The Klan is not alone among hate groups in discovering the utility of new media. All manner of extremist thought is espoused on the Web, and these voices are commingled in a poisonous soup with the latest jihadist groups seeking America's destruction. Unlike the domestic groups discussed in this chapter, the jihadist groups are primarily located overseas, with an occasional appearance in the United States. A recent example is revolutionmuslim.com, run by a (possibly unstable) lone New York City cab driver and former orthodox Jew named Yousef al-Khattab (once Joseph Cohen). The site is no joke but contains a shocking video mocking the beheading of Daniel Pearl, a picture of the Statue of Liberty with an axe in her side, and a video lampooning U.S. soldiers killed in Iraq. A day after Fox News reported on the Pearl video, it was accessible on the site only if a visitor registered (March 28, 2008). In contrast to loner Khattab, organized overseas Middle Eastern extremists such as al-Qaeda, Hamas, and Hezbollah all maintain their own media subsidiaries. Al-Qaeda's al-Sahab media branch not only releases content to the news media, it now delivers policy statements, criticisms of the majority of moderate Muslims, conducts interviews, and disseminates tactical instructions in a variety of ways, including on the Web. Just recently, al-Qaeda's number two, Ayman al-Zawahiri, posted a 90-minute audio statement directly to the Internet defending the group's specific attacks and any civilian deaths. It came in response to some 900 questions posted by users between December 2007 and January 2008 on radical jihadist forums linked to the group. "I would like to thank those who responded to the open debate with me by our production arm al-Sahab and in particular those who operate within the media Jihad" (Adnkronos International, 2008, para. 20).

In mid-September 2008, however, the ability of al-Qaeda to use the Web freely suffered a major blow when four of five online sites used to disseminate the organization's messages and images were disabled—possibly by U.S. and British efforts (Knickmeyer, E., Washington Post Foreign Service, October 18, 2008). "On Sept. 29, a statement by the al-Fajr Media Center, a distribution network created by supporters of al-Qaeda and other Sunni extremist groups, said the forums had disappeared 'for technical reasons,' and it urged followers not to trust look-alike sites." This could indicate that intelligence agencies are scoring key victories in cyberspace: "these sites are the equivalent of pentagon.mil, whitehouse.gov, att.com," said Evan F. Kohlmann, an expert on online al-Qaeda operations who has advised the FBI and others. With just one authorized al-Qaeda site still in business, "this has left al-Qaeda's propaganda strategy hanging by a very narrow thread."

Yet the Web continues to offer myriad chances for militant groups to give like-minded supporters chances to share video content. The latest example comes from Hamas and is modeled after YouTube, this time known as Aqsatube.com. The site glorifies terrorism and allows postings from other Palestinian terror groups, according to a *Jerusalem Post* story (Mizroch, 2008).

There is little evidence to suggest that neo-Nazi or pro-white, patriot groups are pooling forces with foreign terrorists because of their refusal to embrace suicide as a viable tactic (B. Marcus, personal communication, March 5, 2008). This is despite the fact that they share a common enemy: the Jew. "There have been actual conversations online between Jihadist extremists and neo-Nazis where the radical Jihadist extremist would say, 'Until you are ready to strap a bomb around yourself and blow yourself up, you are just talk.'"

Like their foreign counterparts, some American extremists have found their Web operations curtailed recently as well. In October 2008, federal agents arrested William White, a Roanoke-based white supremacist who leads the American Socialist Workers Party, temporarily disabling his Overthrow.com Web site. White was charged with obstruction of justice in connection to a 2004 case against Matt Hale, who was convicted of soliciting the murder of a federal judge (Hammack, L. October 19, 2008). Most recently White's Web site pictured Barack Obama, in the crosshairs of a rifle view made into a swastika under the headline "Kill this N—." White's Web site had also posted a home address of a juror in the case against Hale and personal information of African American youth involved in the Jena 6 case, along with abstract calls for lynching. A couple of days before the arrest, the Web site had been temporarily shut down and White's computer seized (Roanoke.com , October 17, 2008).

Despite events that have reduced the influence of white power media with the death of National Alliance leader Pierce and the placement of Hale behind bars, a vast array of Internet extremism still continues well into the first decade of the twenty-first century. A wide range of Web radicals in addition to white supremacists and al-Qaeda, currently include Hezbollah, Hamas, animal liberation and environmental militants, holocaust deniers, homophobes, black separatists, the Jewish Defense League, Islamophobes, xenophobes, and various conspiracy theorists . The Internet now contains sophisticated locations with detailed text and video instructions that teach visitors step-by-step how to commit assaults, arsons, and bombings for maximum violent effect. Today's global developments and technological innovations make worries of past years and past bad actors appear almost mild and part of a more innocent and trusting era.

So-called lone wolves who are unconnected, and often unstable, like Khattab or Hunt, Wiesel's stalker, act alone to achieve their twisted goals. Thus, law enforcement increasingly monitors words that are otherwise protected by the First Amendment, looking for the instant when they form a genuine plan for violence that justifies enforcement. This chapter examines the use of present-day technology by extremist groups that advocate white supremacy and convince young people that the cause is so important that it justifies breaking the law. The chapter traces the history of the use of new communication technology by extremists, describes the increased sophistication of Web sites run by groups advocating hate, and discusses their use of implicit rhetoric and slick graphics that mimic the multimedia approaches used by more legitimate entities. There is much evidence that these sites deliberately employ such techniques to appeal to a wider audience of young people who have access to computers and money to spend on white power music, Nazi memorabilia, T-shirts, and other items.

The chapter focuses on white supremacist groups because they have made documented efforts from the earliest days of the Internet to reframe their social movement's image, maintain unifying principles, and reeducate other whites using new media in ways that were later used by others (Burris, Smith, & Strahm, 2000; Schroer, 2001). The methods used by white racist Internet sites to attract youth to extreme right-wing politics include video games (Anti-Defamation League [ADL], 2002), white power music, and interpersonal recruitment, particularly by skinheads (Burris et al., 2000). This chapter calls for the close examination of these Internet sites because the technology has developed into a powerful tool, with young people continually adopting it easily and naturally, often much more rapidly than adults (Katz, 2000; Tapscott, 1998; Wallace, 1999). This also means that young people may gain a false sense of competence, control, and belief in the authority of sites that actually have low factual value. The interactive nature of the computer can be seductive in a personal way. Young people use their experiences, virtual and real, to inform their adult lives. The nature of the Internet is well suited to high-risk organizations because the technology can bring scattered racists together instantly for debate, dialogue, and planning. Web sites themselves serve as promotional tools, while many contain encryption devices, requiring users to register and enter codes each time they take part in particular activities for optimal privacy. Often, they create forums that allow people to send messages to one another in private, making it more difficult for law enforcement.

Former skinhead T. J. Leyden called for more regulation of the Internet, despite its legal status as a town square, with the greatest First Amendment protection possible (ACLU v. Reno, 2000). There must be "categories" on the World Wide Web similar to those in public libraries so that young people can verify the validity of what they are seeing and reading. "There is no reason a person should be allowed to pretend they are a doctor and write about breast cancer on the Internet, when they have no credentials," said Leyden (personal communication, March 21, 2008). "On YouTube, there's no librarian," he said.

Leyden further observed,

> Propaganda spinners like Tom Metzger and Louis Farrakhan are alongside a Harvard PhD who has studied the Holocaust and been to Auschwitz. A kid may decide, I like one of those first guys better. White racist music is not labeled as associated with the neo-Nazi movement, and a kid may like the tune so that it becomes a stepping-stone.

The military can be a breeding ground for white supremacy, agreed both Leyden and Marcus. Marcus cited the case of Robert West, whose Web site was taken down because members of the U.S. military, unlike civilians, cannot engage actively in white supremacist groups by law. Marcus said some terrorist groups provide users with cyberterrorism software programs that will infiltrate sites of Jewish groups or other targets. White supremacists are as dangerous as many foreign terrorists, Leyden said. They are engaged in such activities as drug and gun running and murder sprees—but reside here.

Ken Stern (2001–2002), an expert on anti-Semitism with the American Jewish Committee, argued that hate Web sites augment alternative means when it comes to recruitment. His article in the *Journal of Hate Studies* points to past communication methods employed by hate groups: fliers on windshield wipers, books, newspapers, magazines, and newsletters. In the 1980s and early 1990s, the organizations used videotapes, radio shows, and dial-a-hate messages from hotline answering machines. Now these groups use all of the above methods, but more often, they have turned to the Internet, using it as a portal or entry point for other media. According to Stern (2001–2002),

> hate groups understand that this global computer network is far superior to the other modes of communication. . . . The Internet is the most remarkable communication advancement of our time because it is easier, cheaper, quicker, multimedia, immense and interactive. Hate groups no longer have to search for people to hear their message or hope members will distribute newsletters. They now can set up websites that surfers young and old can visit. (p. 58)

Schroer (2001) argues that these hate sites cannot compete with "the overwhelming majority of messages that are presenting their organizations as hate-based, ignorant, violent and the like" (p. 227). Back, Keith, and Solomos (1998) write that

> the numbers of people involved in ultra rightwing nationalist movements are relatively small in most societies. What is significant about the Internet is that it possesses the potential to offer these small, geographically dispersed movements a means to communicate, develop a sense of common purpose and create a virtual home symbolically. (p. 98)

The combination of white supremacists' use of new media, young people's propensity to be early adopters of such technology, and teenagers' struggle to find their place in the world may provide hate groups with a widening window of opportunity to gain young people's attention and potential loyalty by multiple methods.

The intent of this chapter is not to encourage public fears about offensive speech, but to warn against complacency. After discussing particular Web sites, this chapter will explore the historical roots of media use by white supremacists. Hate groups are employing new modalities and addressing a wealthier audience, but it would be a mistake to believe that their messages are also new. On the contrary, white supremacy is deeply rooted in American popular ideology. While many have gotten more skilled at the use of html style sheets, Flash 8, and the posting of video and streaming audio content, these Internet sites often post the same racist and anti-Semitic tracts that have been spread since the eugenics movement declared that blacks were genetically inferior to whites in the early twentieth century and since Henry Ford launched a bitter campaign against Jews using the *Dearborn Independent* in 1920. The problem white supremacists face is that this is not 1925, when the Klan's popularity peaked. The social and historical context has dramatically shifted so that these groups are employing modern techniques to disseminate old hatreds. Today's social context, in which both a woman and an African American sought the U.S. presidency in 2008 and a woman was nominated for Vice President, may provide a springboard for adults to educate young people about the importance of diversity and tolerance.

Hate organizations now see a chance for validation in the virtual world when they are unable to win credibility elsewhere (Berlet, 2001; Lee & Leets, 2002; Levin, 2002; Stern, 2001–2002). The sites contain "libraries" that purport to offer the truth to the Internet's users. An early indication of hate groups' capacity to reach young people was apparent a decade ago in a CNN/Time survey of 13- to 17-year-olds. The survey determined that 44 percent of American teenagers had seen Web sites that were X-rated or had sexual content, 25 percent had seen sites with information about hate groups, 14 percent had seen sites with information about how to build bombs, and 12 percent had seen Web sites that discussed how or where to buy a gun. At the same time, 62 percent said their parents knew little or nothing about the Internet sites they visited (Okrent, 1999).

While teens may be better able than younger children to distinguish between legitimate and unfounded content, "some adolescents appear to take Internet content at face value, suggesting the potential for an immediate message effect," contend Stanford communication researchers Elisa Lee and Laura Leets (2002, p. 927). Their work provides an argument for hate speech restrictions that is blunted by their own finding that most teens they studied saw hate Web sites as not particularly convincing.

Experts disagree not only about the impact of hate Web sites, but also about their actual numbers. The Simon Wiesenthal Center in Los Angeles currently documents the largest number of "problematic" sites at 7,000—more than twice what the organization found in 2001. The result gets criticized, though, for being too broad and inclusive. It includes not only Web sites, but also blogs, newsgroups, YouTube, and other on-demand video sites, and not only pro-white groups but also antigay and antiabortion groups, along with jihadist terror groups. Earlier versions of the annual report cite a growing use of the Internet as "a key propaganda weapon, marketing tool and fundraising engine" by groups including al-Qaeda and Hamas. "Highlights include powerful terrorist videos that recruit young people into the horrific culture of death and Hate on Demand—two flash movies tracing the evolution of how hate and terror groups have manipulated and leveraged the web to promote their agendas" (Web advertisement for the group's *Digital Terrorism* CD, 2007). "The Internet has become as real a battlefield as exists anyplace. It provides a haven and an opportunity for Islamist extremists to recruit, educate, communicate and bond in a secure, protected environment. As a result, in many ways it is the prime factor in the radicalization of many of recruits to the jihadi ideology," said Mark Weitzman, director of the Simon Wiesenthal Center's Task Force against Hate and Terrorism (Weitzman, 2007).

The Southern Poverty Law Center (SPLC) found that the number of hate groups in America grew 5 percent in 2007 to 888. The increase was 48 percent since 2000. Although SPLC's numbers are more narrowly focused, the problems of definition persist. Critics question how Simon Wiesenthal arrives at its estimates, even given the fact that the report includes more than just traditional white supremacists. Marcus is skeptical about the group's method of calculation and any effort to definitively count hate Web sites. SPLC counted 643 U.S.-based hate Web sites in 2007, as opposed to 566 a year earlier. "There are thousands of sites, and internationally, there's an increase, but there is no accurate way of assessing the number of hate sites," Marcus said. "These are just what they can find" (B. Marcus, personal communication, March 5, 2008).

The inroads of hate groups on the Internet come at a time when youth have unprecedented media access. Kraut and colleagues (1998) initially found that young people using the Internet suffered increased isolation, but the results of follow-up studies (Kraut et al., 2002) are less alarming about the Internet's impact, demonstrating that only isolated teens increase their isolation, while extroverts experience greater social benefits. A digital divide—at least initially—appeared to work in favor of white supremacists because Internet penetration was at first strongest among ,wealthier white families. See Table 12.1 for a count of racist Web sites on the Internet.

A SAMPLING OF KEY HATE SITES

Hate sites have taken on the sophistication of legitimate entryways, and they often try to fool visitors looking for other sites by mislabeling theirs as Britney Spears on YouTube, so they can gain access to people who would not otherwise encounter them, according to Marcus. Most Web sites of white supremacists suggest that the whites they target need only be exposed to the wisdom of their textual arguments and compelling images to be brought to a higher level of understanding that the majority, brainwashed by mainstream media and the multicultural education system, somehow lack. In that way, white supremacists invent their potential audience. As such, the images and text of their Web sites are powerful to the extent that they dupe some into believing what they are seeing is socially acceptable or forward thinking.

Table 12.1   Charting Selected Hate Websites Active in 2007

Hate group	Number of sites
Ku Klux Klan	64
Racist skinhead	30
Neo-Nazi	92
Neo-Confederate	31
White nationalist	201
Black separatist	33
General hate	155
Antigay	19
Racist music sites	24
Other	112
Christian identity	37
Total	643

Source: Southern Poverty Law Center, "The Year in Hate," *Intelligence Report*, Spring 2008, pp. 59–65.

"There's still a lot of disorganization in white supremacist and far-right groups," said Marcus. "Pierce died. Hale is behind bars, so there aren't any strong leaders, but there are more groups and more people are joining, particularly around such issues as immigration," he explained. There might be slow periods brought on by the death or jailing of a leader, but now the groups are reorganizing and building backup, Marcus noted. Web sites may be hard to locate or unstable, moving servers regularly, or be forced out of commission, only to reappear.

By September 2008, prompted by calls from Senator Joseph Lieberman and others, YouTube banned terrorism training videos and other extremist videos that incite others to perpetrate violent acts, but with 13 hours of new video uploaded every few minutes, the effort is virtually impossible and the Google-run video sharing site relies on its users to report problematic videos (Sullivan, 2008). Although YouTube is large and popular, it represents a tiny slice of video content on the Web worldwide. Marcus said and cited www.88tube.net as an example of a problematic site (Personal communication, B. Marcus October 13, 2008).

Stormfront

With more than 120,000 members and 4 million individual posts, Stormfront (http://www.stormfront.org) is the largest and oldest hate Web site. Its specialty is its forums, which allow users to communicate with one another, but the site also has streaming radio links, newslinks, and a daily schedule that includes a talk show by organizer Don Black, a convicted federal felon and former KKK leader, and David Duke, also an ex-Klan leader. Users can hear Celtic music and talks on Irish culture, Norwegian beauty, and Islam, among other topics. Members post dating advice, write about upcoming events, and meet other white singles. They read about poetry, politics and theology. Young people form white nationalist school clubs and find others who agree with them in their community. Stormfront, in part to limit liability risk, makes some attempt to monitor its users and those too extreme may find themselves ousted. Black explains on the site, "Do not suggest any activity which is illegal under U.S. law," and then goes on to list a host of other requirements, including no profanity or racial epithets and "no personal flames" or attacks. A town hall talk by Duke and Black suggests that white people must preserve their race or risk becoming a minority (Stormfront post retrieved on March 17, 2008 http://www.stormfront.org/forum/). Anti-hate activists and law enforcement also monitor the site to find potential problems. The site has expanded its technology and contains international links but also has some stagnant and inactive pages.

Many of the content items are simply the same old tracts that white supremacists have used for years to promote their vision (albeit with easy Web shopping carts and the use of Pay Pal). There are still pieces that have not been updated in years, including http://stormfront.org/kids, posted by Don Black's son Derek, who says he's 15 on the site but now is an adult. "I used to be in public school," he writes. "It is a shame how many White people are wasted in that system. I am now in home school. I am no longer attacked by gangs of non-whites and I spend my day learning, instead of tutoring the slowest kids in my class." In late March 2008, near Easter, the site still bid visitors a happy Halloween and contained a link to a discussion of the history of the October holiday.

It is interesting to note that resist.com, operated by White Aryan Resistance (WAR), which, in 2002, used to be the least technologically adept site among the hate movement locations, is now improving its technique with moving flames of Flash 8. It met the definition of a first-generation site and was "linear" and "barebones functional" in its early years (as defined by David Siegel's *Creating Killer Web Sites*, 1997). Its keywords for the page in an html style sheet still include such tricks that will take search engine users to the site when they enter the names of antihate organizations like Simon Wiesenthal Center, SPLC, Morris Dees, ADL, and Morris Casuto, an ADL leader in San Diego. John Malpezzi, who arranges media for Tom Metzger, claimed that the expansion of resist.com is a function of Metzger's personality, which he optimistically claims attracts 10 million hits a month to the site, with an Internet radio show. Malpezzi called Stormfront "a minor concern" and "no big deal." He criticized the fact that Stormfront even could point to its high membership, saying, "Would you want to be a member of anything because if you are, the FBI is monitoring you. If Homeland Security doesn't like what you are saying, you've got problems buddy. Why don't you just check into jail right now and forget about the membership fee?" (J. Malpezzi, personal communication, March 14, 2008). Metzger espouses a fierce brand of racism and is known as a principal mentor of the neo-Nazi skinhead movement. In 1988, he was implicated in fomenting a fatal attack by Portland skinheads on an Ethiopian immigrant that led to a multimillion-dollar civil judgment against him. His legal troubles continued in 1991 for his involvement in a Los Angeles cross lighting and in 1995 for the bulk distribution of racist fliers to supermarkets. Metzger is a major advocate of lone wolf theory, which favors individual or small-cell racist violence (ADL, 2001).

Such sites as Metzger's are extremely dangerous and need to be watched closely by Homeland Security and other law enforcement agencies, according to Leyden, who himself has had WAR encourage followers to pursue him as a "race traitor," listing on the Web the schedule and locations of his speaking engagements against hate.

At Resistance (http://www.resistance.com), run by the neo-Nazi National Alliance, visitors could hear and order white power music as well as sample disturbing video games, read interviews with white power bands, and examine a racist comic book called *White Will* (resistance.com, February 23, 2002). This was all prior to the death of National Alliance leader William Pierce on July 23, 2002 (Retrieved from www.natall.com, April 3, 2008). The Resistance Records site is now less visually appealing. It used to feature Pierce as he spoke about race, the economy, and the 1993 standoff between the Branch Davidians and the Federal Bureau of Investigation (FBI) near Waco, Texas. Pierce wrote *The Turner Diaries* under the pseudonym Andrew Macdonald (1978), about an antigovernment militant who instigated a violent race war. The novel inspired Oklahoma City bomber Timothy McVeigh and the terrorist group the Order in the 1980s. The controversial tract is for sale on the National Alliance Web site, along with the magazine *Resistance*. The site used to compete for teenagers' attention and capitalize on commonly used marketing methods, bringing the company $1.3 million in annual sales before Pierce's death (Hirschorn M. & Tatro S., 2002). By 2008, newsgroups of the National Alliance discussed the politics of the presidential race, particularly the progress of Barack Obama and the trouble he faced from his controversial former pastor Reverend Jeremiah Wright (Retrieved from natall.com, March 19, 2008).

It is not a simplistic, cause-effect relationship, but there is no escaping the fact that the media, as pervasive as they are, have significant sway with the young. Resistance Records is still America's leading supplier of racist music and runs the influential racist Web site resistance.com. There teens and others may purchase white power rock music CDs with racist and violent lyrics that encourage the purported struggle for white rights. Viewers can take the bolder step of subscribing to *Resistance* magazine or attending a concert. The site says that Pierce was a workaholic on behalf of pro-European causes who kept up an 80-hour-a-week schedule before cancer claimed him. While still sophisticated and functional, the site no longer has the look and feel of an old Tower Records aisle that used to appeal to youth. The graphic design is much more basic. It used to play up interviews with top white power music figures and include extensive marketing about why particular young people chose white power music. Now its simplicity may have something to do with Pierce's death and the arrest of a subsequent leader, which have contributed to an erosion in membership of its owner, the National Alliance.

The cautionary note for those worried about young people uncritically embracing hateful rhetoric on the Web is that there is widespread agreement among scholars about the inadequacy of the "effects," or hypodermic needle concept, of media influence (Gauntlett, 1998). Too many factors mitigate the direct path of racist propaganda, from the computer screen to a child's brain, including the content of the message, its repetition, and individual children's upbringing and educational background, to name a few. "The Internet certainly does provide individuals access to the views and ideas of 'extreme' groups, but to say the web had been the main mover in turning a nice young person into a hate-filled killer might just seem to be attributing a bit too much power and autonomy to a bunch of web pages, which are little different in their 'power' to a pile of leaflets" (p. 1). Other scholars, including David Buckingham (2000), discuss children as skeptical consumers of media products, not as innocent dupes.

Plenty of newer racist groups have joined the white racialist fold now and include Northeast White Pride, or NEWP.org, based in Haverhill, Massachusetts, near Boston. The Web site is listed by SPLC as one of 643 racist Web sites active in 2007 (Southern Poverty Law Center, 2008). The group is listed as one of the sites that "actively promotes hate beyond the mere publishing of Internet material" (SPLC, 2008, p. 59). The site has video clips meant to prove the point that all black people want to kill whites and offers free Web hosting, so that members can have their own sites. There are no dues or requirements to join. The organization targets people who live in the Northeast and share similar views and maintains that users may face fewer restrictions than at Stormfront. However, those with racist views also might favor the more extreme NSM88.com, the most technically sophisticated site among the white racialist locations, according to Internet analyst Marcus. The organization touts itself as "dedicated to the preservation of our proud European heritage and the creation of a Nationalist Socialist Society in America and around the world" (http://www.nsm88.org/index2.html, p. 1). Users can easily click on and purchase white racist music, listen to sounds of a 2008 book burning, watch rally videos, and donate money to the cause. There is a P.O. box that traces the headquarters of the organization to Detroit, Michigan. Offerings include Nuke Israel, immigration in the United States and United Kingdom, and video footage of a National Socialist Movement rally in Washington, D.C. One headline reads, "Sub-prime Mortgages: How the Jew Banks Screwed America." The Web site says that membership is open to all Aryans over age 18 and that those under 18 can join the Viking Youth Movement.

One early hate site noticeably missing from the Web is wcotc.com, formerly run by Matt Hale, former head of the now defunct World Church of the Creator. The group gained attention for the violent acts of its members. A 1999 decision by the state of Illinois to reject Hale's application for a law license due to his past conduct is widely thought to have helped trigger a murderous shooting spree by his follower Benjamin Smith, in which two people were killed and nine injured (ADL, 2001). Hale was convicted of one count of solicitation of murder and three counts of obstruction of justice in April 2004. Hale's creativity movement espoused the view that the white race is nature's highest creation and that nonwhites are mud races and natural enemies. Ironically, the wcotc domain is now run by a progressive religious order that features a star of David on its display.

One more sophisticated site is Sigrdrifa (http://www.sigrdrifa.net), which provides advice to homeschooling parents seeking to raise proud white racialists. The site demonstrates the desire of racists to ensure that racism will last. According to the homepage,

> In this day and age, European culture is fading into history, and all the beauty, uniqueness, and tradition is quickly being stripped away. Not only European culture is suffering, all culture is fading. Mono-culture and consumerism is the new culture to replace all cultures. As dismal as things seem, there is hope. Although we cannot save all, Sigrdrifa is here to ensure that our unique and beautiful European heritage is preserved for future generations. (http://www.sigrdrifa.net/about.shtml)

The site is clever and crafty but not as multimedia-focused as some of the others directed at young people. It is more concerned with crafts, age-appropriate heritage games, and other activities for homeschooling parents of young children. A September 2000 newsletter stated Sigrdrifa's philosophy in a veiled way, making a play for the mainstream mother that might lean toward racist views but reject overt racism:

> There is massive amounts [*sic*] of educational materials out there for our children. Anything from Rudyard Kipling to various books on a number of Folkish interests such as the Vikings or Celtic life can be found at the library or bookstores. There might not be books out there that would teach a child the more common (and stunted) politics of our movement; There might not be materials out there in which the characters use words like

"ni**er" etc.; But that is as it should be. Neither of those things are concepts for our kids to ingest. (Sigrdrifa.net September 2000)

Criticizing the movement as stunted and downgrading the use of an ethnic
slur against blacks around children are two obvious attempts to bring more
moderate white women into the white racialist fold. Amid the plethora of mundane parenting material, how would a less astute parent know that this site was
problematic? Such a parent would definitely need to scrutinize the site closely.
After all, a search engine for the lyrics of "Wheels on the Bus" brings up this
site, among others. More reliable information might be gleaned from the fish
food notices at the side of the main page. However, in April 2002, the poster
seemed innocuous, honoring Scottish heritage, another method of constructing
the meaning of whiteness. The month before, unsuspecting visitors could have
found a less stealthy message. The poster on one side of the page, with its fiery
V, was for Volksfront, which professes "neither love nor hate for other cultures"
but seeks "nothing less than a complete and self-sufficient European-American
community." Where everyone else in America should go is left unsaid. Toward
that end, *folk building* is described as the process of creating and maintaining
"our own self-reliant economic structure." In other words, the site employed a
number of implicit messages, saying its goals are not hateful, but at the same
time, it claimed the group wanted to carry on the dream of "patriots like Robert
Matthews," former head of the defunct terrorist group, The Order, which murdered Jewish radio talk show host Alan Berg in Denver among other crimes.
Matthews died in a fiery Washington State gun battle with the FBI in 1984.
Today, Volksfront International at http://www.volksfrontinternational.com/ is
a bit more guarded but positions itself as "at the forefront of the struggle for
White autonomy, White self-determination, and the issues of the White work-
ing class" (retrieved from the organizations homepage on December 12, 2008).
Still, an uncritical parent might have no idea of these facts. A quicker way to
understand the racist leanings of the group making the Web site would be to
determine its allegiances by looking at the Web ring to which it subscribes.
This one, created in March 2002, connects to other racist groups, including the
Southern White Knights of the KKK. Randy Blazak of the Oregon Spotlight, an
antihate group in Portland, Oregon, said that the woman who organizes homeschooling in Washington State for Sigrdrifa also is a member of Volksfront (R.
Blazak, personal communication, April 29, 2002). The current site is not as
complete or current as it was in 2002 and includes a message asking visitors to
"excuse the mess—this website is constantly under revision" (March 22, 2008).

Former skinhead Leyden believed that the Internet has, in the twenty-
first century, become such a popular vehicle for white supremacists that it
has surpassed the appeal of white power music alone. "We have a generation
of MTV kids, and for them, visuals are just as important as audio, and these
websites have dripping blood, they have things that come popping out at you.

It's all multimedia, and a lot of these sites are on the cutting edge." (Leyden, T.J., Personal communications, February 21, 2002, March 21, 2008. This comment by Leyden was during the first interview, when the hate groups were also experimenting with the Internet.)

In Leyden's view, even early Internet recruitment stabilized the white power movement and helped it grow, removing the traditional barriers of space and time. "When you had a kid in Sioux City, Iowa, a kid in Lincoln, Nebraska, a kid in Billings, Montana, these kids if they were lucky got together once a year at an Aryan festival or got together every once in a great while at a concert. These kids now get together constantly, every night on the Internet (Personal Communication with Leyden, 2002).

Hal Turner Show

The New Jersey Web radio show host was among the most virulent racists in America and often suggested killing his enemies. He threatened the life of President Bush, saying, "A well-placed bullet can solve a lot of problems." He also suggested shooting and killing Mexicans as they cross the border and called for killing several judges. However, Hal Turner's Web site (http://www.halturnershow.com) was removed from the Internet when his cover was given away as an informant by a hacker who had found his communications with an FBI agent. Both Turner and the FBI declined comment in an *Intelligence Report* story (Potok, 2008). Almost as soon as the controversial Web site with streaming audio resurfaced, Turner was in trouble again. In response to a Lexington, Massachusetts, superintendent's presentation of a new, more inclusive K–6 curriculum that included gay parents, Turner said,

> I would laugh if some concerned fathers donned ski masks and gloves, took a ride over to this arrogant prick's house and knocked the living shit out of him. I advocate parents using force and violence against Superintendent Paul B. Ash as a method of defending the health and safety of schoolchildren presently being endangered through his politically correct indoctrination into deadly, disease-ridden sodomite lifestyles. ("Honest Talk in a Time of Universal Deceit," www.halturnershow.com retrieved April 4, 2008)

The methods Turner has used, ostensibly to expose violent extremists, were questioned by critics, who said that Turner's extreme rhetoric was an attempt to instigate criminal acts. The Web site section on the superintendent was no different in that it also printed photos of Ash and several of his last known addresses.

HISTORY OF HATE CAMPAIGNS AND MEDIA USE

While new actors have surfaced, what white supremacists seek is not a new America, but an old one that accepts racism and regards tolerance or multiculturalism with resentment. Racist ideologies are still embedded in mainstream society and in the stereotypes of media production, fueling interest in politicians like David Duke, for instance, but they are significantly less prevalent today than in earlier periods. It is important to examine the historical roots of American racism to understand the long-standing intentions of its white supremacists. The original KKK was a right-wing populist entity that followed the left-leaning Jacksonian progressive movement, to uphold the rights of the common man, but it also denounced the federal central banking system and sought the violent expulsion of Native Americans from their land (Berlet & Lyons, 2000). This popular strain in American politics provides a foundation for diverse grassroots citizen movements, including the Klan, the militias, and the Christian Right, contends Berlet and Lyon's *Right-Wing Populism in America*. The rise of both progressivism and populist thought has had a great deal to do with the breakdown of the nation's homogeneous nature, according to Richard Hofstadter (1966) in *The Age of Reform*. Up until 1880, America was rural, Yankee, and Protestant, and the immigrant population was too small to have an appreciable effect on civic life. Americans still had an attachment to what Hofstadter refers to as "the agrarian myth" or "a kind of homage that Americans have paid to the fancied innocence of their origins" (Hofstadter, 1966, p. 2). Yet Hofstadter refers to the coexistence of reform with reaction. This historical legacy lent white supremacy much of its psychic power and mainstream support.

Today, this legacy persists, but with racism more covert, the Internet is used as a tool by a more discreet and scheming set of white supremacists. Examining the ideas of white supremacists and their creation of virtual spaces on the World Wide Web involves investigating earlier media use during the historical periods in which their views have enjoyed the greatest popular appeal, particularly the early twentieth century, when new immigrants created unforeseen tensions and the second KKK was in its peak. Ideas of white Protestant superiority have been ingredients of America since its first days.

Nancy MacLean (1994), in *Behind the Mask of Chivalry*, describes the broad appeal of the Klan in the 1920s, when as many as 5 million white men signed up, the most ever. It was "a form of populism that combined hostility to established elites with dedication to white supremacy, support for conservative family values, enthusiasm for 'old-time religion' and antipathy to welfare recipients, trade unionists, immigrants, liberals and leftists" (pp. xi–xii). The campaign of the Klan in those years resonated not with single or unemployed white men, an idea espoused in some other scholarly reports, but with the very foundation of the Georgia communities that MacLean studied, namely, highly respected, solidly middle-class citizens, including church-going and civic-minded shop owners, ministers, politicians, and law enforcement officers. Berlet and Lyons (2000) agree with MacLean's (1994) assessment that the second Klan attracted ordinary people:

Despite widespread popular rhetoric, it is neither accurate nor useful to portray right-wing populists as a "lunatic fringe" of marginal "extremists." Right-wing populists are dangerous not because they are crazy irrational zealots—but because they are not. These people may be our neighbors, our co-workers and our relatives. (p. 3)

In this way, the Internet must be viewed as part of American society, not as a threatening, foreign element outside of it, and its ideological risks must be considered based on the successes and failures of past media campaigns using technologies that were new at the time.

Georgia was the birthplace and national headquarters of the second KKK. As farms suffered from economic blight and the federal government expanded, the success of African Americans moving north as well as Harlem radicalism inspired fear and loathing in conservative white southerners, MacLean (1994) shows. She painstakingly details how William J. Simmons, the second Klan's founder, reinvigorated the organization—with the help of the media— by hiring marketers Mary Elizabeth Tyler and Edward Young Clarke of the Southern Publicity Association. Within months, membership swelled from a few thousand to 100,000. Tyler expertly diffused an early scandal, the *New York World's* investigation that tied the Klan to 150 incidents of violent vigilantism and prompted a congressional investigation. Tyler turned this messy situation into a mass recruiting opportunity, and membership increased to 1 million, with 200 new chapters. Particularly, the two marketers built on the postwar fears of white men. The group railed against organized blacks, Jews, Roman Catholics, and Bolshevism, declaring itself a defender of American purity and patriotism, traditional religion and morality. The Klan pledged to fight challenges to the rights and privileges of people who were of the same stock as America's founders. MacLean (1994) writes,

> The message took. Although Tyler and Clarke had expected only South-erners to respond, men from all over the country did. "In all my years of experience in organization work," Clarke told Simmons, "I have never seen anything equal to the clamor across the nation for the Klan." (p. 6)

Thus white supremacists learned early that the media were a critical factor in their support or marginalization.

The Klan also capitalized on a fundamental facet of American life at the most successful point in its history—the popularity of more than 600 secret, fraternal organizations, which had a membership of more than 30 million by the mid-1920s. Americans were joiners. The Junior Order of United American Mechanics (JOUAM), an anti-Catholic nativist group, shared its weekly publication, *The Searchlight*, with the Klan, until the Klan took it over in 1923. MacLean (1994) notes that members of JOUAM included President Warren

Harding. Among those who shared members with the Klan were such trusted American social organizations as the Shriners, the Elks, and the Masons, among others. It is an embarrassing truth of the nation's history that Protestant clergymen were often respected Klan members. This type of mainstream support was no accident. The Klan reveled in the rewards of its media savvy. Its outreach included the formation of a national lecture bureau, which addressed audiences of more than 200,000, according to MacLean. These public addresses were bolstered by a Klan press that, in addition to the national publications, included 40 weekly newspapers produced by state and local KKK chapters. Clearly, then, the Klan has not always been an organization to gawk at when a handful of marchers paraded down main street. Instead, it has stood at the core of American life. In Athens, Georgia, MacLean shows, the Klan was made up of family men, a three-term mayor and a tax receiver, a county commissioner and a justice of the peace, as well as the president of the Lions Club.

The call for this second Klan first came not from Simmons, the self-appointed grand wizard, but Tom Watson, a leader of the Georgia populist movement of the 1890s. In *The Age of Reform*, Hofstadter (1966) quotes Watson as fueling nativist prejudices and antimanufacturer sentiment:

> We have become the world's melting pot. The scum of creation has been dumped on us. Some of our principal cities are more foreign than American. The most dangerous and corrupting hordes of the Old World have invaded us. The vice and crime which they have planted in our midst are sickening and terrifying. What brought these Goths and Vandals to our shores? The manufacturers are mainly to blame. They wanted cheap labor and they didn't care a curse how much harm to our future might be the consequence of their heartless policy. (pp. 82–83)

By 1915, anti-Semitic sentiment was running high, and vigilantes kidnapped and hanged Leo Frank, a Jewish factory supervisor whose death sentence had been commuted by the Georgia governor in the murder of Mary Phagan, one of Frank's white employees. MacLean (1994) and others, including Levin (2002), have pointed out that during 1915, Simmons painstakingly orchestrated the KKK's second revival so that it would happen at the same time as the release of the racist and pro-Confederate *Birth of a Nation*, the world's first, full-length feature film. Simmons held a rally and cross burning ceremony a week before opening night and must have been pleased that an Atlanta newspaper ran his ad for "The World's Greatest Secret, Social, Patriotic and Beneficiary Order" directly alongside the advertisement for the movie (Chalmers, 1981).

The film was based on Thomas Dixon's 1905 bestseller, *The Clansman: An Historical Romance of the Ku Klux Klan*. MacLean (1994) writes,

> In this racist epic of the Civil War, Reconstruction and the restoration of white rule, [D. W.] Griffith harnessed all the emotive power of modern

film-making technique to convince viewers that black men were beasts and white vigilantes were the saviors of American civilization. Given the right to vote and hold office, the film averred, African-American men dragged society into chaos; worse, they used such power to stalk white women. Griffith left no doubt about how this fate had been averted. In the final climactic scene the hooded and robed members of the Ku Klux Klan rode in to save his young white heroine from rape by castrating and lynching her black, would-be assailant. (pp. 12–13)

The Klan, in another move that showed the value of the media to the organization, made repeated use of this film to recruit new members over the years, for, as Walter Lippmann (as cited in MacLean, 1994) remarked in 1922, "No one who has seen the film will ever hear the name [Ku Klux Klan] again without seeing those white horsemen" (p. 13).

The Klan has always been distinct in that it has painted itself as an army, ready to do battle to save the white race from its otherwise inevitable extinction, ready to defend America as the Klan defined it. The Web sites of a variety of white supremacist groups contain this same age-old anxiety, as they issue a call for RAHOWA (or Racial Holy War). White supremacy grew strong as America became less isolated and increasingly less homogeneous, moving from the agricultural life to an industrial one; women secured the right to vote; and Woodrow Wilson moved to form the League of Nations. White supremacy appeared to be more tenuous than ever so that Klan membership seemed something of a necessity to the white male mind. MacLean (1994) points to "the rise of divorce, feminism, black radicalism, white racial liberalism, and the post-war strike wave" as "the birth pangs of a new kind of social order" (p. 33) that threatened to erase the security of white males. Despite the fact that these phenomena have been with us for the better part of a century, Internet sites continue to capitalize on similar racist fears and add paranoia to the mix, wherever convenient. Klan membership proved particularly attractive to the lower middle class of the 1920s, who felt trapped between the demands of capitalism, including monopolies and high finance, and those of labor. Populist leaders like Watson provided support for these causes by adopting racist language against Jews, Roman Catholics, and other minorities. The typical Klansman was petit-bourgeois, a small property owner or skilled laborer, but also less economically secure for his class, MacLean argues. Hofstadter (1966) agrees with her evaluation that pro-white forces in society felt adrift both economically and socially: "The Anglo-Saxon Americans now felt themselves more than ever to be the representatives of a threatened purity of race and ideals, a threatened Protestantism, even a threatened integrity of national allegiance—for the war and its aftermath had awakened them to the realization that the country was full of naturalized citizens still intensely concerned with the politics of Europe and divided in their loyalties" (p. 292).

At the time that the Klan's influence had been rising, Henry Ford's anti-Semitic rantings in the *Dearborn Independent* marked another major attempt to sway American public sentiment against Jews using the tool of the media. Ford, who had purchased his weekly the previous year in 1919, ran a story titled "The International Jew: The World's Problem" on the front page of the May 20, 1920, edition. It reproduced the long-standing myth of a worldwide Jewish conspiracy. That article was based on the book *The Protocols of the Elders of Zion*, an invention of the Russian secret police at the turn of the twentieth century, which alleged that Jewish devils were plotting to undermine Christian civilization. The book was published in London in early 1920, with an American publisher's version titled *The Cause of World Unrest*. Both *The Protocols of the Elders of Zion* and Ford's writings are available on the Web sites of white supremacists today. Ford's initial offensive inaugurated 91 straight weeks of anti-Semitic articles, and such writings continued to appear sporadically until 1927, according to Leonard Dinnerstein's (1994) book *Anti-Semitism in America*. Interestingly, the stories are believed to have spurred the newspaper's circulation from an initial 72,000 copies weekly to a peak of 700,000 in 1924, just 50,000 copies fewer than the largest newspaper in circulation in the United States at the time, the *Daily News* in New York City (Dinnerstein, 1994). Some Klan Web sites still contain the complete International Jew series online as well as *The Protocols* and other notorious anti-Semitic readings.

Ford's series on the International Jew was a conscious attempt to "have some sensationalism" that would boost sales. A consultant had suggested capitalizing on growing anti-Semitic feeling in the United States. According to Dinnerstein (1994), Ford said he was

> only trying to awake the Gentile world to an understanding of what is going on. The Jew is a mere huckster, a trader who doesn't want to produce but to make something out of what somebody else produces. (p. 81)

In this, Ford's tone is imitated by white supremacist Web pages today, which claim they have special knowledge of looming disastrous consequences if Jews are allowed to continue imposing their poisonous liberal vision of the world on other Americans. "The outlandish tales of alleged Jewish vices were read by millions of Americans, mostly in rural areas, who knew little or nothing about Jews, except what they had already absorbed from religious teachings, gossip and *The Dearborn Independent*," Dinnerstein (1994, p. 81) writes. He traces Ford's anti-Semitic attitudes to his failure to convince the European powers to end World War I, which he blamed on Jewish radicalism.

By 1918, when he ran and was defeated as the Democratic nominee for U.S. senator from Michigan, Ford was blaming nearly everything that upset his political aspirations on Jews. Yet Ford's anti-Semitism did not damage his popularity with the American people, write Berlet and Lyons (2000): "In 1923 with his anti-Semitic views by then well-known, a national poll by *Collier's* magazine nonetheless listed Ford as the front-runner for president, 14 percentage points ahead of incumbent Warren G. Harding. 'Ford for President' clubs sprang up across the country" (p. 109).

According to the *Dearborn Independent* (as quoted in Dinnerstein, 1994),

> Most of big business, the trusts and the banks, the natural resources and the chief agricultural products, especially tobacco, cotton and sugar, are in the control of Jewish financiers or their agents. Jewish journalists are a large and powerful group here. "Large numbers of department stores are held by Jewish firms," says the Jewish Encyclopedia and many if not most of them are run under Gentile names. Jews are the largest and most numerous landlords of residence property in the country. They are supreme in the theatrical world. They absolutely control the circulations of publications throughout the country. Fewer than any race whose presence among us is noticeable, they receive daily an amount of favorable publicity which would be impossible did they not have the facilities for creating and distributing it themselves. (p. 82)

The attacks on the Jews and other ethnic groups were well received but did not win universal approval. Still, the International Jew is very important to understanding the history of hate in America. It is credited with influencing Adolf Hitler's *Mein Kampf,* another tract easily available on today's Internet. It can be purchased at resistance.com. "Hitler kept a picture of Ford on the wall of his office in Munich, praised the automobile magnate in *Mein Kampf,* and later told a *Detroit News* reporter, 'I regard Henry Ford as my inspiration,'?" writes Dinnerstein (1994, p. 83). "On Ford's 75th birthday in 1938, Hitler sent personal greetings and bestowed on him the highest honor the German government could grant a foreigner: the Grand Cross of the German Eagle" (Dinnerstein, 1994, p. 82).

Berlet and Lyons (2000) note that Ford's philosophy was an outgrowth of producerism, which defined white farmers and slave-owning planters as "productive," while bankers, monopolists, and people of color were not. Ford attacked "parasitic Jews," their financial conspiracy, and evil Wall Street. According to Hofstadter (1966), "It was chiefly Populist writers who expressed that identification of the Jew with the usurer and 'the international gold ring' which was the central theme of the American anti-Semitism of the age. From Thaddeus Stevens and Coin Harvey to Father [William] Coughlin, and from Brooks and Henry Adams to Ezra Pound, there has been a curiously persistent linkage between anti-Semitism and money and credit obsessions. . . . Henry Ford's notorious anti-Semitism of the 1920s, along with his hatred of 'Wall Street,' were the foibles of a Michigan farm boy who had been liberally exposed to Populist notions" (p. 81).

Ford's *Dearborn Independent* was by no means alone among the press in its anti-Semitic writings. Dinnerstein reports that Detroit newspapers as early as 1850 called Jews "mysterious," "cursed," and "wanderers." The April 6 issue of the *New York Herald* actually "ran a front-page story accusing Jews of bleeding a Christian missionary to death in the Middle East, grinding up his bones, and mixing his blood with unleavened bread for the Passover feast." Around Yom Kippur that year, rumors that Jews had killed a Gentile girl for the holiday prompted 500 men, led by the police, to vandalize a synagogue on the high holy day, according to Dinnerstein. Part of this receptivity, even a thirst, of Americans for such anti-Semitic fables had to do with the ancient myth of Jews' culpability for the murder of Christ and their rejection of Jesus as their savior. Such outrageous stories sound much like the words of the defunct World Church of the Creator's Matt Hale, who publicly has accused Jews of using the blood of babies for religious ceremonial purposes (Matt Hale, *Court TV*, July 1999, Brian Levin, personal communication, April 4, 2008). Jews were viewed as outsiders in America, and the contributions they made to the communities in which they settled were not to be praised, but distrusted, Dinnerstein argues. In fact, hatred of Jews has been incorporated into the English language as *jew* often has been used as a verb meaning "to bargain unfairly or cheat." The Jew, like the Shakespearean character Shylock in *The Merchant of Venice*, was supposed to lust after riches and gold (Dinnerstein, 1994).

The mainstream press—as well as advertising, popular literature, and cartoons—shared complicity for anti-Semitic feeling in this country, and anti-Semitic media appeals specifically targeting youth were a part of American popular tradition, starting with the public education system. McGuffey readers told schoolchildren that America was a Christian country. According to Dinnerstein (1994), "schoolbooks throughout America reiterated Protestant homilies while portraying Jews as crafty, greedy, dishonest, sly, selfish, unkind, unethical, disobedient and wicked. . . . Children learned how the Jews were the bitter enemies of the early Christians, that they rejected and killed the Savior and that even in the nineteenth century, they still denied their responsibility for the crucifixion of Jesus" (p. 18). Even Mother Goose rhymes, first published in England in the seventeenth century, expressed anti-Semitic sentiment meant for children's ears: "Jack sold his egg / To a rogue of a Jew / Who cheated him out / Of half his due" (Dinnerstein, 1994, p. 18).

Policies toward immigration reflected sharp racial distinctions, based on the pseudo-scientific reasoning of eugenics, with Nordic races considered to be at the top of the racial hierarchy. Immigration law had long limited newcomers from many Asian countries but allowed Mexican immigrants because of the needs of Western agriculture. Those who lobbied for tighter racial restrictions won a major victory starting in 1917, when Congress required immigrants to be able to read and write because Southern and Eastern

Europeans were thought to have high illiteracy rates. Madison Grant and Henry Fairfield Osborn, authors of the best-selling *The Passing of a Great Race* (1921) went beyond support for immigration restrictions on undesired groups to advocate state-imposed sterilization of the unfit:

> This is a practical, merciful and inevitable solution of the whole problem and can be applied to an ever widening circle of social discards, beginning always with the criminal, the diseased and the insane and extending gradually to types which may be called weaklings rather than defectives and perhaps ultimately to worthless racial types. (Grant and Osborn, p. 51)

By 1931, 28 states had laws allowing institutionalized people to be sterilized involuntarily. Women were ultimately the majority of those sterilized because they were considered by eugenicists to be breeders for racial ends. The tenets of the eugenics movement and American social policies influenced Nazi laws on sterilization, and many American eugenicists supported Nazi "racial hygiene" policies during the 1930s—so some of the most offensive Nazi tactics actually had their start in America, and not in Germany (Berlet, 2001, p. 93).

The idea that people from different countries could be graded along a continuum of quality was embedded in the minds of typical people and was considered common sense. "Public fairs often included 'fitter family' contests in which judges reviewed human pedigrees to determine the most eugenically positive families, just as the best cattle, chicken and pigs competed for blue ribbons," writes Berlet (2001; quoting Saxton from *The Rise and Fall of the White Republic*, 1990).

The Klan's power reached its peak in 1924 and 1925 and began to wane after that amid sex and corruption scandals. By 1936, the Klan sold its Imperial Palace. Later media campaigns took over, further fostering early racist and anti-Semitic attitudes in the country. However, it almost did not matter that the Klan was no longer a significant force. By the mid-1930s, precepts about the inferiority of blacks and other minority groups were part of the American mind-set so that much of the raw materials of hate in this country were firmly established. According to Levin (2002), Father William Coughlin "gained a national following through a xenophobic and increasingly anti-Semitic radio program broadcast from coast to coast. The power of Coughlin's message and the radio medium, however, was no match for the changing sentiments of the American public, which had shifted with America's entry into World War II in 1941" (p. 960 see also Walker, 1994). The fascist Silver Legion had taken over for the Klan, and its magazine *Liberation* had a circulation of 50,000 in 1933, with the organization itself gaining a peak membership of 15,000 in 1934, but the membership declined to 5,000 by 1938, when its middle-class support evaporated. The Friends of New Germany and its successor, the German-American Bund, founded in 1936, supported Nazi rule, denouncing the "melting pot" as a Jewish concept and calling on German Americans to remain racially pure. The Bund had only 8,299 members, but its ability to draw some 22,000 people to a pro-America rally in 1939 shows that it still retained a significant support base, according to Berlet (2001). The Bund actually promoted American Indians, showing that racial politics in America cannot be viewed narrowly. This was based on Hitler's romantic notions of nature versus evil Jewish industry and demonstrated the shifting ways certain cultural groups were treated in the United States, depending on the social context, geographic locale, and year. Berlet (2001) writes,

> Nazi cultural pluralism took an added twist when Hitler's government declared that American Indians were members of the Aryan race. The Bund made serious (but virtually fruitless) efforts to recruit Indians as members. In 1937, Pelley, calling himself "chief Pelley of the Tribe of Silver," promised American Indians that he would free them from reservations and place Jews in reservations instead. (p. 134)

As Americans absorbed the outcome of the war and the Nazi shame of racial discrimination became embodied in the Holocaust, racism began to receive much less public approval.

The short history of computer-based communication reveals that white supremacists are not ready to give up, but rather have seized on the Internet with intensity reminiscent of 1920s zeal. It has provided an outlet for them, despite a disenfranchised social status. As early as 1985, the Aryan Liberty Net system began with a revealing message:

> msg left by: system operator—finally we are all going to be linked together at one point in time. Imagine if you will all of the great minds of the patriotic christian movement linked together and joined into one computer. All the years of combined experience available to the movement. Now imagine any patriot in the country being able to call up and access those minds to deal with the problems and issues that affect him. You are online with the aryan nations brain trust. It is here to serve the folk. (Berlet, 2001, p. 1)

The computer bulletin board system (BBS), which was among the earliest to go online, was spearheaded by Louis Beam, a notorious Texas KKK leader who worked with Aryan Nations' Richard Butler in Idaho, and George Dietz, a prolific publisher of neo-Nazi materials (ADL, 1999; Berlet, 2001; Levin, 2002). Before the Internet became available to the public, bulletin boards allowed any person with a computer, a modem, and a phone line to dial up and log in to a computer containing public postings. Extremist groups quickly saw the potential rewards of such electronic communication (Berlet, 2001).

After Dietz and Beam, Metzger—the leader of WAR—utilized an early bigoted BBS system, along with the monthly WAR newspaper, videos, books, pamphlets, audiotapes, a national network of telephone message banks, and a cable-access show. According to Levin (2002) "Metzger's goal of inciting random acts of racial violence, particularly by young neo-Nazi skinheads, however, eventually proved costly" wrote Levin (2002, p. 963). "In October 1990, Metzger, his son and his WAR organization were found tortuously liable in the amount of $12.5 million by an Oregon civil court jury in the killing of a young Ethiopian immigrant by Portland skinheads who were linked to the California bigot" (ADL, 1996, p. 1). The WAR Web site continues to run racist cartoons that may attract the younger set, as described by Stern (2001–2002), who reprinted some of them in his article on Internet hate sites. One pictures a young white man beating up a black man with the caption, "Believe it or not White man, in the long run, it costs far less to take a stand now. Get busy . . . Defend your way of life . . . or lose it."

By the turn of the twenty-first century, there was heightened concern in the civil rights community over the growing number of white supremacist Web sites because racists could potentially benefit from the fact that Web sites are cheap, fast, global, uncensored, and immediate. "The Internet is the greatest thing to ever happen to hate," said David Goldman (2001, available at http://www.splcenter.org/intel/intelreport/article.jsp?sid=193) who monitored hate sites for HateWatch for six years. Many white supremacists, including David Duke, have made the hyperbolic prediction that the Internet might become the tool for a coming white revolution (Goldman, 2001).

Black, the creator of Stormfront, learned about the political power of the Internet early on by creating the first neo-Nazi site, just as he had come to join extremist groups early in life. He signed up with Virginia's neo-Nazi National Socialist Party when he was only 17 and still in high school.

Later, he tried to adopt David Duke's less obvious approach to hate, hoping to attract more people to a toned-down version of white supremacy. Duke himself became active in racist groups as a youth when he attended Louisiana State University, but he eventually left the Klan to lead the National Association for the Advancement of White People, which he called "a Klan without robes," and won election to the Louisiana State Legislature. His own writings are blatantly racist, raising fears about the rising nonwhite birthrate, intermarriage between the races, and immigration. Black, a former computer consultant, honed his technical skills while in federal prison (1982–1985) for trying to establish an all-white enclave by overthrowing the government of the island of Dominica. "There is the potential here to reach millions," Black said of the Internet. "I think it's a major breakthrough. I don't know if it's the ultimate solution to developing a white rights movement in this country, but it's certainly a significant advance" (ADL, 1999, p. iii). By the late 1990s, Stormfront had more than 1 million visitors (ADL, 1999). Pierce, of the National Alliance, was no less enthused about the Internet's power to advance his racist goals. He called it "the one medium where we are on an equal footing with CBS, NBC and all the rest of them" (ADL, 1999, p. 15).

Just as violence is advocated today, albeit more surreptitiously, on the Internet, violence served to enforce white supremacy throughout America's history, from the mass killing of Native Americans to the vicious lynching, rapes, torture, and murders of African Americans and other minority groups. America's legacy of racism still has a muted presence in cases of job discrimination and racial profiling. Once in a while, this racist and heterosexist legacy spills over to cases such as that of James Byrd, dragged from behind a truck in Jasper, Texas, or Matt Shepard, the gay youth beaten to death in Laramie, Wyoming. The shock that the media say most decent people feel belies the shame of America's past, when unprovoked violence appears to have been a much more commonplace and acceptable facet of social life. In this way, the white supremacy advocated on Web sites is a throwback to an earlier age and nothing new. What is new and daunting is the fact that so many Americans have profoundly easier access to this material. Whether that will mean anything in light of America's more enlightened social context remains to be seen. The most dangerous aspect of the white supremacist Web pages lies mainly in the potential, perhaps especially among some of our young, to ignore history and mistakenly view the materials as a fresh and new call to action.

REFERENCES

ACLU v. Reno, U.S. 844 (1997).

Adnkronos International. (2008). *Terrorism: Al-Zawahiri says al-Qaeda does not kill innocent people.* Retrieved April 3, 2008, from http://www.adnkronos.com/AKI/English/Security/?id=1.0.2035420505

Anti-Defamation League. (1996). *Danger: Extremism: The major vehicles and voices on America's far-right fringe.* New York: Author.

Anti-Defamation League. (1999). *Poisoning the Web: Hatred online.* New York: Author.

Anti-Defamation League. (2001). *Extremism in America: A guide.* New York: Author.

Anti-Defamation League. (2002, February 19). *Growing proliferation of racist video games target youth on the Internet.* Retrieved April 6, 2008, from http://www.adl.org/PresRele/extremism_72/4042_72.asp

Back, L., Keith, M., & Solomos, J. (1998). Racism on the Internet: Mapping neo-fascist subcultures in cyberspace. In J. Kaplan & T. Bjorgo (Eds.), *Nation and race: The developing Euro-American racist subculture* (pp. 73–101). Boston: Northeastern University Press.

Berlet, C. (2001, April 28). *When hate went online.* Boston: Public Research Associates.

Berlet, C., & Lyons, M. (2000). *Right-wing populism in America: Too close for comfort.* New York: Guilford Press.

Bostdorff, D. (2004). The Internet rhetoric of the Ku Klux Klan: A case study in Web site community building run amok. *Journal of Communication Studies, 55,* 340.

Buckingham, D. (2000). *The making of citizens: Young people, news and politics.* New York: Routledge.

Burris, V., Smith, E., & Strahm, A. (2000, May). White supremacist networks on the Internet. *Sociological Focus, 33:* 22, 215–234.

Chalmers, D. (1981). *Hooded Americanism: The history of the Ku Klux Klan.* Durham, NC: Duke University Press.

Dinnerstein, L. (1994). *Anti-Semitism in America.* Cambridge: Oxford University Press.

Garland, C. (2008). Klan's new message of cyber-hate. *New Zealand Herald.* Retrieved March 27, 2008, from http://www.nzherald.co.nz/topic/story.cfm?c_id=177&objectid=10500415

Gauntlett, D. (1998). Ten things wrong with the "effects model." In R. Dickinson, R. Harindranath, & O. Linne (Eds.), *Approaches to audiences* quote available at http://www.newmediastudies.com/effects1.htm, Introduction. London: Arnold.

Goldman, D. (2001, Spring). Cyberhate revisited: A long-time monitor of hate sites on the Internet argues that they are less important to extremists than is commonly believed [Interview]. *Intelligence Report,* Retrieved November 14, 2008, from http://www.splcenter.org/intel/intelreport/article.jsp?sid=193

Grant, M., & Fairfield, H. (1921). *The Passing of a Great Race.* C. Scribner's sons.

Hammack, L. (2008, October 19). "Neo-Nazi arrested, jailed on federal charge." Retrieved November 12, 2008, from http://www.roanoke.com/news/roanoke/wb/181018

Hofstadter, R. (1966). *The age of reform: From Bryant to FDR.* New York: Mass Market Paperbacks.

Katz, J. (2000). *Geeks: How two lost boys rode the Internet out of Idaho.* New York: Villard.

Knickmeyer, E. (2008, October 18). Washington Post Foreign Service, Page A1.

Kraut, R., Kiesler, S., Boneva, B., Cummings, J., Helgeson, V., & Crawford, A. (2002). Internet paradox revisited. *Journal of Social Issues, 58,* 49–74.

Kraut, R., Patterson, M., Lundmark, V., Kiesler, S., Mukhopadhyay, T., & Scherlis, W. (1998). Internet paradox: A social technology that reduces social involvement and psychological well-being? *American Psychologist, 53,* 1017–1032.

Lee, E., & Leets, L. (2002, February). Persuasive storytelling by hate groups on-line: Examining its effects on adolescents. *American Behavioral Scientist, 45,* 927–957.

Levin, B. (2002, February). Cyberhate: A legal and historical analysis of extremists' use of computer networks in America. *American Behavioral Scientist, 45,* 958–988.

Macdonald, A. (1978). *The Turner diaries.* Hillsboro, WV: National Vanguard.

MacLean, N. (1994). *Behind the mask of chivalry: The Making of the second Ku Klux Klan.* Oxford: Oxford University Press.

Martin, A. (2007, February 13). Elie Wiesel attack suspect identified. *San Francisco Examiner Reader,* Retrieved November 14, 2008, from http://www.examiner.com/a-556256~Author_attacked_in_S_F__hotel.html

Mizroch, Amir. (2008, October 15). "AqsaTube glorifes terrorism online." *Jerusalem Post.* Retrieved October 19, 2008, from http://www.jpost.com/servlet/Satellite?cid=1222017532579&pagename=JPost%2FJPArticle%2FShowFull

Okrent, D. (1999, May 10). Raising kids online: What can parents do? *Time,* pp. 38–43.

Potok, M. (2008, Spring). Russian roulette: The FBI's alleged use of an informant who regularly suggested killing his enemies comes under fire as reckless endangerment. *Intelligence Report*, pp. 12–13.

Reuters. (2007a, February 17). *Police identify suspect in Elie Wiesel attack*. Retrieved October 12, 2008, from http://www.reuters.com/article/domesticNews/id USN1734673820070217

Reuters. (2007b, February 18). *U.S. police arrest Holocaust denier suspected in Elie Wiesel attack*. Retrieved March 27, 2008, from http://www.haaretz.com/hasen/spages/827037.html

Schroer, T. (2001). Issue and identity framing within the white racialist movement: Internet dynamics. *Politics of Social Inequality, 9*, 207–231.

Siegel, D. (1997). *Creating killer Web sites* (Rev. ed.). Upper Saddle River, NJ: Pearson.

Sigrdrfa.net. http://www.sigrdrifa.net/about.shtml Retrieved October 8, 2008.

Simon Wiesenthal Center. (News releases), *Digital Hate & Terrorism 2001–2007: Interactive report on the Internet*. Los Angeles: Author: SW Center. http://www.wiesenthal.com/site/apps/nlnet/content2.aspx?c=fwLYKnN8LzH&b=4423615&ct=3876867

Southern Poverty Law Center. (2008, Spring). Hate Websites active in 2007. *Intelligence Report*, p. 59.

Stern, K. S. (2001–2002). Hate and the Internet. *Journal of Hate Studies, 1*, 57–107.

Sullivan, E. (2008, September 12). *YouTube bans terrorism training videos*. Author: Associated Press.

Tapscott, D. (1998). *Growing up digital: The rise of the Net generation*. New York: McGraw-Hill.

U.S.-based revolution Muslim Website spreading messages of hate. (2008). Retrieved March 29, 2008, from http://www.revolutionmuslim.com

Walker, S. (1994). *Hate speech: The history of an American controversy*. Lincoln, NE: Bison Books.

Wallace, P. (1999). *The psychology of the Internet*. Cambridge, UK: Cambridge University Press.

Weitzman, M. (2007). *Using the Web as a weapon: The Internet as a tool for violent radicalization and homegrown terrorism*, Testimony before the U.S. House of Representatives Committee on Homeland Security, November 6, Par. 17.

Weitzman, M. (2001). The Internet is our sword: Aspects of online antisemitism. In J. Roth & E. Maxwell (Eds.), *Remembering for the future: The Holocaust in an age of genocide*, New York: Palgrave.

(Executive Producers: Hirschorn M. & S. Tatro (executive producers)). (2002, January). *Inside hate rock* [Television broadcast]. New York: VH1.

ABOUT THE EDITOR
AND CONTRIBUTORS

Brian Levin is a civil rights attorney and professor of criminal justice at California State University, San Bernardino, where he is the director of the Center for the Study of Hate and Extremism. He has testified before Congress and various state legislatures. He is also the principal author of various U.S. Supreme Court *amici* briefs on hate crimes. Professor Levin formerly served as associate director of the Southern Poverty Law Center's Klanwatch/Militia Task Force and as a New York City police officer. He is the author or coauthor of books and articles on hate crimes and extremism. He received his JD from Stanford Law School, where he was awarded the Block Civil Liberties Award, and his BA, summa cum laude, from the University of Pennsylvania.

Sara-Ellen Amster, PhD, is an assistant professor of communication at National University in Costa Mesa, California, where she focuses on fostering media literacy and respect for the value of the press. A Pulitzer-nominated journalist, she is also the author of *Seeds of Cynicism: The Undermining of Journalistic Education* (2006). She has degrees from Cornell and Harvard universities and received her PhD from the University of California, San Diego.

Heidi Beirich is the director of research and special projects for the Southern Poverty Law Center's Intelligence Project, which tracks the activities of hate groups and domestic terrorists.

Susie Bennett, MS, MA, is a research associate at West Virginia University. Her current research focuses on inner-city gangs, hate crimes, and community policing. She received graduate training at Northeastern University in Boston and the University of California, Irvine.

Randy Blazak is an associate professor of sociology at Portland State University, where he is the director of the Hate Crime Research Network (http://www.hatecrime.net). He earned his PhD from Emory University in 1995, after completing a long-term ethnographic study of racist skinheads. His research has been published in journals and books, including chapters in *Home Grown Hate: Gender and Organized Racism* (2004) and *Hate and Bias Crimes: A Reader* (2003). He is the chair of the Coalition against Hate Crimes in Oregon and is writing a textbook on juvenile delinquency. He is currently researching the development of a program for paroled hate group members and the role of Serbian nationalism in the skinhead movement.

Norman Conti, PhD, is an assistant professor at Duquesne University. His research and teaching foci are in police socialization, hate crime, and community policing. His graduate training was at the University of Pittsburgh.

Bill Dixon is senior lecturer in criminology at Keele University, England. He is the joint editor, with Elrena van der Spuy, of *Justice Gained? Crime and Crime Control in South Africa's Transition* (2004).

David Gadd is senior lecturer in criminology at Keele University, England. He is a coauthor of *Psychosocial Criminology* (2007), with Tony Jefferson.

Mark S. Hamm is professor of criminology at Indiana State University. He has published widely in the areas of terrorism and hate crime. He is the author of nine books, including *American Skinheads: The Criminology and Control of Hate Groups* (1993) and *In Bad Company: America's Terrorist Underground* (2002). His work is frequently used as primary source material for media representations of hate crime and terrorism.

Jessica S. Henry is an assistant professor at Montclair State University, where she teaches in the Department of Justice Studies. She received her JD from New York University School of Law in 1995. Her teaching and research areas include hate crimes and capital punishment.

Kevin Hicks serves as director of the Writing across the Curriculum program at Alabama State University, where he also teaches English and humanities courses.

Jack Levin, PhD, is the Irving and Betty Brudnick Professor of Sociology and Criminology at Northeastern University in Boston, where he codirects its Center on Violence and Conflict. He has authored or coauthored a number of books, including *Why We Hate* (2004), *The Functions of Prejudice* (1975), *Hate Crimes Revisited* (2002), *Serial Killers and Sadistic Murderers—Up Close and Personal* (2008), and *The Violence of Hate* (2002). Levin has also published more than 150 articles in professional journals and major newspapers such as the *New York Times, Boston Globe, Dallas Morning News, Philadelphia Inquirer, Christian Science Monitor, Chicago Tribune, Washington Post,* and *USA Today.* His most recent work focuses on two areas: animal abuse in relation to sadistic murder and the prosecution of hate offenses.

James J. Nolan, PhD, is an associate professor of sociology and criminology at West Virginia University. His research and teaching focus on group relations, crime, and social control. Dr. Nolan was a police officer in Wilmington, Delaware, for 13 years and then worked for 5 years with the Federal Bureau of Investigation. He received graduate training at Temple University in Philadelphia.

Barbara Perry is professor of criminology, justice, and policy studies at the University of Ontario Institute of Technology. She has written extensively in the area of hate crime, including two books on the topic: *In the Name of Hate: Understanding Hate Crimes* (2001) and *Hate and Bias Crime: A Reader* (2003). She has just completed a book manuscript for University of Arizona Press titled *The Silent Victims: Native American Victims of Hate Crime* (forthcoming), based on interviews with Native Americans, and one on policing Native American communities for Lexington Press. Dr. Perry continues to work in the area of hate crime and has begun to make contributions to the limited scholarship on hate crime in Canada. Here she is particularly interested in anti-Muslim violence and hate crime against aboriginal people.

Timothy Pytell is an associate professor of history and director of graduate studies in social and behavioral sciences at California State University, San Bernardino. He earned his PhD from New York University in 1999 and is the author of numerous articles on Holocaust survivors, and a book on the famous Holocaust survivor and psychotherapist Viktor Frankl, titled *Viktor Frankl: Das Ende eines Mythos?*.

Gordana Rabrenovic, PhD, is an associate professor of sociology and education and the director of the Brudnick Center on Violence and Conflict at Northeastern University. Her substantive specialties are in the areas of community studies, urban education, and intergroup conflict and violence.

Her publications include books such as *Community Builders: A Tale of Neighborhood Mobilization in Two Cities* (1996), *Community Politics and Policy* (1999), and *Why We Hate* (2004), and she has edited [two] special issues of the *American Behavioral Scientist* on "Hate Crimes and Ethnic Conflict" (2001) and "Responding to Hate Violence: New Challenges and Solutions" (2007). Her current work focuses on violence against immigrants in the United States and Europe and on violence on college campuses.

Carolyn Turpin-Petrosino is associate professor of criminal justice at Bridgewater State College, Bridgewater, Massachusetts. She has published several articles on parole decision making, community policing, juvenile diversion, and, most recently, hate crimes. Her current projects involve the antiblack hate crime patterns and the investigation of community responses to hate crime events. In addition, Dr. Petrosino is investigating the utility of ethical theories in policy analyses.

INDEX

ADL. *See* Anti-Defamation League

African Americans: alleged inferiority, 3–4; discrimination against, 20; incident reports, 17, 170–71; lynching, 29; segregation, 30–31; stereotypes, 48. *See also* Racism/racial violence

African slavery, 26–27, 29

Allport, Gordon, 41–42

Almaguer, Thomas, 3

al-Qaeda terrorists, 136, 223, 224, 227

American Holocaust: The Conquest of the New World (Stannard), 209–10

American Nazi Party, 33, 97, 109–10, 139

American Renaissance (magazine/movement), 112, 113, 116, 122, 124–25

American skinheads, 103–4

Amster, Sara-Ellen, 221–48

Animus-based violence, 5, 26, 29, 189–90, 197

Antibisexual, antigay, and antilesbian (anti-BGL): assault, 197; categorizing, 143; civil rights exclusions, 57; cultural imaging, 72; hate groups, 153, 158–59, 227; heterosexism, 56–60, 88, 143; KKK, 148; legislation, 188; SO bias, 189. *See also* Lesbian/gay/bisexual/transgender

Anti-Defamation League (ADL): anti-Semitism, 163; bias-crime legislation, 9, 186–87; as hate group, 153; hate group monitoring, 139, 140–41, 222; institutional vandalism, 187–88; SO crimes, 13; statistical reports by, 169

Antidiscrimination, 7, 10

Anti-Muslim prejudice, 44, 103, 148, 154

Anti-Semitism: ADL, 163; history, 4; the Holocaust, 213–16; KKK, 96–97; lynchings, 30; media value, 239, 240, 242, 243; Muslims, 154; Nazism, 43, 44–45, 97; white nationalism, 124–25, 134

Apartheid, 44, 78

Apprendi v. New Jersey (2000), 185

'A Problem from Hell': America and the Age of Genocide (Power), 207

Armenian genocide, 206, 212–13, 217, 218

Aryan Liberty Net, 244

Aryan Nations, 65, 98, 139, 148

Aryan Republican Army (ARA), 105–6, 149

Asian Americans, 13, 27–28

Axis Rule in Occupied Europe (Lemkin), 207

Aztlán conspiracy, 123–24, 141